DESPITE
GOOD
INTENTIONS

Despite Good Intentions

WHY DEVELOPMENT ASSISTANCE TO THE THIRD WORLD HAS FAILED

Thomas W. Dichter

University of Massachusetts Press
AMHERST & BOSTON

Copyright © 2003 by University of Massachusetts Press
All rights reserved
Printed in the United States of America
LC 2002010178
ISBN 1-55849-392-1 (library cloth); 393-X (paper)
Designed by Jack Harrison
Set in Electra with Novarese display type by Graphic Composition, Inc.
Printed and bound by Thomson-Shore, Inc.

Library of Congress Cataloging-in-Publication Data

Dichter, Thomas W.
    Despite good intentions : why development assistance to the third
world has failed / Thomas W. Dichter.
        p.   cm.
Includes bibliographical references and index.
ISBN 1-55849-392-1 (cloth : alk. paper) — ISBN 1-55849-393-X (pbk. : alk. paper)
1. Economic assistance — Developing countries — Evaluation.
2. Poverty — Developing countries.   I. Title.
HC60 .D485 2003
338.91'09172'4 — dc21
                        2002010178

British Library Cataloguing in Publication data are available.

For Susan

Contents

Preface

I can't recall exactly when I began to have doubts about the value of development assistance. But I know that those doubts crystallized through contact with colleagues. Development workers, naturally enough, get to know and work with other development workers. Because we spend much of our working lives traveling, we end up still together after work is over, on planes, in jeeps, in restaurants, hotels, hostels, and huts. And over a beer we talk, not about our ideals but about the day-to-day business of development. We talk about raising money, plot strategies for getting grants and contracts, and compare notes about salaries and jobs. Sometimes we loosen up more and note some of the silliness we put up with, the compromises we are forced to make, the efforts we make to cover for others' incompetence. And, of course, we gossip. In short, we are like others in any industry.

In my naïveté I was not used to thinking of development assistance as an industry. I had for years genuinely believed that we could meaningfully help foster others' development, and for me that meant we occupied a different realm of endeavor from commerce or government. The more I saw that we — the professionals and the organizations for which we work — behave as self-interestedly as any other industry or field and those in it, the more uncomfortable I became. My doubts became concrete a few years ago when some neighbors asked me for my "professional" opinion. They were starting to have considerable disposable income and wanted to contribute money to a good cause, preferably something that would help third world people. My neighbors traveled and, unlike most Americans I'd known, were interested in the third world and sensed how complex the world had become. They wanted to help, but they wanted their money to be used effectively and efficiently. Whom would I recommend, they asked me; which organization did the best work in alleviating poverty?

I could not give them the assurance they wanted. I knew of no organization that really accomplished much in the way of sustained alleviation of poverty. Still less, I knew of none that promoted what I had come to see as real development. Moreover, I was not aware of any organization which did exactly what it told the public it did or which used public moneys or charitable contributions really wisely. I hemmed and hawed. Finally I told them that I felt like a restaurant critic asked by good friends if he could get them in to see the kitchen of one of their favorite spots: "You don't want to know what goes on in there," I said, and left it at that.

But it was my youngest son who pushed me to begin this book. At the time I was an officer of a medium-size foundation. When I wasn't traveling, my time was spent in front of a computer screen writing reports and memos, manipulating budget numbers, trying, as I had come to realize, to sell something, not on behalf of the poor or necessarily in the interests of development but on behalf of the organization for which I worked.

My son, then aged nine, began to drop by my office after school, a short walk away. He was at the stage where he was becoming conscious of his parents as people whose being did not revolve only around him, but who had lives, filled largely with work in the outside world. As children will, he had come to think, or more accurately to want to think, that what his father did was important. He knew that I went off to work wearing a tie and that I traveled; he had heard that some people seemed to think highly of me and that I was trying to do something that was "good." So after a few visits to the office, it must have taken some courage for him to admit his frustration at the gap between what he had imagined and what it looked like I was doing. He would see me before the computer screen typing away or answering the telephone and talking in a voice that must have been unfamiliar. One day he asked me, "Dad, is this all you do?"

Because this book is critical of development assistance, the reader might like to know whether my experience is sufficient to back up my case. It is. Over more than thirty years, I have flown a million and a half miles, bumped along countless dusty and muddy roads, gotten dysentery at the most inconvenient times, and seen poverty on every continent, in more countries than I dare to count. I've sat on the ground in the sun and the rain and talked with thousands of people. More to the point, I have multiple perspectives on the development assistance industry because in my checkered career I have worked for virtually every type of organization in the business and in a wide range of functions.

My interest in the developing countries began in 1961 when the Peace Corps was formed. In December 1963, in my senior year of college, I applied to the Peace Corps. After graduating, I went. By 1966 I knew that I wanted to continue working in the third world, and it seemed to me that a graduate degree would help. After finishing a Ph.D. in anthropology, I taught, briefly, and then again got involved with the Peace Corps, training other volunteers, writing manuals, and, fourteen years after being a volunteer, directing the Peace Corps program in Yemen.

Another perspective came from my time as a practicing anthropologist, when I looked at how countries and people became "modern" and in Morocco studied several different school systems to understand the role of education in what we used to think of as the "process of modernization." I worked for several years for a think tank on similar issues in central Asia and the Middle East. I lived in Tunisia working on a World Bank project. For six years I was a senior officer of a nongovernmental organization (NGO) and helped design, raise money for, and evaluate development projects in Africa and Latin America. Employment with a profit-making development contractor put me in close touch with the workings of the U.S. Agency for International Development (USAID). I got a job with a large foundation and for several years found myself giving out money instead of writing proposals to get it. And, finally, I spent four years on a long-term consulting contract with the World Bank. In between these "employed" positions there were several periods, one as long as three years, when I lived as a freelance consultant, taking on all manner of work for scores of organizations, big and small, in many countries. Throughout these years I also taught, did research, and wrote articles on a number of development-related topics.

The prospective reader might also wonder where I come from politically. Those to the left of center might hope that I would add another voice to individuals who say the problem is that poor people's own needs and talents have been left out of the development mix, that the big institutions such as the World Bank are agents of self-interested capitalism and thus exploit the poor, that much of development funding goes to corrupt governments, that one of the keys now is massive debt relief, and so on. The "greens" might hope that I would add fuel to their view that development has ridden roughshod on the environment, that the third world has been a dumping ground for the dregs of our irresponsible behavior, and so forth, while conservatives might hope that I am arguing for neo-isolationism and a massive reduction in foreign aid, or a much more conditional use of it. And advocates of the "third way" might hope that this book will add to their argument about more trade and less aid.

While I cannot claim to be completely apolitical, my argument in this book does not line up comfortably alongside any particular stance. Political stances usually come complete with a built-in solution to the problem being analyzed. Thus if X is deemed to have failed because policymakers were too naïve or too ignorant to take Y into account, then the obvious solution to the problem is X plus Y.

But I do not have a coherent solution, certainly not one that lends itself to realistic implementation. My concern is to show not so much why development assistance does not work, though I think I do that as well, but how it does not work. And my conclusion is that development assistance cannot really accomplish what we have hoped it could, no matter how it might be restructured or reengineered or even no matter how much we try to change the "paradigm" (to use the jargon of the 1990s).

If there is a stance in this book, then, it is pragmatic rather than political or ideological. Simply, our efforts have not worked. Little lasting good (and some harm) has come from all the money and energy we have expended. And the purpose of this book is to show what keeps getting in the way. But let us be clear. I am talking about development with a capital *D* — a set of intended changes of such magnitude as to result in measurable and lasting material improvements in masses of people's lives. I am not talking about whether it is worthwhile to help people in need. We can and perhaps should give of ourselves and our goods to others. But that is different. Humanitarian effort should not be confused with development or poverty alleviation.

A word about the eighteen stories in this book. They are not closely linked to the analytic chapters in the sense that each pair is intended precisely to illustrate the points made in each chapter. Rather, they are meant to ground the analysis in the realities of development assistance as it is practiced day to day, year by year, and especially at the field end of things where projects and the poor meet. That is why ten of the eighteen stories are about NGOs, which have become our field practitioners. Naturally, the stories, which follow a four-decades-long chronology, reflect my own experience. But as I have had the privilege of a number of different perspectives over the years, I believe they are a fair representation of the way things are and of how things were at different times.

In the stories, every substantive detail, every event, every direct quote, and every fact and figure comes from something that I was personally involved with or saw. I did not borrow from others' experiences whether told to me or written about.

At the same time, the stories are fictionalized. I have created a character, Ben Rymaker, whose career and changing sensibilities run through the chronology. And though he gets more involved in some of the stories than in others, Ben is not what the stories are about. He is a witness, a means to convey what really can and does happen. Because of that role, I have felt free also to fictionalize some of the details of where and how he moved in his career. The most convenient way to make him present in so many places and times is to cast him often as a consultant.

I have also changed the names of people and organizations and, in very few instances where I felt it did not matter, moved a date by a year or disguised (probably too thinly) the location of an event. There are some minor legal reasons to do this — in one case I actually signed a contract with an employer promising not to reveal any proprietary information about the organization — but mostly I have done it, in the fashion of the old *Dragnet* police show on television, to "protect the innocent." In keeping with my apolitical argument, I do not feel any of the organizations in development assistance, despite different motivations and some of the foolishness they perpetrate, are truly blameworthy. To identify the organizations in the stories would therefore be a gratuitous act. They are well meaning, like count-less others. And certainly most of the people who work in them have good intentions. Most development professionals I have met possess very high ideals about the work they do.

But because no one has to date been funded to do development work out-side the structure of an organization, those good intentions and ideals get twisted, bent, and reshaped.

Development professionals have, almost all of us, become caught in the evolution of a set of increasingly self-serving structures whose imperatives, stakes, and incentives have snuck up on us, sometimes so quietly that we have not noticed. If we haven't seen how much those structures limit and compromise development, it is partly because we are in fact so sincere and partly because it is not in our interest to do so.

Finally, I apologize to the reader for the awkwardness of the repeated use of the phrase "development assistance" and "development assistance in-dustry." Unfortunately, the lexicon of development, like that of so many other fields, is studded with jargon and marbles-in-the-mouth acronyms, and there's nothing to be done about it. But when possible I have tried to re-duce the use of the phrase by using the pronoun "we," appropriately enough because I have been part of this field for much of the last forty years.

This book rests on years and years of interaction with countless people in many places. Some of their names I never knew; quite a few of those whose names I once did know, have slipped into the outer reaches of my blurry memory. All of them are to be thanked, whether they would like it or not. But there are a few people who were directly involved in the book and whose names I do have at hand.

Bruce Wilcox of the University of Massachusetts Press had the courage to see possibility in the hybrid style of the book and urged me to make more of it. Several friends from both inside and outside the development business contributed valuable comments, perspective, and encouragement. I thank Libby and Larry Alson, Joan and Linc Diamant, Kevin Dwyer, Vijay Maha-jan, Albey and Alicia Reiner, and Ian Smillie.

My children, Alex, Megan, Max, and Paul, lived through many of the experiences related in this book and, inadvertently or otherwise, helped me see things more clearly as I worked and lived development, especially dur-ing the 1980s. My wife, Susan, lived much of my development experience with me and shared my frustrations. Her tough questions, coming always from a high critical standard, encouraged me — no, often forced me — to try to transform my discomfort into analysis. I hope she will think I have done so.

Abbreviations

AICPA	American Institute of Certified Public Accountants
CARE	Cooperative for Assistance and Relief Everywhere
CGIAR	Consultative Group on International Agricultural Research
DAC	Development Assistance Committee
EEC	European Economic Community
Danida	Danish International Development Agency
DFID	Department for International Development (U.K.)
FAO	Food and Agriculture Organization
FASB	Financial Accounting Standards Board
IFAD	International Fund for Agricultural Development
IFPRI	International Food Policy Research Institute
ILO	International Labour Organization
IMF	International Monetary Fund
NGO	nongovernmental organization
ODA	official development assistance
OECD	Organization for Economic Cooperation and Development
PCV	Peace Corps volunteer
SCF	Save the Children Federation
Sida	Swedish International Development Cooperation Agency
SIPA	School for International and Public Affairs (Columbia University)
UNDP	United Nations Development Programme
UNICEF	United Nations Children's Fund
USAID	United States Agency for International Development
WHO	World Health Organization

DESPITE
GOOD
INTENTIONS

The Great Paradox of Development Assistance

> We are six on the mission to the North-west Frontier: an old Japanese, a
> Korean, an American, a Bangladeshi, a Dutch girl, me. . . . None of us
> have been here before. . . . The Korean who brought us together does not
> know us either. He got my name from an Indian I once worked with in
> Manila. . . . How did the world get this way? . . . OK: the Japanese,
> because Japanese money is becoming important; a Bangladeshi, because
> they are cheap and brown; a Korean, because the mission organiser is
> Korean; an American to punch statistics; a Dutch girl sociologist for the
> soft and warm. A mix of people because this time it's an international
> agency. I'm in charge; I make the big decisions. We've got four weeks to
> come up with a project for, say, thirty million dollars. Routine.
>
> —LEONARD FRANK, "The Development Game"

Thirty judiciously spent minutes in a small-town public library will provide
enough random facts to dramatize the plight of the world's poor:

- In 1998 more people were living on less than one dollar a day than in 1996.
- In 1999 the assets of the world's two hundred richest people were greater
  than the combined incomes of the lowest 40 percent of the world's
  peoples.
- The world's rich-poor gap has more than doubled since the 1960s. The
  rich world at the end of the 1990s earned about sixty times what the poor
  world did; in 1999 the top 20 percent earned seventy-four times as much
  as the bottom 20 percent.
- In 1999, 1.3 billion people were breathing air that did not meet minimum
  World Health Organization standards.
- In 1997 there were over 100 million street children in the world's cities.
- In 1997 there were 1.5 billion people without access to medical care.
- In 1999 almost 1 billion people lived in urban slums.[1]

---

1. Various sources were used for these data, including World Bank, *World Development Report, 2000–2001* (New York: Oxford University Press for the World Bank, 2001), and Chandrika Kaul and Valerie Tomaselli-Moschovitis, *Statistical Handbook on Poverty in the Developing World* (Phoenix: Oryx Press, 1999).

For more than fifty years the international development assistance industry has tried to alter the conditions behind these dismal numbers with hardly any lasting success to show for it. And where there has been success, surprisingly little evidence exists that it can be attributed to the interventions of the development assistance industry. The once impressive economic growth of "Asian Tigers" such as South Korea, Taiwan, and Singapore, along with a significant improvement in the quality of life of their people, was largely the result of government policies, location, private sector initiative, and perhaps some historical luck.[2]

But dramatic statistics are a cheap device. They can just as easily make a glass look half full as half empty. And so the defenders of the development industry can make it seem they have many accomplishments to cite. For example, more access to primary education has resulted in more people with basic literacy, and under the World Health Organization a decade-long effort to wipe out smallpox succeeded. In the 1990s for the first time we saw a decline in the fertility rate of the developing countries owing to a lowering of infant mortality and a decrease in death rates.

Yes, these *are* achievements, and some are attributable to the development industry. But large questions surround these achievements and put them in perspective: Could they have been had for less money? What unintended and negative consequences came in their train? What new problems are posed by more people living longer and better educated, but with fewer opportunities and maybe even more miserable prospects? And why, despite such achievements, is worldwide poverty at least as widespread as ever?

Why has an industry that since 1960 has spent over $1.7 trillion on development assistance, by any commonsense cost-benefit calculus, produced negligible results (if not made things worse)? No other large-scale publicly funded effort of such duration could have got away with such poor performance, certainly not in the private sector or even in the ranks of government. Yet all the players in development assistance are still in business. Not only are all the organizations that were formed to help the emerging nations develop and to alleviate the plight of the world's poor still functioning (and in some cases thriving,) but more and more organizations, big and small, have been founded along the way as well.

I am far from the first to be critical of development assistance. There have been other critiques over the years — quite a few, in fact. A number have been written by outsiders who want to expose the development industry as a bunch of neocolonialists in disguise, promoters of growth at the expense

2. In the late 1950s, South Korea and Ghana had almost exactly the same ranking in world statistics on poverty and economic status.

of "well-being," or cynics who do not really care about the poor.[3] But the critique that has come from *within* the development industry itself is more revealing. Its style is an interesting mix of innocence and naïve optimism. Much of this internal critique says: "We realize we have made mistakes, but they've been honest mistakes, mistakes that we've learned from, but now we've figured it out and have answers to the question of how we can do better."

The World Bank, the most prestigious player in the development industry, provides an excellent example of the chronic tendency in development assistance to say that if certain (largely obvious) propositions can be taken on board, we are now ready to do it right. In 1992 the Bank, disturbed by the growing failure rate of its projects, produced an internal document titled "Effective Implementation: Key to Development Impact," which begins with this introduction:

> As a development institution, the Bank has continuously broadened its activities. Increasingly ambitious goals and development priorities have expanded its reach. . . . The projects the Bank supports — as a lender of last resort — of necessity entail substantial risk taking. This calls for vigilance, realism, and constructive self-evaluation. The Bank must be no less restrained in diagnosing and seeking to remedy its own shortcomings than it is in seeking to help member countries recognize and address theirs. For only through rigorous and continuous self-assessment based on exacting standards can a large and influential institution such as the Bank maintain its effectiveness."[4]

The report details the Bank's "declining portfolio performance" in the 1980s and early 1990s. The Bank's own staff assessments, done after the "completion of disbursement" (i.e., when projects are over), showed that the number of projects judged unsatisfactory increased from 15 percent in 1981 to 37.5 percent in 1991.

---

3. Graham Hancock's *Lords of Poverty* (London: Macmillan, 1989) is an excellent example of the latter. Pascal Bruckner's *The Tears of the White Man* (New York: Free Press, 1986) is an example of the neocolonialist argument, and Gilbert Rist's *The History of Development* (London: Zed Books, 1997) is a classic example of the anticapitalism, antigrowth critique. There have also been occasional journalistic pieces critical of development assistance (some use the term "foreign aid," which can include military aid). Some important pieces from the last fifteen years, in chronological order, are "When Foreign Aid Fails," *Atlantic Monthly*, April 1985; "The Perversion of Foreign Aid," *Commentary*, June 1985; "Modernizing Aid," editorial, *Toronto Globe and Mail*, March 11, 1988, about the failures of NGOs in development; "Foreign Aid Largely a Failure," *Washington Post*, February 21, 1989; "The Twilight of Foreign Aid," *Financial Times*, September 28, 1992; "Why Aid Is an Empty Promise," feature story, *Economist*, May 7–13, 1994; "Taming the Beast of H Street," editorial, *Financial Times*, September 26, 1994, about the World Bank; "Africa Is Dying," cover story, *New Republic*, June 16, 1997.

4. World Bank, "Effective Implementation: Key to Development Impact," confidential Portfolio Management Task Force report (Washington, D.C., September 22, 1992), i.

And what are the report's conclusions? "Five conclusions are basic to the recommendations of the Task Force":

- The Bank's success is determined by benefits "on-the-ground"—sustainable development impact. . . .
- . . . Successful implementation requires commitment built on stakeholder participation and local "ownership."
- . . . Quality at entry into the portfolio is a critical determinant of success in project outcome. . . . Results-oriented implementation planning as a basis for later monitoring is essential.
- . . . The project-by-project approach to portfolio performance management needs to proceed within a country context to address generic problems of implementation and . . . to focus accountability with the Bank for portfolio results.
- If the Bank is to remain effective, portfolio performance must be taken into account in the Bank's country assistance strategies, business processes, and personnel policies.[5]

Besides the often anodyne content of such promises to do better, what is important about these inside-the-industry critiques is that most of their prescriptions are for changes in technique or, at best, emphasis. Few development insiders are willing to entertain the possibility that there may no longer be any really good reason for this industry to exist at all. To suggest this would mean taking a look at development *as an industry*, as having its own imperatives, as having its own survival at stake, more, increasingly, than the survival of its putative raison d'être—the poor people of the underdeveloped nations.

This last proposition—that aid has become a business whose main stake is its own survival—begins to explain why there has been so little apparent learning or fundamental change in how things are done, despite all the evidence of failure, all the studies (countless retellings of the "operation was a success, but the patient died" sort) and the many expensive evaluations and retrospective looks at this half century of work, the majority of which show depressing if not always negative results. That the World Bank in 1992 (almost fifty years after its founding in 1944) had to remind itself that "sustainable impact," "on the ground," is the determinant of success is a big clue to the almost willful myopia within the industry.

To me, this combination of large-scale failure and persistently unselfconscious pride in an industry whose self-proclaimed responsibility is to do something about poverty is as mind-boggling as any of the dismal poverty statistics cited earlier. But other than in this introduction, I do not want to wring my hands too much about how the development industry should

5. Ibid., ii. In 1998 the World Bank produced a more comprehensive review of development assistance called *Assessing Aid: What Works, What Doesn't, and Why.*

have done better. I do not think it could have, and that is why this critique is different.

The explanation has to begin by recalling the deep moral basis for development assistance, for this is not a malevolent field. And while it is true that behind the development assistance programs of many of the industrial nations there has often been selfish national interest, former colonial loyalty, and/or political conditionality, especially at the height of the cold war, there has always been these nations' conscience. From its first thin efforts before the Second World War through its serious beginnings in the late 1940s, development assistance has been driven by the question, How can we stand by and allow poverty in our midst?

In the early postwar years of development assistance, the conscience of many of the Western nations was strongly bolstered by their confidence. The United States especially, with its action-oriented, problem-solving culture, led the early development organizations to take on the task of helping others develop and did so with considerable self-assurance.

And because in the rich industrial nations responsibility and accountability, not to mention efficiency, are high values when it comes to taking on big tasks, development assistance got itself organized. Organizing development within structures of accountability also fit with another implicit model — the modern firm.

While getting organized seems like a sine qua non for any complex endeavor, in the case of development assistance the side effects of organization have been counterproductive and sometimes harmful. It is those side effects which begin to explain the many failures. That is the great paradox of development assistance.

The first of these side effects is a set of organizational imperatives that the structure of any organization, by its very nature, demands. These begin with the mundane systems that have to be built: an accounting system, a personnel system, a system for decision making, a system to describe what the people who work for the organization are supposed to do every day — in short, a set of systems designed to take action, to *do* something that can be sufficiently measured or accounted for so that those who put up the money for the work can be satisfied that it was not wasted.

Not long after these systems are set up, a more subtle imperative evolves — the organization begins to become a set of stakes, beginning with its jobholders. Employees want to maintain their jobs and the responsibilities and authority that come with them. The organization itself, while an abstraction in any literal sense, becomes a real stakeholder; the stake being self-preservation and perpetuation. It "wants" to keep going, to stay alive. In fact, in today's world merely staying alive is not enough; the organization has to learn to "want" to grow.

The second side effect of organization in the modern context is that organizations in the same line of work have a tendency to form industries. The word "industry" today is no longer a passive descriptive for a number of firms producing similar things or doing similar work. Today, industries are in themselves active entities, engaged in preserving, promoting, and guarding the interests of their member firms.

These side effects of organization all make sense in the world of commerce. Moreover, in the world of commerce the side effects and the main effects are not even distinct, or if they are, the distinctions (*and* the side effects, for that matter) are moot. The goal in commerce is clear and singular: to make money.

But even though much of the financing for development assistance is made up of loans and some development assistance institutions even make money from lending, development assistance is not a commercial venture. It exists in the publicly financed realm — development assistance is financed ultimately by people's taxes or contributions. In any case, whether money is "made" here and there in development assistance is beside the point. Development assistance, by definition, is not in the money-making business. It has an altogether different aim.

For fifty years, no matter how the terminology has shifted, the ultimate aim of those who take development seriously has been a significant reduction in poverty. Additionally, only when the majority of people in a country sense enough choice to be in some degree of control of their daily existence, if not of their lives, can it be said that development is occurring. Given how elusive such success has been, development professionals increasingly acknowledge development as a highly complex series of interactions between and among virtually all aspects of existence: from the physical to the human; from the psychological to the economic; from the political and social to the cultural. Development is indeed a process, something we who work in this field have (perhaps too glibly) come to accept. What has been less often accepted is that it is also a historical process, in that it is linked to the past and generally takes historical kinds of time — not weeks, months, or years but decades and centuries.

I think we in development understand these propositions implicitly. The problem is that when we make the leap between that understanding and what we do, we slip off into a deductive mode of thinking rather than an inductive one. Our general principles about poverty tell us how things should be, instead of allowing the particulars of time and place to tell us how things are. Thus we do not follow the implications of what we have come to understand but act as if development were something else. And that is where these organizational imperatives and side effects come in: They not only make it easy for us to act as if development were something other than the complex (and often opaque) set of interactions that we know it to be but also box us in to that collective illusion, such is their power.

For example, because of our urgency to end poverty, we act as if development is a construction, a matter of planning and engineering. While we rarely use the term "engineering," we do regularly use an engineering lexicon: such words as "plan," "objective," and "implement." And we talk much about measurement and "indicators."

We seem to know that development is not measurable or easily quantifiable in any reasonable time frame, yet we measure many things anyway, in wholly unreasonable time frames (e.g., two years, three years, five years), acting as if these measurements are proxies for development. This seems innocuous enough. But as much as it seems intuitively correct that the number of wells drilled or kilometers of road built or water lines laid are proxies for development, they are in themselves not development. Isn't what counts the whole complex set of institutions and habits that keep those roads maintained and the wells clean? Ditto the number of children inoculated, and ditto especially the number of farmers trained to use a new kind of fertilizer or the number of poor rural women in Bangladesh who have been given a small loan to buy a cell phone. By themselves, can we say that these interventions are development? Can we with assurance even honestly say they are building blocks of development?

Because development is complex and intricately integrated, there are myriad unintended consequences from every "intervention" we make. And yet we continue to act as if these managed and organized individual interventions — we call them "projects" or bundle the projects into programs — will, when "completed," add to the overall "process" of development.

The keys to development increasingly lie in the realm of the policies, laws, and institutions of a society, and to change these requires indirect kinds of approaches — stimulating, fostering, convincing — rather than doing things directly. Why is it, then, that the majority of development assistance organizations continue to "do" things? And why do more and more come into existence every day with funding to do still more things?[6]

We skirt around the edges of the larger question of whose role development is anyway (if it is a role). We acknowledge that in theory the government of Niger or Haiti or Sierra Leone should be building the roads, providing tax moneys for schools, protecting the environment, providing well-trained public safety personnel, and, more important, ensuring property rights and a rule of law, the very core set of institutions that a respectable modern society must have, or at least toward which it must show some evident progress. But the truth is, we say, that they cannot (they are undertrained, inept, or at war) or they will not (there is no government or it is corrupt). Of course, this being the twenty-first century and not the nineteenth, the option of recolonizing such failed states or "basket case" countries is out,

6. Most of these are nongovernmental organizations (NGOs).

as is the option of making them into "protectorates." And so we, the development assistance organizations, get involved in their development, and our industry lobbies for more moneys to do so.

And when we notice these contradictions and try to change, we end up tinkering with technique or go on retreats to learn to be more "relevant." Yet no matter what we have tried, we seem to get stuck in the same trap. Nongovernmental organizations (NGOs) now recognize, for example, that "we" cannot do development for poor people. We say they have to be part of it; they have to make decisions; they have to do it. And so we design techniques, such as Participatory Rural Appraisal, to help them (make them?) be part of it. We may sometimes sense the irony in our active engagement in helping "them" become actively engaged in their own development or in our efforts to intervene directly in a process we know to be indirect, but we do not seem to be able to do much about these contradictions. We get stuck in what are essentially the same old roles.

The kind of development assistance our industry provides is increasingly counterproductive (and harmful) because it acts as if all the things we have come to know — like the inappropriateness of projects — are not so. And the question asked in this book is whether the development assistance industry does so (and seems destined to continue) because of the imperatives of our organizations and, increasingly, our industry. We are caught in a cycle of moral impulse and responsible accountability to our donors which leads us to want to help people in direct ways. This has meant using the moneys at our disposal to show measurable if not always visible results, which in turn reinforces our tendency to "do" things directly. We continue today, after fifty years, to carry out projects and programs that procure personnel and supplies, distributing wheelbarrows, hoes, seeds, small loans, advice, or technical assistance. It does not matter what the projects and programs do as long as they are time bound, have measurable indicators that seem in the very short run to alleviate poverty, and use lots of our own labor. We have built thousands of substantial organizations employing hundreds of thousands of professionals to manage all this work. And for years we have spent between $50 billion and $60 billion per year and have always lamented that it is not more.

Today almost all organizations in the development assistance industry, from small but increasingly savvy NGOs to the World Bank, talk about results, about the poor as "clients," about effectiveness and accountability. In the interest of accountability we have become more professional. Our industry, like those in the world of commerce, now has specialized training institutes for our profession. We have our own journals, our own associations, and our own vocabulary. All this is well-meaning, but in this book I ask whether ultimately, as in the world of commerce, most of these "improvements" seem to be about staying in business.

The first five chapters of this book take a historical approach. I try to show how development assistance became an industry in response to the evolution of the development idea, how little we have taken from the history of the world's actual development, and how we tend to avoid some universals of human nature. The remaining chapters are an examination of why the industry does not change. I try to get across the complex interactions between our own good intentions, our need for other people's money and what we do to get it, our language and thought, and our jobs and careers and the organizations in which we develop them.

Am I saying that no answers or solutions exist to the dire problems of the developing countries? No. I am saying that the development assistance industry is not the answer. The problems of development are far too complex for any organized and deliberate effort to solve in any lasting way. Development is not a set of obstinate problems the way cancer is but a historical process that cannot really be engineered or controlled. At the least, finding a set of techniques to make it happen is unlikely. In short, development is not a "challenge," something we can deliberately "attack" the way finding a cure for cancer can be. Certainly an industry set up to engineer change through an endless series of short- and medium-term direct interventions ("projects" and "programs") is, to put it mildly, a gross mismatch of means and ends.

In the year 2000 in the western United States, forest fires raged through the summer. For the first time the U.S. Forest Service, the National Parks, and the ecologists all began to admit that perhaps nature was bigger than they were, that the idea that fire was bad needed to be revisited. More and more professionals began to entertain the notion that for one hundred years the instinct to put out fires may not have been in the best interest of the forest. This counterintuitive approach may be an apt analogy to what we face now after all these years of trying to help the third world develop.

Now may be the right time to be counterintuitive. There is not much we can do directly that seems to work in any lasting way. We would be of better service by going home and closing down all projects that do not directly save lives or relieve the sufferings of war and political ostracism. But the discipline to do nothing "developmental," to intervene only minimally and with a light hand, to take direct action only in the humanitarian realm, flies in the face of our action-oriented culture, not to mention our instinct to help. I do not deny how hard it is to reconcile good intentions and the organization to carry them out with the evidence that much of what has been or could be done directly is counterproductive. But the ending of poverty — which has become the goal of the industry that has evolved since the 1940s — is a different kind of prospect than helping others and does not lend itself very well to the helping intuition. Just as we can help specific people who are poor without making much of a difference in the development of the country in which they live, development can likewise occur without making an immediate difference in people's lives. What may be needed is restraint — a tempering, if not a wholesale repression, of our good intentions.

Does this mean that we say "Well, then, let's leave well enough alone, let them (the poor of the developing nations) be. Let the forces of the international marketplace bring on development. Let globalization reign"? (As if it could be so easily stopped.) Yes, it might mean that. But that answer is less gloomy than it seems. For there are some positive and hopeful trends; they just do not fall within the ambit of the development assistance industry. The first lies in the nexus now forming between the poor people of the world and one of the most significant drivers of globalization — telecommunication. The poor are not and have never been as passive as we often think. When they catch on to possibility, they try do something with it. And more and more, the poor, aided by telecommunication that enables them to "catch on," are taking development into their own hands. Telecommunication in the form of everything from radio and television to cell phone technology and the Internet offers perhaps the one real bridge to a sense of possibility that the poor can access everywhere. Of course, it does not always work — there are many formidable obstacles, such as war, violence, and despotism.

The second positive trend is the growing tendency among many of the poor simply to move to another place. A significant portion of the income they make in so doing generates what the professionals refer to as "remittance income." Unfortunately, we do not have accurate global statistics to chart the trend in detail. But we do know enough to say that the amount of money poor workers earn away from their home country and either save to reinvest or send back to relatives has the potential to equal and surpass all official development assistance, and may have done so already. More money may come to poor people from the remittance income they earn as voluntarily displaced workers than the development industry has provided or could realistically provide annually. There is a difference, to be sure. The people's own money has both the advantage and perhaps the disadvantage of being used outside the architecture of the development assistance industry. But it is no more uneven and rough around the edges, and it achieves automatically and instantly one of the goals the development industry has never been able to reach: full "ownership" of the goal of poverty alleviation by the people themselves.

What should our role be, if anything? What could a formally organized, publicly paid for, outsider-driven development industry accomplish? Well, very little, and most of it indirect. And whatever few things it may make sense for "us" to do for "them," must be done with a light hand. These things, moreover, will have few easily measurable effects, will surely take far *less* money than is presently being applied, and will involve far fewer and much smaller organizations to manage them.

Romance

Morocco, Thanksgiving 1964

B EN R YMAKER was so excited he hadn't minded the eighteen hours on rickety buses. The mountain town he'd arrived in was quiet at eleven in the morning. The air was cold, and the bright sun made the poplar trees silvery.

This would be his chance to see his friends from training, to be an American again. Turkey, stuffing — he couldn't imagine how Bing had put it together but believed the promises he'd made in his letter.

The two months since he'd begun his job at the ancient Koranic university to which he'd been assigned seemed like a long time, though he knew it wasn't. What an adventure it had been. For the first time in Ben's twenty-two years, he was happy and knew he was happy, both at once.

Ben's house in the medina of Marrakech, across the street from the old palace of the pasha, his landlord had said, once had a tunnel under the street to connect it to the palace. The house had been built for the palace guards. It was a big beige cube, unassuming from the outside, invisible among the others in the street, but huge and ornate inside.

The street in front of his house was a Hollywood film set to Ben. Every morning when he opened his door he was stunned. Every form of wheeled vehicle moved by: donkey carts and men pulling makeshift wagons made of parts from junked vehicles with tires so worn they weren't round anymore. People on mobylettes, people driving black Solex bikes, men on mules and horses, driving old cars. Black Citroens from the late forties, Peugeot group taxis filled with ten men and women arriving from their villages in the High Atlas Mountains, and buses blurting awful black smoke and tilting as they went by, their frames teetering on top of bent axles and barely supported by springs gone flat.

This was one of the main thoroughfares of the old city. Weaving through it, on foot, were women in djellabas, heading to the vegetable souk nearby, veiled, the outline of their mouths in the black gauze of their veils, and men too, as well as clumps of boys and girls dressed in blue smocks on their way to school.

Everyday Ben dragged his red Schwinn bicycle out of the house and locked the door behind him. The Peace Corps had issued him the bike. He felt lucky to get it, since there were only a few available. Indeed, he felt lucky in other ways too. He was one of only a handful of volunteers to be assigned to Marrakech, the most traditional city in Morocco's south. He loved it. He was far from the capital city, far from the Peace Corps headquarters, and the only foreigner teaching at Koutoubia University. He had learned his way around the medina, one of the largest in the country, without even realizing how complex it was. He took in so much color, so much detail, that in three weeks he could find his way to almost any corner of it.

He'd get on the bike and begin his trip to the school, through the western side of the medina. In the United States, Ben had been shy. He had no experience being seen or noticed, having always shied away from attention, his fear of embarrassment more than overwhelming his secret hopes for recognition. But here he was, riding a one-speed, red, American-made Schwinn, with high chrome handlebars, a monster compared with anything made in Europe or Africa. People were aghast, staring at Ben and the bike, so odd in its size, color, and shape and, to their eyes, so laughably cumbersome. The children did laugh, point, and throw small stones at Ben, every morning, all along his route.

But he didn't mind it. He loved it. It did not, it could not, occur to him that people might be in any way hostile toward his presence. He had come to Morocco to help, to teach English, to be an agent of modernization and development. He had had choices, like all the people in his group of thirty-two volunteers. The United States in 1964 had a booming economy. Less than half of high school graduates went on to college, and virtually all those who finished had entry-level jobs in many fields for the asking, or opportunities to go to graduate or professional schools. On the moral plane there were also choices, more and different from the ones available to people coming out of school in the 1940s or 1950s. The civil rights movement was gripping many in the country, and John Kennedy's New Frontier had struck strong chords with so many people who wanted to play a role in the new world. Ben's generation was eager to do something that made a difference.

But Ben had no clear view that he was going to save the world. He had wrestled with the question during the group's training at Princeton when the Goodman, Schwerner, and Chaney murders had occurred that summer. Many nights were spent with his fellow trainees asking out loud whether it was right to go off to Africa then. One of them was quitting the Peace Corps to go to Mississippi and point blank said to the group that they ought to face up to the problems in their own country first. "When they are solved," he had said, "you can all go off to play Lawrence of Arabia."

Honest with himself up to a point, Ben admitted that Morocco, a country he had hardly heard of before his assignment arrived in the mail, was far more romantic than Alabama, far more exciting, and offered a window to a larger world. He wanted, after all, to gain something for himself, to have an adventure, to grow, to learn a new language. Secretly, he wanted to get away from the familiar. It was too harsh, he understood its reality too well. The civil rights struggle, for all he didn't know and understand about it, represented for Ben a very layered history; its origins and its grievances cried for redress, a goal too enormous for Ben to believe in any easy solution. Morocco, though Ben did not articulate it to himself in this way, offered adventure plus a chance to believe one might make a difference in a setting that was fresh. Ben, a foreigner and an outsider, could conveniently ignore that Morocco too had a complex history. Anyway, he was not made of the same stuff as Chaney, Schwerner, or Goodman, and he knew it.

The training program was rigorous. Most of the trainees had been good students at good schools. They knew the Peace Corps standards were tough and were made aware that they were being judged and could be "terminated" from the program. Yet the structure and the curriculum during their training were familiar, as was the setting, being little different from college. They knew that some Peace Corps volunteers, or

PCVs as they were called, elsewhere were being trained in boot camp–type circumstances, but those trainees were being sent to rural assignments in jungles and rain forests. Ben's group were to be teachers. Teachers going to Morocco needed to learn to teach, to understand the history and culture of the country.

The Peace Corps, now in its third full year of operation, had already begun to take on some of the new learning that U.S. government agencies, especially in the development assistance realm, were now espousing, particularly the idea of subcontracting as a more efficient way to do the government's business. The Peace Corps could not handle all training directly, especially now that the number of volunteers was expanding so rapidly. Thus training for different groups was contracted out, sometimes to a private agency but more often to a university. Princeton was under contract to design and provide the training program, and because French was the language being taught to the trainees, the head of the training program was a faculty member in the French department.

This struck only a few of the trainees as odd, since at that time Morocco had been independent of France for only eight years. As the trainees would be teaching English in secondary schools, the reality was that these schools were still being run by the French.

Two Moroccans had been hired to offer other parts of the training, one a graduate student in political science, the other a linguist who had just finished a degree in the United States and would soon be returning to Morocco as an inspector with the Ministry of Education in Rabat.

Every day the trainees heard lectures from both and found themselves passive witnesses to an increasingly volatile debate between the two Moroccans, who did not share similar politics. One was a radical and a closet atheist, the other a conservative and a devout Muslim. The former conveyed to the trainees how far Morocco had to go to become modern, and the latter, what a wonderful place Morocco was right then and now. The trainees welcomed both messages and liked the two men equally.

Missing was discussion of whether the Peace Corps was wanted in Morocco. Nor did anyone at any time raise or entertain doubt about the trainees' role as PCVs in Morocco. It was simply assumed that the three goals of the Peace Corps — to make friends for America, to help others develop and modernize, and to bring knowledge of other cultures back to America — were legitimate and sensible.

The days were full, and friendships were made quickly, bound by the shared sense of going off on a mission far away. The Atlantic was wide in 1964, and of the thirty-two trainees, all college graduates, all middle

class, only two had crossed it before. If he had given much thought to jus-
tifying the experience, and he had not, the anchor of Ben's rationaliza-
tion — what gave his choice intellectual coherence — was his belief that
relations between people were paramount and would always be the
foundation of development. Though he had been a history major in college, the subject was unconnected in his mind to development. And so
he had little interest in applying history to the larger forces in development, not to mention economics, trade, climate, or natural resource endowments. Development, in Ben's inchoate theory, was a matter of psychology — a function of attitude. Modernization was to him a good thing
in and of itself; furthermore, it was inevitable. But it could be fostered
and made a healthier process if people could be influenced, helped to
be less afraid of change, more open to it.

He didn't believe in differences. He thought what people carried in
their heads and hearts was fundamentally the same everywhere, and if
he himself had been malleable, open to learning new things, then he
believed others could be helped to be so. His own background also
explained his motivation and his inability to entertain any but the most
magnanimous view of Moroccans. The son of European refugees from
Hitler, Ben had had hardly any religious upbringing but still identified
with Jewish culture. He was not only aware of the perversity of being a
Jew in a Muslim land, of studying Arabic when he had never spent ten
minutes learning Hebrew, but he also got a kick out of it and told himself he was an exemplar of the New Frontier — a citizen of the world.

On his bike riding through the medina, smiling and laughing as he
dodged the small stones the kids threw at him, he would yell *"sir f'halek,
red'd ban,"* from his bike, "make way, get out of the way," throwing out
the phrases in a Marakchi accent. How different he was from the Ugly
American. How different even from the nice embassy people he and his
group had met during their week of orientation in Rabat, Morocco's capital. Here he was, not even in the country ten weeks, and already fear-
lessly speaking the language, living among the people. And at every moment, on duty as well as off, he was doing his job. Not only was he
exposing Moroccans to something new, he was entertaining them too.
All Marrakech was his stage.

Arriving at the school, he'd walk into his classroom. The students were
older than he was, and many wore beards. They had never in their lives
been exposed to another language besides Arabic. This was an experiment. In the 930-year history of this institution, only Koranic studies
were taught. The Koutoubia University was one of a line of institutions

throughout the Islamic world where men became scholars of Islam. Ben knew, at the same time, that while these students certainly had a genuine interest in Islam, they were here in part because they had not succeeded in making it in the French-oriented system, that instead of being tracked into LM (Lettres Modernes), they were tracked into LO (Lettres Originelles). Ben found no irony in this. To him, Lettres Modernes was the better system. This was where Moroccans would learn French *and* English, where they would prepare to run the country in a modern way and thus contribute to Morocco joining the community of nations. LO, he knew, as did the students, was a backwater. When the Ministry of Education decided to offer English to LO students, it seemed to Ben a great concept, rightly democratic. It isn't right to track students who did less well and lock them forever in a system with no connection to the real world. So when his assignment was explained to him, he was eager and enthusiastic. Here was a chance to make a difference, to be the first English teacher in 930 years! But his Peace Corps director in Rabat had been apologetic about the assignment. For Ben would be given eleven classes to teach, each with over forty students, and required to prepare for and teach each class for two hours per week. This load was considerably greater than the average. Ben said he'd take it on, gladly.

But he had not reckoned with the daily frustration of trying to apply an utterly modern method of teaching a foreign language (only just coming into use in the United States) in a context where students had spent their entire learning lives (in some instances thirty years) learning by rote, memorizing words and sentences, hadith and Koranic sura written out painstakingly in whitewash on a wooden board called a *luh*.

Ben began by doing what he had been taught to do. Indoctrinated in the new Oral/Aural method, a true believer in the purism of English Only, Ben began on the first day by walking in and saying "Hello, my name is Ben. What's yours?" He repeated this over and over again, as he had been taught to do, going to each student, pointing to himself when he said the name "Ben" and touching the student on the shoulder when asking "What's yours?" He would act out the response, saying "My name is Mohamed," "My name is Abdulkarim," "My name is Hassan," waiting patiently, though with a slightly reddening face, for someone to take the bait. Fifteen minutes passed slowly. Nothing. Blank stares. Undaunted, Ben continued all week, trying to get through. Nothing.

Abruptly, he threw in the towel and reverted to using the little Arabic he had, explaining, as best as he could, what he wanted them to say. The "method" went out the window, and while this sat uneasily with him, indeed it gnawed at him, Ben had seen that he had to adjust to the particular circumstances he was faced with. By the fifth week, Ben had virtually abandoned the teaching of English. The days became sessions filled with broken conversations in which the students lectured him on Arabic and Islam and plied him, assaulted him, with questions about America, the questions always laced with opinions they wanted verified.

It had dawned on Ben that if the tracking system was wrong, then the reality was that the linguistic road to modernity, in 1964 at least, was French first and foremost and only then, perhaps, English. By the seventh week Ben had concluded that the ministry had no business trying to foist colloquial English — American English! — on bearded thirty-year-olds who knew no French.

When Ben arrived at Bing's, he felt like a veteran. This would be the first get-together of the trainees since they had gone to their assignments. Travel in Morocco was slow. A bus ride of a few hundred miles could take a day and a half, and time was short, since Thanksgiving was not a Moroccan holiday. Those who were able to attend Bing's dinner had had to juggle their teaching schedules, at some risk since the *proviseurs* of their respective schools tended to be tough old Frenchmen who did not take the Americans seriously to begin with.

Six PCVs were gathered at Bing's house when Ben arrived. There were slaps on the back and bear hugs and laughter as he arrived. Two of the volunteers Ben hadn't seen since the day they'd all landed — they were posted deep in the south, the most remote area in the country.

The little group's greetings became a raucous din. Recounting their adventures, in rapid-fire speech, already peppered with French and Moroccan phrases and words, everyone burst forth with anecdotes, laughing and talking all at once. They all told stories, all of them hilariously funny, about their students, their encounters with the school administrators, and the funny ways of some of the Moroccans they had come to know. As the afternoon went on, the stories turned inward, and people began admitting more personal things. The time the kids threw stones at Joe because he didn't know he was not to enter the girls' side of the school. The time Rob got invited to the provincial governor's house and was forced to eat a sheep's eye, only to discover later that none of the Moroccans present would touch them. The time Ben got sunstroke hitchhiking to Ouarzazate, like an idiot, at midday without a hat on. And other faux pas they had made before they had learned the ropes and the language. A few admitted how lonely they had been, how much they missed home.

There was gossip and an obligatory catching each other up on family happenings at home in Minnesota, Boston, California, Virginia, on siblings and parents whom no one else had met. There was much comparison of diseases — who had become sick and for how long, who had lost the most weight, who looked the most ravaged by dysentery. Somehow there was this sense of survival, as if they had all come through a battle in a war. Everyone was smoking cheap Moroccan cigarettes and drinking. The wine flowed. Love was in the air — self-love and love for these friends, friends who felt so close that day, so much like oneself, so on the same plane, so proud. When the turkey arrived, it brought everything together.

Bing had raised it himself. A farmboy from western Massachusetts, he had planned this meal since the day he arrived. The *bibi* (Moroccan Arabic for turkey) was huge, twelve or thirteen kilos. It had had to be taken to the skeptical local baker, the only one with an oven big enough to hold it. Bing had arranged to have the whole group go to the oven with great fanfare to pick up the cooked bird, and as the little group of friends accompanied him and the turkey, the town's onlookers cheered, or seemed to. No stones were being thrown here. Bing was the town celebrity.

Everyone was hungry. Ben and the others sat around the low Moroccan table. The turkey was to be served, as were all the dishes, in Moroccan style. Nothing had been easier to adapt to than this. Everyone was by now adept at eating with their hands and, like converts, were strict about the rules. Never use your left hand, place the most succulent pieces of meat away from you, preferably to be given to others seated near you, feel free to express yourself by burping, and so on.

Ben ate ravenously. Someone took a picture. He still has it. It shows a young man with thick black wavy hair, a handsome face, holding an enormous drumstick away from his mouth, pausing to smile into the camera, mouth slightly rimmed with brown gravy, giddily satisfied, wildly happy.

Illusion

Marrakech, Morocco,
December 1964

By the middle of December, Ben's days had become so routine that he began to feel he had lived in Marrakech as long as any old-time resident. Not only did he know his way around the medina, but he also began to believe that he knew what was going on. He had a regular vegetable seller, knew the man who picked up his garbage in a donkey-drawn cart, chatted amiably with the butcher, knew how to choose mint for his tea from the man who sold ten kinds of it, and even had a regular spot at a café in the ville nouvelle where he met with three other foreigners once a week. A delicate balance between his "work" at the school and the pleasure he gained from the interaction with his students — really a long, friendly conversation in which he was the center of attention — had now been achieved. He loved being greeted as "Ustad Ben," an honorific that in the school's context had overtones of religious respect, of learnedness. Ben was beginning to be engulfed in a warm cocoon embellished and constructed in his imagination.

One morning Ben rode his bike to school, taking his usual route. As he approached the walled compound of his school, he sensed commotion, heard noise, saw dust rising in the air. As soon as the school was in sight, Ben saw fire trucks and, through the dust, incredibly, army tanks and troops. The school was surrounded by police and soldiers, not in a tight circle but in a casual formation, as if waiting for orders to get organized.

Ben slowed as he approached, then sped up. Something was happening here, something was wrong with this picture, something totally new to Ben. But it did not occur to him that whatever was happening could affect him or was noteworthy or serious. The scene had no references in Ben's experience. Army troops and tanks simply had no sensible association with schools and students. Further, this was not the U.S. Army but the Moroccan Army. Ben would have felt trepidation had it been the U.S. Army or, even worse, New York cops. But this was the Moroccan Army, and somehow, without realizing it, the soldiers were to Ben as picturesque as Marrakech's ocher buildings and the blue sky over the Atlas Mountains. Thus immunized, Ben rode his Schwinn right through the troops to the gate of the school, smiling wonderingly. There he was stopped by two soldiers. "Go away," they gestured to him. Ben ignored them. He searched to the left and the right, looking for someone who appeared as if he might speak French. He spotted an officer, perhaps a lieutenant, and went up to him, leaving his bike leaning against the wall.

"Good morning, sir, could you tell me what is going on here?"

The young officer looked at Ben coldly: "Who are *you*? You shouldn't be here. Foreigners are not allowed here today."

"But I'm a teacher at this school," Ben replied, "and I have classes to teach this morning."

"There will be no classes today. You'd better go home and keep away from the school. There will be trouble later on."

Unsatisfied with this reply, Ben turned and walked back to his bike. Without hesitation, he opened the small wooden door that allowed people to go into the courtyard without opening the main gates, and went in.

In the courtyard, hundreds of students were milling about, busily moving back and forth between the classrooms that surrounded the square hard-mud court and dragging all the desks, chairs, and anything movable from every classroom. These were growing into an enormous pile in the center of the courtyard, one now at least ten feet high.

Ben could not understand what was happening. He looked for other teachers, for the supervisor, for anyone from the school administration, but not one of them was in sight. Only students. No one noticed Ben. He spotted two of his favorite students carrying a desk. These were young men in their midtwenties who spoke a smattering of French.

"What are you doing, Hsein? What are you doing, Mohamed?" he asked, his voice rising.

Both young men stared at Ben, with a look that made him think they were much older and wiser than he had realized, perhaps considerably older and wiser than Ben himself.

"You'd better go home," they said, without addressing Ben by name, but with great courtesy. "You don't belong here. This has nothing to do with you. It could be dangerous for you to be here. Please leave."

"But what is happening?" Ben yelled. "I want to understand what you are doing. We are supposed to be in class. What are you doing with the desks and chairs? They belong in the classroom. We must all go in and have our class."

The two young men stopped. "M'sieu," they said, "the students all over Morocco are on strike. We are going to burn the chairs and desks. Then the soldiers will come inside the school and beat us. Some of us will go to the hospital. Some of us may be killed. You must leave. There will be no classes."

"Killed!" "On strike!" Ben was incredulous. What an idea — students on strike? What insanity, students burning chairs and desks, expecting soldiers to beat them. This was absolutely incomprehensible. He turned to the two students and said, the frustration in his voice tinged with outrage: "But you cannot strike. You are students. This is a school. No one will hurt you. You must go back to the classroom."

At this, the older of the two young men, Hsein, put his arm on Ben's and gently but firmly began leading him to the gate of the school. "M'sieu," he said in his broken French, "you must leave, and you must leave now."

Ben went back through the gate, picked up his big Schwinn bike, and slowly walked to the road facing the school. Now he could see that a crowd had begun to gather at the road's edge. Silently, the onlookers, including many women, perhaps the mothers of some of the students, were settling in, as if for a long wait. They, the soldiers, and the fire trucks, with their water hoses trained on the school gates, were all standing there, waiting.

Confused, stunned, humiliated, angry, Ben began peddling furiously, turning left onto the widest boulevard in the city, Blvd. Mohamed V. He was heading three miles northward to the ville nouvelle the French had built, parallel to but far away from the medina, which the French thought of as the "native" city. The French built their parallel cities in part for strategic reasons. Here, in the tree-lined avenues of the ville nouvelle, the French administrators and their families, the merchants, and the professionals would feel at home, in a replica of France, and be free to live life their way and be safe.

Ben went to the Café Tout Va Bien. His twenty-minute bike ride had brought him to France, to a corner café in Provence, with palm trees, shade, and *pastis*. Hoping he would find a few foreigners to talk to, some old-timers who could explain what was going on, Ben sat down at a table and ordered a Flag Pils, the locally made beer. As he drank, he began to realize how shaken he was. This country was not so familiar now. Had he made too many assumptions about Morocco that were really convenient avenues for his own unfulfilled hopes? It struck him that he had built a Morocco that existed only for Ben, that had no life of its own. The truth, which he was beginning to see — was that the students at the university had no particular love for him. They had not asked Ben to come from America. No one had. Perhaps the stones the little kids in the street threw at Ben and his red Schwinn were not thrown with such gaiety and fun as Ben thought. Were the friendly smiles of the butcher and the vegetable seller real? Ben was now not so sure.

CHAPTER ONE

The Developing World and Its Condition

An inveterate observer of poverty whom I knew in the late 1960s used to calculate how much time it would take for a cigarette butt dropped on a city street to be picked up by someone else. When he dropped a butt on a busy street in Fès, Morocco, and it just sat there for minutes, attracting no interest, he declared definitively that Morocco was not poor.

Academics and development professionals would not be content with such a method, though it does establish, albeit crudely, the idea of thresholds of poverty. In any case, classifying the developing countries has evolved as the development assistance industry has. Many ways now exist to measure and judge which countries count as poor and which are less poor.

Before "political correctness," the "third world" was the commonly used term for poor countries. Even though "third world" was originally intended to signify a world that was neither the West nor the communist "East," the subtext naturally enough took on the sense of a ranking: to be first is a good thing; to be third, less good. Within the development assistance profession, the term has dropped from official use in recent years in part because of this invidious connotation, but also because the cold war has ended and, even as a rough ranking, "third" is no longer terribly descriptive. The world, even the old "third world," is now much more segmented than it used to be.[1]

Nonetheless, the manner in which the International Monetary Fund (IMF) classifies countries still begins with a convenient threefold broad typology. There are the "advanced economies," which the IMF counted in 1999 as numbering 28; the "developing countries," which despite their differences are considered as a group (of 127); and the "countries in transition" (largely the former Soviet Union and Eastern European countries), which number 28, for a total of 183 countries. Current shorthand refers to the advanced economies as the "north" and the developing countries as the "south."

Within the 127 "developing countries" there is great variety, as there is in

1. I continue to use "third world" in the text because it has become a convenient short phrase that many people inside and outside the development industry still use.

the methods used to measure how they are doing on their path to development. Gross national product (GNP)—the Dow Jones index of development—used to be favored. But the descriptive value of GNP has begun to fade, partly because it does not capture the dimensions of poverty, or "quality of life." To do so requires such measures as the Human Development Index (HDI), which statistically combines life expectancy, adult literacy, school enrolment, and per capita gross domestic product (GDP).

Another shorthand way to capture poverty differences between rich and poor is to note the causes of death. Organizations such as the World Health Organization track the changing causes of death and morbidity in the developing nations, as well as infant mortality rates. Heart disease is a rare cause of death in poor countries and a leading killer in the north. This is in part due to diet but it is also a statistical artifact—in the "north" people live long enough to get heart disease in the first place, whereas in the "south" they do not. What we in the north might call "mundane" diseases (e.g., respiratory infections and diarrhea) are the leading causes of death in the developing world. Measles, whooping cough, and typhoid, despite lowering rates of these diseases owing to immunization programs, are still on the top-twenty lists. Acquired immunodeficiency syndrome (AIDS) is, of course, a new killer.

Among the establishment economists, how the developing countries derive their export earnings is one ranking that has gained currency in recent years. Export earnings are important because they are a proxy for the degree to which a country is part of a global market. And since the world is becoming global, if a poor country is not competing successfully in it or, worse yet, not part of the global market at all, it is not merely isolated but also likely to be and remain poor.

A little over 30 percent of the developing countries (forty of them) derive their main source of export earnings from primary products—natural endowments that come from the earth. About the same number (thirty-nine countries) get their export earnings from what the IMF calls "services," "factor income," and "private transfers." This group would include Jamaica, the Dominican Republic, Jordan, Panama, and so on. "Services" might include tourism; "factor income" means such things as commission income from shipping agencies or income derived from any agent type of function; and "private transfers" (a growing part of many economies in the developing countries) is everything from an immigrant dishwasher in New York sending money home, to temporary workers in the Persian Gulf, who'll spend two years, five men to a room, earning enough to start a business when they return home. The smallest number of the developing countries (six) make their export earnings from manufacturing. This elite 5 percent includes China, India, Malaysia, Pakistan, Thailand, and Brazil.

It is among the first two groups (a total of 79 countries) that we find the poorest countries, those which are on the edge of survival. Many of them need foreign aid to subsist, and to them development assistance represents significant money. For example, Burkina Faso had an annual government budget of $492 million in 1995 and received about $485 million in foreign aid, or roughly 98 percent of its budget. Laos in 1997 received over 80 percent of its budget in aid; Benin, about 60 percent; Nepal, about 50 percent; Ethiopia, about 25 percent; and Kenya, 15 percent. A handful of the very poorest receive more in aid than their annual budgets, the champion being Haiti, which received over $730 million in aid (1995) and had an annual budget of about $360 million. In fact, between the mid- and late 1990s, Haiti, with a GDP almost two hundred times smaller than India, received between a quarter and a half as much foreign aid as did India.[2]

There are still other ways of categorizing the developing countries. At the bottom of the heap are what many in the development profession refer to privately as "basket case" countries or "beggar" nations. Some are in this state because of civil strife and intermittent war and were not always so badly off (Liberia and Sierra Leone are recent examples). Academics have begun to refer to such countries accurately as "failed" or "collapsed" states. Others simply have few resources of any kind, including the resource of geography itself. Chad, Niger, and Mali are completely landlocked and have large proportions of desert and few people. In terms of their potential in a rapidly evolving global marketplace, it is hard to see these states having a bright sustainable economic future anytime soon.

The increasingly complex classifications of countries and poverty depend on increasingly sophisticated statistics. Thousands of things are now routinely measured, from the share of smallholder farmers in total crop production to food staple self-sufficiency, to daily caloric intakes, to the percentage of the population with access to services such as health, water and sanitation, to rural-urban differences in access to those services, to the ratio of the proportion of the agriculturally active population to that of the general rural population, to the rate of the spread of landlessness. These measurements have lent themselves to numerous and different indexes of poverty, such as the Relative Welfare Index, the Food Security Index, the Basic Needs Index, the Human Development Index, and the Integrated Poverty Index (IPI). The IPI requires some math skill; it "is determined on the basis of the percentage of the rural population below the poverty line, the income-gap ratio (difference in GNP per capita income of the country from the highest in the sample of total countries expressed as a percentage of the latter), the distribution of income below the poverty line as reflected

2. *World Factbook* 2000, online ed. (Washington, D.C.: Central Intelligence Agency, 2001); see <http://www.cia.gov/cia/publications/factbook>.

in the life expectancy at birth, and the rate of growth in GNP per capita."[3] The debate about how best to categorize poor countries remains perennial, if not very spirited. Still, it is generally accepted that the international poverty line is $1 per person per day (at 1985 prices). Using that measure, between a fifth and a sixth of the world's population (over 1 billion people) are poor. And the next group up on the ladder (who might have double the income, or $2 per person per day) are not dramatically better off in real terms. Indeed, if $2 per person per day were the cutoff point for poverty, then three times as many people (3 billion), or half of the world, would officially be considered poor.

Another accepted criterion for determining which countries are the "poorest" is a per capita income of $785 or less in 1996 dollars. The Organization for Economic Cooperation and Development (OECD) in Paris still uses per capita GNP to create five categories of poor countries and territories. In 1998 these were (1) least developed (called "LLDCs," they have well under $765 in 1995 dollars), of which there were 48, most of them in Africa; (2) low income (under $765), of which there were 24, including Albania and Mongolia; (3) lower middle income (called "LMICs," $766 to $3,035), of which there were 53, including Morocco and El Salvador; (4) upper middle (called "UMICs," $3,036 to $9,385), of which there were 27 countries, including Malaysia, Gabon, and Uruguay; and (5) high income (over $9,385).

These typologies remain at best a dry compendium of numbers. They serve an illustrative purpose but are, in any case, "temporary." Who is on which list changes constantly, not just with how poverty is measured but year to year, even month to month, as prospects change (such as discovering oil), wars end, and aid begins to flow again — or as other countries fall into collapse. For example, in 1998 the poorest five countries in terms of life expectancy at birth, infant mortality, and adult literacy rates (from most poor to least) were Mozambique, Ethiopia, Somalia, Malawi, and Bangladesh. But the 1999 rankings based on the Human Development Index (which takes per capita GDP into account) list the poorest five as Sierra Leone, Niger, Ethiopia, Burkina Faso, and Burundi. Or, if only GDP per capita were used, in 1999 the five poorest (again from most poor to least) would be Democratic Republic of the Congo (formerly Zaire), Rwanda, Ethiopia, Sierra Leone, and Chad.

These last five countries all had GDP per capita in the $400 to $670 range. These are, of course, averages, which means that many people have much less annual cash than these amounts. Nonetheless, what Americans spend per household (on average) for food outside the home (restaurants, fast food, coffee at Dunkin Donuts on the way to work) is equal to the per

3. Idriss Jazairy, Mohiuddin Alamgir, and Theresa Panuccio, *The State of World Rural Poverty* (Rome: IFAD, 1992), 35.

capita GDP of Congo, Rwanda, Ethiopia, and Sierra Leone combined; what Americans spend on average per household on entertainment is equal to the GDP per capita of Ethiopia, Sierra Leone, and Chad combined.

How do the poor themselves define poverty? In the 1950s, when my grandfather was in his eighties, he would sit on the porch waiting for a slightly younger, septuagenarian acquaintance of his to pass by. The other man, who was born in the 1880s, forty miles from Manhattan, but had never seen New York City or gone past the third grade, would look at my grandfather and say, "Hey, Pops, got money in the bank?" And my grandfather, who knew little English, would nod and reply, "Yah, money in the bank."

What seems to count most in defining poverty to the poor themselves is the degree of control they have over their lives. That can simply be security, knowing that if something bad happens you have a secure safety net. And security can be land, lots of children, or safe savings.

Or control can be choices — not just the freedom to choose but also the actuality of the options themselves, having them and knowing about them. For a poor person in southern Sudan, choices are severely curtailed or nonexistent. If you are a woman, you may have no choice about who or when you marry or about when and how often you become pregnant. You have little or no choice about what kind and what amount of food you give to your child. If your child becomes sick (which is almost a given), you likely have little choice about what to do, just as you had no options about preventing the illness in the first place. Nor can you choose when you work, how you work, or what work you do. If you farm for subsistence and bad weather wipes out your crop, your choice is to starve, beg, or walk. If you farm to have a salable surplus after meeting your own needs and bad weather does not wipe out your crop, you have little choice about the selling price of your surplus, since you cannot store the surplus and you cannot transport it very far to find a different "market." If someone threatens you, you do not have the choice of going to the "authorities" or getting a lawyer. And so on. All the examples of measures and statistics which were put forward at the beginning of this chapter, particularly the old standbys on infant mortality, life expectancy at birth, and other social indicators such as adult literacy rate, are simply ways to express with some scientific rigor poor people's limited ability to exercise real choice over their fate.

In the 1890s Mark Twain described poverty in India by mixing his own rudimentary statistical analysis with a sardonic eye:

A farm-hand's wages were only half a rupee (former value) a month — that is to say, less than a cent a day; nearly $2.90 a year. If such a wage-earner had a good deal of a family — and they all have that, for God is very good to these poor natives in some ways — he would save a profit of fifteen cents, clean and clear, out of his year's toil; I mean a frugal, thrifty person would, not one given to display and ostentation. And if he owed $13.50 and took good care of his health, he could pay it off in ninety years. Then he could hold up his head, and look his creditors in the face again.

Think of these facts and what they mean. India does not consist of cities. There are no cities in India — to speak of. Its stupendous population consists of farm-laborers. India is one vast farm — one almost interminable stretch of field with mud fences between. Think of the above facts; and consider what an incredible aggregate of poverty they place before you."[4]

To put it another way, very poor countries are places where most people's lives suffer the essential condition Mark Twain observed a century ago — no matter what you do, even if you possess those wonderfully protestant quali-ties of frugality and thrift and are not "given to display and ostentation" — the options to change your condition are few or none.

Why are some countries poorer than others? In 1957 the per capita GDP of South Korea was $491 and that of Ghana was $490. At the end of the 1980s Ghana's GDP per capita stood around $400 and that of South Korea had moved up to $2,000. Whenever any of us in the development profession began to lose faith, it was "miracles" like those of the Asian Tigers that re-kindled it. These numbers also rekindled the interest in the primus inter pares of all development questions: Why are some countries poorer than others? or Why do some grow, while others do not?

It would seem to follow that if this huge question had easy answers, then development assistance could and would be effective. The surprise is that there *are* answers; moreover, they are not inaccessible. The development industry's failure to reduce poverty and foster real development attests to how ill equipped it is to do much about what it knows.

The factors which explain poverty (and wealth) and with which no one much argues exist on a spectrum that extends from the physical to the ephemeral — from hard to soft. These factors follow below. The very real problem for the development industry is that no one of these factors alone explains very much; they operate in interaction with each other in ways that make it close to impossible to "engineer" the development process.

Geography, topography, size, climate, soil, natural resources (water, min-erals, fauna and flora such as forests, and so on), population growth, and density are what could be called "hard factors." These "hard factors" make a big difference in whether a country is going to be wealthy or will have to struggle to come out of poverty.

Moving toward the softer end of the spectrum, other factors begin to com-bine with this first set and with each other. These include:

---

4. Mark Twain, *Following the Equator* (Hartford, Conn.: American Publishing Company; New York: Doubleday and McClure, 1897), 360.

- History. Has the country been in isolation, had some contact with others, or had much contact with others? What was the nature of the contact — for example, was contact as the result of benign migration, conquest, colonialism, war, or linguistic or cultural interchange? Answers to such questions help explain a country's wealth or poverty, as do the questions under the factors below.
- Trade. What kind, with whom, under what terms, and how intense? Is the country strongly outward-looking or only moderately so in its trade relations?
- Internal movement. Can things and people move around the country? By river, canal, or road? What sort of infrastructure has there been/can there be? (Sometimes a mountain just cannot be moved.)
- Human factors. Historical factors interact over time with such human factors as culture, language, and identity. Is the country more or less homogeneous? If not homogeneous, then do people get along with each other? Is there stability and security? Stability and security in turn have to do with government. What is the history and form of government?
- Health. How healthy are the people in the country? Though obviously a complicated matter, health is an important prerequisite for development. If everyone is sick all or part of the time, productivity, and much else, is affected. If many people die young, culture and society have adjustments to make. Whether the people in a country are healthy depends on historical and physical factors too. Epidemiologists now know that one of the most important interventions people can make to improve their own basic health is washing their hands with soap. But that requires water and soap, or the basics from which soap can be made. The causal loop becomes more intertwined.

Further yet toward the soft end of the spectrum are the institutions of society: law, justice, finance, government, and formal religion. Is there what is today called "good governance"? (Are those who govern the institutions of society responsible to the ostensible goals of those institutions or to themselves? Are they disinterested or self-interested?) How widespread and how deep does corruption go? If people have the wherewithal to pay taxes, do they do so? Is there democracy and a free flow of information? What are the institutions of what is now called "civil society," and how do they function (voluntary associations, organized religion, and so forth)? Are there systematized human rights, legal rights, and property rights?

In the economic institutions, are the policies conducive to wealth creation? Do they enable or do they repress entrepreneurship? Are price incentives "right"? What about other incentives?

Today it is the soft factors that reign in the thinking about why some nations remain poor. Rather than asking about poverty, we are coming back to asking about wealth and about growth. Adam Smith in 1776 wrote *An Inquiry into the Nature and Causes of the Wealth of Nations*, establishing an enduring analytic model. But growth theory has not been sexy during much of the last few decades of the development endeavor and has only relatively recently come back into vogue, with some embellishments. We have added to the Smithian neoclassical model a recognition that human capital is as significant (if not more so) than physical and financial capital, and we have woven into the model an essential element from psychology — namely, that people respond to incentives. Hence there is a new interest in the conditions that would increase incentives for productivity and wealth accumulation. "Getting the policies right" has therefore become one of the mantras for development interventions. Likewise, both the size and relative weight of the government's hand (Is the government light- or heavy-handed?) are major points of reference in the debate. Finally, we are adding to the debate such factors as a country's ability or inability to use resources (physical and human) well or poorly. With this last point we are at the threshold of recognizing that the development profession itself—the mere promise of financial aid and the presence of outside experts — can exacerbate inefficiencies (e.g., Has the country gone into debt to the IMF and World Bank to become "developed"?). But official development assistance agencies as a group have not yet dared to admit that official development assistance itself can be a disincentive for development.

At the most ephemeral end of the hard-soft continuum we come to culture. There are many questions to ask here, including: Does the culture emphasize the individual, the collectivity, or community? Do women have the same opportunities as men? What are the components of the "national character"? Is there an ethic of accumulation? Is great value attached to the extended family? How is "social capital" formed and maintained? And, as all cultures adapt and change, how is that change taking place? Back the loop goes to history and the "hard" physical factors.

It is easy to see why the development industry suffers from the blind-men-touching-the-elephant problem, where each man, touching a different part, describes a different animal. Development assistance practitioners may understand *that* all these factors are intertwined and may even grasp *how* they are intertwined, but such understanding does not translate into a blueprint for making it happen.

A Straw in the Wind

The Middle Atlas Mountains,
Morocco, 1971

BEN DID NOT BEGIN to understand poverty until Karim died. Or at least he had not yet realized that its essence lay far deeper than surface effects such as the cardboard paper slums he'd seen. Every week Karim's father, Abdulhaq, whom Ben had hired to supplement his regular Arabic lessons, came into town from his village to sit with Ben for ninety minutes and converse in colloquial dialect. Ben had returned to Morocco as a twenty-eight-year-old Ph.D. candidate to do his anthropological fieldwork in a small town in the Middle Atlas. In that quiescent period in Morocco between the end of colonialism and before mass tourism, only a dozen or so foreigners would pass through town each year, and only one foreigner, an aging Dane, was a longtime resident. When Ben arrived, word had quickly got around that another foreigner was in town who might be a source of income. He'd hired Abdulhaq because he had been aggressive enough to come to Ben's door and knock. Abdulhaq had come to offer his services, any service Ben could use that might earn Abdulhaq a bit of money.

Abdulhaq was a thin man in his thirties. His wore his hair just shy of being shaved completely bald. His nut-brown triangular face, with its high cheekbones and almond-shaped eyes fit the common image of the Berber lineage. Abdulhaq's village, one thousand meters higher in altitude than Ben's town, was fifteen miles away but took almost two hours to get to by car, and that was when the steep, rocky track was dry. Before there were motor vehicles, people came to Ben's town on market days by mule or on foot. Several times Abdulhaq walked to see Ben, arriving the evening before their lesson, saying he had stayed the night with a friend in town whom he never named.

Abdulhaq's village was the burial site of a famous saint, whose tomb was visited seasonally by pilgrims from many parts of the country. These people, poor themselves, provided a small but steady income to supplement the meager amount of cash that a few people made from olives, the principal crop. Villagers subsisted, planting grains on odd-shaped stony plots one hundred square meters in size and raising a few sheep and goats, living pretty much as had their ancestors during the saint's lifetime in the seventeenth century.

The forty-four-year-long French colonial period (1912–56) had brought neither modernity nor prosperity to Abdulhaq's village. Indeed, there had been little contact with the French even though Ben's seemingly nearby town had been a local administrative center and housed one of the oldest French-run modern secondary schools in Morocco. But Abdulhaq had not gone there, nor had anyone else from his village. It was, in every sense, too far away. He had, however, been an excellent student of the Koran, which he had learned, like most male Moroccan children, at the feet of the religious master whose itinerant rounds included Abdulhaq's village.

While people did trade goods back and forth between his village and a cycle of weekly markets in a ten-mile radius, such commerce was measured in the Moroccan equivalent of pennies; it was certainly not enough to alter a centuries-old way of life. Without access to paved roads, local economic life remained just that: local. Needless to say, Abdulhaq's village had no electricity, no telephones, and no running water.

Abdulhaq was a deadly serious man. During the eighteen months he came to Ben's house for conversations, he never laughed and hardly smiled. His grave formality made him seem old and dignified.

In the beginning, Ben taught Abdulhaq how to teach him, managing to get across that while Ben did not care what the two of them talked about, he cared how they did. Ben wanted phrases and new words purposefully brought forward from one conversation to the next, to ensure that he would absorb them. Abdulhaq's intelligence quickly jumped the gap between Ben's pedagogic notions and his own, and by the third or fourth week the method began to work.

Abdulhaq's world was limited, but his knowledge of it was encyclopedic. There was nothing local he did not understand or could not explain. He knew about the weather, about olives and their names, about all the crops, plants, and animals in the area. He could explain festivals, the significance of customs and costumes, the reasons why prices fluctuated in the marketplace, and how to tell a high-quality mint leaf from one that was not, just by looking at it. He knew also how to make and do things. He could weave a basket, carve a walking stick, make a rope from sisal fiber, cure a sick goat, and preserve olives in twenty-five ways. If holes in his knowledge remained, his religion filled them in, especially when it came to answering the large questions in the nonmaterial realm.

But for all this, Abdulhaq was not content. He desperately wanted to change the conditions of his life. He saw himself as poor and did not want to be. And this became one of the topics he and Ben talked about. When they did not talk about olives and goats and the mysteries of the weather, they talked about Abdulhaq's life.

He lived in a rectangular mud brick house about ten feet wide by twenty-five feet long. There were two small windows and a rough homemade wood door. The roof was flat and made of mud-covered wattle. The floor was smooth, even though it was dirt. In one corner stood a small blue wood chest with painted flowers on it that held Abdulhaq's possessions. Unlike many of his neighbors, who had large families, Abdulhaq's was tiny. He had a wife, whom Ben glimpsed so fleetingly and rarely that he continued to think of Abdulhaq as if he were a widower, and a son, Karim.

Karim was about two when Ben first visited Abdulhaq in his village. The first thing that struck Ben about the relationship between Karim and his father was Abdulhaq's embarrassment. Karim sat on the floor, almost naked in October, a season when the wind in the low mountains can make forty-five degrees feel like twenty. His nose ran continuously. Even his eyes looked mucousy. His head was blotchy with scabs and dirty tufts of thin hair. The windows let in just enough light to see the permanent grayness of the dirt on Karim's hands and face. Abdulhaq would ask Ben to sit on the banquette against one wall. In front of this was the ubiquitous round tea tray, aluminum having recently replaced the traditional brass. On it was the tea service, also in cheap aluminum. He did not pick up Karim or hold him. At the same time, it became obvious to Ben that Abdulhaq loved his son. After awhile, Abdulhaq would look at Ben, point his hand and move it around the room, ending outstretched at Karim on the floor, and then he would sigh: "Look at this, look at him."

At first Ben would expect this to be followed by "Woe is me" or something designed to elicit pity, but it didn't come. Abdulhaq would pour the tea, and they would talk. Ben would glance at Karim. He did not move much, but he was not sick. In fact, he seemed fat and round.

Had Abdulhaq been less relentlessly grave, Ben might have suspected he was using a subtle long-term strategy to get something from him, other than the few dirhams per week Ben paid him, even though he never asked Ben for anything, for himself, his wife, or Karim. But his contact with Ben, his aggressive proposition when he first came to Ben's door, had already singled him out as different from an ordinary supplicant. He was ambitious to go somewhere in his life but unclear where that was or what route to take. He wanted to take charge of his life, to be in control over much more than his mere local skills and lore.

It was with Karim that Ben saw how much Abdulhaq's fatalism pulled at him, dragging him back to a condition against which he railed but was prepared to accept forever. For Abdulhaq was inexorably connected, if not tied, to his roots and its traditions. And this emerged as Ben began to understand what lay behind his seeming aloofness from his son.

A strange calculus about life and death, perhaps born of necessity, had been part of Abdulhaq's folk religion. Crudely put, Karim's life was, at two years old, not at all a sure bet. Of course no one's life is, but in Abdulhaq's tradition, a child can be called back to Allah very easily, and every family history he knew of demonstrated how often this occurred. Therefore a father such as Abdulhaq might be less willing to invest in a "natural" love for his child. Because the odds improved as the child grew older, the investment of self that the parent was willing to make increased accordingly.

Did the weight of these beliefs make Karim's death eight months later a self-fulfilled prophecy? Was Abdulhaq trying to break out of this harness of meanings, or was he being supported by it?

Their conversations provided some clues to answer these questions. But they remained too small and too infrequent to make much of. Abdulhaq would occasionally knit his forehead and narrow his eyes in anger as he criticized the limitations of his fellow villagers. "They" were ignorant, and even worse, "they" were afraid of foreigners and things foreign. "They" would never change.

To this he would sometimes add considerable derision about the false comforts of being part of such a venerable community, one that was known far and wide because of the saint. He would suggest that behind the appearance of village harmony were feuds, jealousies, and resentments that always remained on a low boil. He, Abdulhaq, was above such things. He followed the precepts of his religion seriously.

But such conversations were not the norm. The week following one of them, Ben and Abdulhaq would again be talking about crops and the weather or about olives. That winter was particularly gray, damp, and cold. To keep warm, they began to walk while they conversed. There were olive trees in Ben's yard and all over the town. Olives alone could occupy their ninety minutes. Ben was filled with questions from the botanic to the economic, and Abdulhaq, ready with answers. He not only knew everything there was to know about olives but also had a vast store of olive-related epigrams, and even riddles: "Our servant is green. Her children are born white and then grow black. Who is she? An olive tree." And so they continued, meeting weekly in the space between Ben's research and the other activities Abdulhaq engaged in to makes ends meet (his own olive trees, some petty trading, and basket making).

In June Ben received a call saying his father had had a heart attack, and he immediately flew back to the United States to see him in the hospital. Sometime in the middle of the three weeks that Ben was away, Karim became ill. At first he was just feverish and listless, but after a couple of days, Abdulhaq came into town looking for Ben. He thought perhaps Karim was in danger and wanted Ben to come in his car to Abdulhaq's village to take Karim to the main hospital in Fès, the only city in the region with modern facilities. He did not trust the local clinic in Ben's town, as it was run by the government. Abdulhaq wanted Karim to be seen by a French doctor.

Of course, Ben was not there when he came. Abdulhaq had no money to hire a taxi and felt Karim could not handle the long bus trip. He went back to the village and brought Karim reluctantly back to the government clinic in Ben's town. The next day Karim died of spinal meningitis.

When Ben returned from the States and heard the news, he felt guilty. Despite Abdulhaq's unusual entrepreneurial overtures to a foreigner, despite his ambitions, despite his insights, however tortured, into his own lot, and despite the extraordinarily finely detailed grasp of his surroundings, he was stuck. There was no security. He was right up against it — at the full mercy of a minor bit of bad timing. Ben had many hedges available to him when bad luck came. Abdulhaq had recently acquired only one, and Ben had proved to be a straw in the wind.

Being Useful or Being Used

San'a, Yemen, 1979

A SHOWER OF KHAT leaves lands with a smack on the windshield of Ben's Mitsubishi. It is early afternoon and the national ritual — khat chewing — is under way. The leaves come from the truck in front of him. Ben can't see the driver, probably because he's a twelve- or thirteen-year-old child. In this unregulated land, no one cares that half the truck drivers don't have licenses. As long as they can see above the bottom of the windshield — even if they need a cushion to prop them up — kids can drive the heavy rigs. But all drivers, young and old, big and small, about to head to the Red Sea and the port of Hodeida (150 miles on the map but a treacherous six-hour mountain drive from San'a's 7,500-foot elevation to sea level) fortify themselves with the narcotic green leaf, chucking the stems and outer leaves of the plant out the side window as they chew.

Ben's is one of the vehicles on the dusty Ring Road surrounding this remote, ancient capital. The traffic moves chaotically, plying between the airport on one side of the city and the three main roads leading out of town: one, to Taiz, near the border with Marxist South Yemen; one straight north to the Saudi border; and the Chinese road (a gift of the People's Republic) down to Hodeida. New Toyota jeeps dominate the passenger vehicles, and Peugeot station wagons, the intertown taxis. The thousands of trucks are British and Japanese made. There are a few traffic lights, but either they don't work or are ignored.

There is no industry on the Ring Road, nor much of it elsewhere in Yemen. A Sheraton Hotel is under construction north of the Ring, a sign of things to come, but the few buildings to be seen here and there along the Ring are the headquarters of the international aid organizations that serve Yemen — the United Nations Development Programme (UNDP), United Nations Children's Fund (UNICEF), World Health Organization (WHO), USAID, and the Yemen American Language Institute (YALI) — and so on, as well as many government ministries, recently established in modern quarters. Beyond the Ring Road lie the barren mountains and terraced fields of a country living in the fourteenth century. Further inside the road is the "old city."

This inner city, ancient and dense, is a National Geographic photographer's dream. Its narrow five-, six-, and seven-story stone buildings, constructed by hand without any steel or wood inner framework, are dotted with irregularly sized and placed windows and doors, the wide frames painted white. From a short distance away the mass of buildings looks like an apprentice pastry maker's first efforts at applying icing: the white painted window frames of the towers show an unsteady hand. In an increasingly uniform urban world, old San'a in 1979 exudes so much strangeness and difference that a visitor could palpably imagine himself Richard Burton coming into Mecca in 1853.

Ben, director of the U.S. Peace Corps program in Yemen, occasionally takes his children to the old city. They don't experience it the way he does. They focus on the smells, the open sewers, and the carcasses of dead dogs lying here and there in the narrow lanes. There are even more dead dogs lying at dusty intersections on the edge of the old city, killed by the new cars and trucks driven by inexperienced drivers. The climate is dry, so after a few days of stench, the dogs mummify, ignored by the "locals." Ben's son Max, age eight, has dubbed the place "dead dog city."

Old San'a is simply too old and inappropriate for the offices of the international agencies that have set up shop in Yemen since the country began to "open up" in the early 1970s and accept foreign aid. One exception to the general rule that international agencies be on the Ring Road is the Peace Corps. Faithful to its 1960s-style commitment to represent the opposite of the ugly American, the Peace Corps office is in a rundown four-story stone tower in the old part of the city. Ben's office is on the top floor; he gets double the exercise he would in climbing the stairs because not one of the fifty steps is the same height as the next.

Ben is on his way to visit Jane, a PCV who is one of two lab technicians the Peace Corps has provided to the Ministry of Health of the YARG (in U.S. Embassy lingo, the Yemen Arab Republic Government). She has threatened to resign after six months in the country, a quarter of the way into her twenty-four-month commitment. She works in the ministry's "Central Laboratory" near the university, also on the Ring Road. Central Lab is by far the largest and best-equipped medical lab in the country.

Ben parks his car outside the low, unfinished building. Like much in modern San'a, it has been put into use as soon as the functional minimums (one electric wire, jury-rigged in from a street pole, and a roof) are in place. Steel reinforcing rods stick askew out of the concrete roof — it's impossible to tell whether they are waiting for the second story to begin or left over from the completion of the first. Dirt and debris are everywhere, the detritus of rapid, unplanned, and uncoordinated development, fueled by a volatile and unusual mixture: first, official development assistance supplied by many industrial nations, several UN agencies, the Soviet Union and several Eastern bloc countries, and second, vast amounts of new private money in Yemeni hands, money sent home to the country by 1 million Yemeni workers abroad, most of them in Saudi Arabia, Yemen's neighbor to the north.

Ben has lived and worked in many third world countries. But Yemen is something new for him. The garbage and dirt are especially bizarre: There are hundreds of metal automobile parts sticking out of the ground, as if some modern artist had been commissioned to do a "sculpture garden" as a contribution to San'a's art scene. On closer examination, these bizarre bits of metal are recognizable as transmission cases, engine blocks, rear axles, differentials, and leaf springs. Twenty years ago there might have been one hundred motor vehicles in the whole country. But since the mid-1970s Yemen has been booming, and cars and trucks, almost all brand new, have been rolling in. Road conditions are poor, and service being absent, both in fact and in concept, vehicles fall into disrepair quickly. As they do, "mechanics" work on them on the spot, the bad parts dropped left and right on the ground. The vehicle moves on, the rains come, the silt covers up a portion of the discarded part, the rains end, the part is implanted in the now dried mud. Besides the twisted metal, there are tens of thousands of plastic bags, discarded in the street by their users, people who until five years before had never seen a bag of any kind, let alone plastic. Not used to having anything that could be discarded, much less things that would not turn to dust, these bags are also dropped in the street.

The street, itself a new concept, is "just out there," counting as neither a public nor a private place. If it is anything it is apparently a good place in which to discard used things. But unlike the auto parts, the bags are not indifferent to the wind, and as it swirls in and out of San'a's high valley, periodically forming tiny "dust devil" tornadoes (the U.S. embassy newspaper is called the *Dust Devil News*), it picks up the bags and deposits them on the thorny branches of every tree and bush in the city. There they are arrayed permanently — pale green, pale pink, and pale yellow — like so many deflated balloons on a desert Christmas tree.

Ben walks through the Central Lab building. He knows his way, and the few people he passes in the corridor ignore him. The floors are dirty, and the San'a dust is everywhere. Coming to a glass door, Ben enters Jane's lab.

Jane is twenty-three and comes from Idaho, where she was trained as a medical lab technician. She joined the Peace Corps because she wanted both to get out of Idaho and, quite sincerely, to help poor countries develop. People like her, with specialized technical skills, are the new breed of Peace Corps volunteer. Eighteen years after the Peace Corps (founded in 1961) began sending liberal arts graduates to the third world armed with a smile and six to ten weeks of training in agriculture or forestry, third world countries — even the most destitute — are no longer willing to accept just anybody. They would like people with skills. Yemen is no exception. Indeed the YARG would prefer to have many people come and simply apply their skills in perpetuity. PCVs are, after all, free to the YARG. While the government ministries have said to Ben that PCVs should work alongside Yemeni "counterparts" so that these might in turn learn the same skills (which is one of the main objectives of the Peace Corps), in reality very few such counterparts exist, and the ministries are not really behind the idea. Anyway, as Ben has been told in confidence by several Yemeni officials who have studied abroad, young Yemenis don't want to do the kind of work the Peace Corps volunteers do.

This is the first of Jane's complaints: She has no counterpart. Instead, she is running the Central Lab's bacteriologic section alone. She found things in a mess when she arrived. Straightening them out took up her first few months to such an extent that she didn't have time to think about the lack of a counterpart. Now, with hundreds of samples coming into the lab daily, she is overworked. Yet her boss, Dr. Yacoub, wants still more from her. He tells Ben that he has never had a lab tech who works so hard. He is delighted. She complains that she cannot get enough supplies (slides, cleaning equipment, petri dishes, test tubes, centrifuges). Some of this equipment is to be supplied under a grant from the Dutch government. (The Dutch cannot afford to give development aid to every country so they pick a strategic few in which to concentrate their assistance. For some reason, Yemen is one of these.) The Dutch make good on their promises, and the donated equipment is now in the country somewhere, probably at the Hodeida port, but the YARG bureaucracy has held up its arrival at Central Lab.

Jane goes on. Having been well trained, she is upset about the difficulty of getting accurate lab results. The samples come in contaminated with other matter so often that it is impossible to tell which of the many bacteria under the microscope belongs to the patient. The refrigeration system is nominally up-to-date (the refrigerators were donated by UNICEF), but one of the night watchmen in the lab keeps turning them off. Jane has spoken to the director about this, but it continues to happen.

And even though Jane works behind closed doors, keeping her eyes to the microscope, she has learned something about the health system in Yemen. She has begun to suspect that when she does manage to get reasonably clear tests, the lab results lead to little. She has heard from one of her fellow PCVs who works in the main hospital that the doctors (mostly trained in the Soviet Union) have little idea of what to make of the results or, if they do, will choose the treatment that brings them the most cash.

Finally, and here Jane's voice begins to break, she feels terribly lonely and isolated. She has hardly spoken to the few people in this building, much less the Yemenis outside it. The others who work in the lab seem to ignore her. The Yemeni women are inaccessible. She feels it is dangerous to talk to the men lest they get the "wrong idea." Because most of the other PCVs are scattered around the country, with few in the capital city, she has little interaction with them.

But she knows she is tough and can take the loneliness. In the end she is more angry than depressed. "I didn't come here for this. I really did believe I could do something, accomplish something. But this, . . . they are simply using me. Even if I stay my whole two years, what will I leave behind? Will Yemen be better off?" Will Yemen's health system be better off?" Will Central Lab be better off?"

Ben hears something like this almost daily. The Peace Corps in Yemen is a backwater post of an agency that is itself a backwater in Washington, D.C. Peace Corps/Yemen (PC/Y) has one of the highest attrition rates in the North Africa, Near East, Asia, Pacific (NANEAP) region. Ben came with ambitions to lower this. He learned quickly why the rate is so high and that not much can be done to change it. The country does not really want or care to make use of the Peace Corps as an agent of development. There are too many conflicting stakes at levels higher than Jane's or Ben's and too many external factors impinging on the Peace Corps's position in the country. The Peace Corps's presence, Ben had learned early on, was part of a quid pro quo. The Yemenis wanted U.S. foreign assistance (especially military assistance). In turn, the United States saw Yemen as important for its cold war strategy — the Soviets and the Americans are training Yemeni military pilots in, respectively, MIGs and F-14s, in two buildings at the airport within five hundred yards of each other — and was willing to put in money. Someone looking out for the interests of the Peace Corps (then facing a dwindling "market" after almost twenty years of existence) required, as a condition of the deal, that Yemen accept a Peace Corps program. Moreover, Yemen's internal politics, for all their impenetrability to Ben, clearly show that the Peace Corps is at best laughably free and fungible labor and at worst a nuisance or an imagined threat.

The threat part became clear a few months after Ben's arrival, when the civil war between the North and the South heated up and Ben was called into the Ministry of the Interior. A square-headed iron block of a man sat behind a desk with a .45-caliber pistol lying to his right, aimed at Ben, and pointedly made clear to Ben that no foreigners were to be allowed anywhere near the disputed border zones. The next week the minister of planning (the Planning Ministry is the one that signs off on and issues visas to the PCVs) called Ben in to warn him that, while they understood that Americans had rules about nondiscrimination, just between the minister and Ben, Ben was to make sure that no American Jews would be allowed to come to the country as PCVs. The Yemenis knew, he reminded Ben, that the Israelis find ways to make use of them as spies.

But Ben is thinking about Jane. By now he has seen so many cases like hers that he has begun to ask why the Peace Corps does not simply pull out of Yemen.

He tries to comfort Jane. Lamely he says: "It could be worse, Jane. You know, over half the PCVs in the country are so underworked they are bored silly. At least you're not spending your monthly allowance buying khat and wasting your time and ruining your health chewing it." (Khat is legal in Yemen, and most serious business in the country, including much of the government's business, gets done around afternoon khat "chews," during which men sit for hours, talking and chewing on the leaves of this plant.) Jane smiles faintly. "Yeah, really."

"Look," Ben says, "I'll talk to Dr. Yacoub again, but you know as well as I do that it's not going to change things. I've gone to the minister himself; I've spoken to the ambassador about the situation. The best I can offer you is to try to get you transferred to another project — maybe the Brits could take you."

Ben is going through the motions, and both of them know it. Jane picks up Ben's part of the dialogue and continues: "Yeah, sure, I know, remember what you said during training — development in Yemen is a 'slim pickings' business if ever there was one. . . . Don't expect too much to happen before your eyes. . . . It takes time . . . OK, Ben, I know, it's my decision."

Ben leaves Jane and makes his way to the headquarters of the Extended Program of Immunization, or EPI, a worldwide immunization project run by the World Health Organization. The project is the successor to the famous smallpox eradication effort, which after a decade of concerted work had recently found and eliminated the last known case of smallpox on Earth. Rather than dismantle the infrastructure and systems that they had developed for this massive campaign, WHO decided to expand to childhood immunization.

Ben has been talking to the head of the project about placing a couple more of his health volunteers there (most of the EPI centers are in towns outside San'a). He has already placed two, and if he can open up a couple more spots, he might be able to offer Jane an option. The advantage would be that she'd be working under an expatriate boss and assigned to a major international organization. She would be assured of better management, someone she could talk to, relate to, and because there are other PCVs assigned to the project, she might be less lonely.

Ben has sympathy for the volunteers. Having been one himself, he identifies with them, and while his job description talks loftily about his liaison role with the YAR government, his role on the U.S. "country team" in Yemen, his leadership in designing new and meaningful programs, and his administrative duties, he takes his job to be mostly guardian and mentor, with time out to be an employment agency. The volunteers are his first concern. He has long understood that the Peace Corps's original hope cannot really be met. JFK had said in 1960, "Think of the wonders skilled American personnel could work, building good-will, building the peace. . . . I therefore propose . . . a 'peace corps'. . . of young people eager to serve the cause of peace in the most useful way." Ben had seen and still saw signs that goodwill was possible to build. Every person-to-person contact provided such an opportunity. But he did not think such contacts built peace, and as for the "wonders," they had not, so far, been forthcoming.

Two weeks later, Ben sets out for Sadah, a town in the north of the country, to visit one of the EPI volunteers. It's Ben's first visit to the town, and his driver has to ask directions at one of the kiosk stalls on the "main" street (the road passing through the town).

As always, Ben is struck by the weird assortment of goods for sale in the shops, all of it imported. Cheap plastic toys from Taiwan and the Philippines, fabrics from India, frozen (and probably defrosted and re-frozen) chickens from Brazil — God knows how they got there — and Kelloggs Corn Flakes (with sell-by dates suggesting that the route from Battle Creek to Yemen was long and circuitous). Only the cases of Pepsi, Fanta, and Coke are produced in Yemen, in the new San'a bottling plants. The throwaway culture that has developed so quickly here has been taken into account by the bottlers, who charge a bottle deposit three times the price of the contents. But people everywhere are clever, and Yemenis have found a way around the deposit with a result that creates even more pollution.

Midafternoon is hot, and the kids walking by the drink kiosk naturally don't want to pay four rials for a one-rial Coke. One of the storekeepers rouses himself from the back of the shop where he and a few friends have been sitting on the floor chewing khat and smoking Rothmans cig-arettes, and empties a bottle of Fanta into a plastic bag, which he hands to one of the children, who pays him a rial. Holding the bag to eye level, the child punctures a small hole in the bag and guides the stream of orange liquid into his mouth. Finishing the drink he drops the bag to the street.

Ben's driver asks directions to the EPI clinic. The low stone building has a sign in front, in Arabic, but with the WHO logo in United Nations light blue. Ben walks in and finds the volunteer, Louise, a licensed prac-tical nurse from Seattle, and the director of the clinic, Lars, a young Danish doctor under contract to WHO through Danida, the Danish bilateral development assistance agency. On a long bench outside sit six women holding babies. They are the only ones (of seventy-five who came several weeks before) to return for the second set of shots in the three-set series.

The EPI program provides the common early childhood inoculations familiar to every American: typhoid, typhus, diphtheria, tetanus, paratyphoid, and polio. In two short years, clinics have been set up throughout Yemen. Program personnel have designed and put in place systems to transport and maintain the vaccines (including the all important refrigeration "cold chain"), as well as training for Yemenis to become vaccinators and vaccination supervisors. WHO had learned much from the smallpox campaign about the physical challenges of such a program in the developing countries. Keeping the vaccines from spoiling, solving power failures in the refrigeration system, and replenishing supplies — above all, not breaking the "cold chain" — was a matter of applying old-style military quartermaster corps management: money, men, and matériel. The cold chain does break in Yemen, but by and large that is not the main problem. What no one anticipated was how to get the women to bring their children to get them vaccinated, not once (as with smallpox) but three times, on a scheduled basis.

Getting across a health message that people both understand and respond to is a worldwide problem. But Yemen has its twists. For now, Yemen was flush with cash (this would change radically by the end of the 1980s). One of the twists was that people preferred to pay the local medicine men twenty dollars for a shot than come into the free EPI center. Part of this is convenience and familiarity, and part is the human universal that you value something when you pay a high price for it. Or they waited until their child was sick and then sought the help of shamans and medicine men. In 1979, Yemen does not have a strong central government (the joke in San'a was that the government's writ extended ten kilometers beyond the Ring Road; from there on out it was tribal dominance or anarchy, depending on whether your head was inclined toward anthropology or political science). In fact EPI originally tried sending mobile vaccination units to the villages, but these were quickly hijacked and robbed by tribal gangs.

Modern drugs are imported privately and sold openly on the marketplace without regulation. Virtually any prescription drug can be bought on the street. During the past few years, it has become routine for Yemenis with externally earned cash to ship in cars, heavy equipment, and drugs; make contract with private foreign companies to drill water wells

(Ingersoll Rand has a representative in San'a just to respond to these requests); hire local bulldozers to carve out rough roads (which fall apart
after the rains, eroding the thin top soil); and set up their own gasoline-
powered generators to run fluorescent lights, VCRs, and especially TV
sets. A remote village of stone houses perched on an almost inaccessible
mountaintop has dozens of TV antennas.

But despite the twentieth-century consumerism, Yemenis cannot buy
health. Their problems are those of the fourteenth century, and the statistics prove it.

Infant mortality (at age one and under) is 24 percent. Thirty-five percent of children die before they are two years old, and 46 percent die before reaching 15 years of age. For a population of almost 7 million people,
there are 234 doctors in the country (of which 47 percent are foreign)
and a total of 10 dentists!

Lars tells a story that he thinks is funny. Two months earlier, one of his
colleagues had a McLuhan-esque inspiration. Thinking "the medium is
the message," he managed to get a twenty-minute film from WHO on
children's diseases put on national TV, following it with an announce-
ment of the EPI program. The next day tens of thousands of parents
trucked their kids to every center in the country demanding vaccinations. The centers were overwhelmed. Fights broke out. Vaccinators quit
in frustration, doors were barred, guns drawn. One week later the centers were back to normal, the event half forgotten, and the previous pattern of twenty-five to forty vaccinations a day resumed.

Louise is well adjusted. She is happy. She doesn't think about these
things. The contact with the women and children is as much satisfaction as she needs. She is the ultimate one-to-one goodwill builder.

Louise brings in one of the women on the bench. Louise smiles and
begins to speak to her in Arabic. The woman is young, about twenty, and
illiterate. She was married at fourteen and has had six children, two of
whom died. She cannot say precisely when they died, though she remembers one of them was perhaps four or five months old and the other
between one and two years old. As for the cause of their deaths? She responds shyly to Louise: "It was their time. Allah willed it."

Louise is patient. She holds the woman's six-month-old baby as she in-
oculates him. Business is slow, so she can spend more time with the
mother. She asks if she is breast-feeding. "No," the mother replies,
proudly. She pulls a plastic bottle from under her black chador. It is half
full with a yellowish liquid. Louise asks, "NIDO?" "Yes," the mother
replies. She has been buying NIDO (a Nestle product) sold in cans.

Many in the international health community have begun to mobilize against Nestle and such products. The campaign hasn't reached Yemen, but Louise is an unofficial advance guard.

"You know," she lectures gently, "this bottle looks nice, but your breast milk is better. If you mix NIDO with dirty water, you are putting sickness into your child. Your own milk can never put sickness into your baby." The mother seems confused. The bottle is convenient for her and for the baby. He can hold it, lie down with it by himself. Louise smiles and repeats the lecture, hands the baby back to the mother, hands the mother her vaccination card, and reminds her when to come back for the third visit. Louise waves good-bye and goes out to the bench to bring in the next woman.

Maybe Louise has it right, Ben thinks. Do your job and don't worry about saving the world. But would Jane be happy here? Is it worth the effort to change her job and get her out of Central Lab? Ben plays God and decides Jane is just as well where she is. Besides, moving the volunteers around too much only gives comfort to those "elements" in the YARG who are hostile to the Peace Corps. Ben too has a job to do.

Jane ended up staying in Yemen, but mainly because she learned to have a good time. In her second year she became engaged to one of the Marine guards at the U.S. embassy, and four weeks before the end of her "tour," when he was posted elsewhere, she left Yemen. Later on, in the mid-1990s, so did the Peace Corps.

CHAPTER TWO

The Evolution of the Idea of Development

If we learn anything from the history of economic development, it is that culture makes all the difference. . . . Yet culture, in the sense of the inner values and attitudes that guide a population, frightens scholars. It has the sulfuric odor of race and inheritance, an air of immutability. In thoughtful moments, economists and social scientists recognize that this is not true, and indeed salute examples of cultural change for the better while deploring changes for the worse. But applauding or deploring implies the passivity of the viewer — an inability to use knowledge to shape people and things. The technicians would rather do: change interest and exchange rates, free up trade, alter political institutions, manage. Besides, criticism of culture cuts close to the ego, injures identity and self-esteem. . . . Benevolent improvers have learned to steer clear.

. . . On the other hand, culture does not stand alone. Economic analysis cherishes the illusion that one good reason should be enough, but the determinants of complex processes are invariably plural and interrelated.

—DAVID S. LANDES, *The Wealth and Poverty of Nations*

There has always been some kind of development. American history — or, for that matter, ancient Roman history — attests to that. It has usually been slow, often sporadic, and sometimes it "just happened," a shorthand way of saying it resulted from such a complex interaction of forces that it is impossible to determine that any single one made it occur. Most important, almost no one in the past really saw where they or their nations wanted to develop toward, as in "What we need is the institution of property rights" or "We'd like to become modern."

Reading history reveals two distinctions to be kept in mind when looking at the modern development industry. The first is that between development as something which occurs and development that is intended as such. The second is that between development which is intended but done by primary agents for their own societies, and development that is intended and done by secondary agents to, for, or on behalf of others.

Development with a Big *D* and Development with a Small *D*

Most of the long sweep of human prehistory and history was a case of development with a small *d* — development that was not deliberately intended or planned. And when there was development that was intended or planned, it was done by primary agents, interested parties who stood to benefit directly from those developments. For the most part these examples come from military conquest of territory and the expansion of empires. As Rome, for example, expanded around the Mediterranean, its aqueducts, public monuments, and coliseums, whether in Lixus or Volubilis in what is now Morocco, Thystrus in what is now El Djem, Tunisia, or Arles in what is now France, were "development projects" planned and executed by the Romans for their own benefit, not to better the natives of Morocco, Tunisia, or France. We certainly have a continuous thread of this type of development, albeit with some subtle changes, through the heyday of colonialism in the late nineteenth and early twentieth centuries to the present day.

Development with a capital *D* is different. Almost entirely a mid–twentieth-century invention, one of its key characteristics is that it is intended by secondary agents (seemingly disinterested parties) on behalf of others. At its core is an ironclad faith in a way of life, one that the rich countries after the Second World War were just beginning to enjoy on a massive scale. For while the seeds of modern development work were planted before, they did not germinate until the end of the war, during the beginning of a period, for America certainly, of remarkably unselfconscious confidence.

Fifty years later, embedded as we are in our postmodern ambivalences, it is hard to remember how optimistic and how sure we were at midcentury about development. Here is C. P. Snow in 1959: "Life for the overwhelming majority of mankind has always been nasty, brutish and short. It is so in the poor countries still. This disparity between the rich and the poor has been noticed. It has been noticed, most acutely and not unnaturally, by the poor. Just because they have noticed it, it won't last for long. Whatever else in the world we know survives to the year 2000, that won't. Once the trick of getting rich is known, as it now is, the world can't survive half rich and half poor. It's just not on."[1]

This surefooted faith in our knowledge of the "trick of getting rich" led, broadscale, to the evolution of development into an industry. The idea of helping the poor, along with the idea of social justice, is at least as old as the Bible. But Snow was talking about scientific progress and technology. To him this was the future, and despite our rather egregious failure to make

---

1. C. P. Snow, *The Two Cultures and a Second Look* (Cambridge: Cambridge University Press, 1959), 41–48.

good his year 2000 guarantee, he was more prescient than he knew. For the threads of capital, technical assistance, and expertise run steadily through the last fifty years of the development industry, far more than the old biblical thread of social justice and just plain charity.

Snow's answers to the question of how to alleviate the condition of a half-poor world reflects his faith in technology. His solutions were as brassy and unequivocal as his predictions about the year 2000. Development could be, quite simply, planned and engineered. To do it, we would need, "first and foremost, capital: capital in all forms. . . . The second requirement, after capital, as important as capital, is men. That is, trained scientists and engineers adaptable enough to devote themselves to a foreign country's industrialisation for at least ten years . . . men who will muck in as colleagues, who will pass on what they know, do an honest technical job, and get out."[2]

Obviously, Snow was not alone. The years immediately after World War II were a time when many in the rich nations agreed that poverty was "just not on." For the first time, "Poverty, ignorance, and disease were not to be accepted as our inescapable mortal lot but to be viewed as evils removable by human efforts. . . . Nations everywhere assumed the responsibility of attacking these evils in their own countries, and an international obligation of the richer nations to help the poor was proclaimed. Development is the word that came to describe these obligations and efforts. It quickly became a major feature of international relations, nations being classified as "developing" or "developed," the poor nations to try bettering themselves and the richer, developed nations to help them without intruding on their sovereignty."[3]

As modern development evolved over the last half century, that initial optimism and commitment became increasingly battered in the face of day-to-day reality. Rather than being discouraged, the intention to do development on behalf of others (the capital D) became stronger still, and all the while development evolved into an industry. We shall see whether that evolution was in part a way of protecting itself from the disturbing complexities the industry had begun to face.

Five Antecedents of Big-D Development

The modern development endeavor could not have arisen without five key ideas. The first is progress. Since the Enlightenment, the West has believed in progress. The idea deepened and spread so well that even the common man by the nineteenth century and certainly by the early twentieth could think it applied to his own life as well as to nations and civilizations. Emile

2. Ibid.
3. "A World to Make: Development in Perspective," *Daedalus*, special issue (Winter 1989).

Coué individualized progress as permanent self-improvement in his pop-ular 1920s mantra, "Every day, and in every way, I am becoming better and better."

But for most of history the majority of people did not think about the idea of progress, nor did they count on positive change in the future or even be-lieve there was such a thing as "the future," which is, incidentally, essential to the idea of progress. There was no commonly shared sense, in preindus-trial society, that things could get better in a permanent way. Of course, life was not entirely or bleakly lived in the moment. There were, even for the common folk, good times and bad times, and in good times ordinary people may have had what we would today call "surpluses" that were in a sense "in-vested" or "saved," suggesting that life was not entirely devoid of the idea of a future. But by and large, most people did not have a regular daily vision of the future, and certainly not one that held great promise — not a future that was bound to be, in our parlance, a "brighter" one. If good things hap-pened, it was Providence that explained them, not progress.

The second, equally early antecedent for the modern development idea is the notion that humans can make their own history — we can be the agents of our destiny. This notion also derives from the Enlightenment, and the shift from being acted on to being an actor in history is a key ingredient in modern development.

The third and later antecedent is the beginning of a change in what might be called the "designated beneficiary" of development. Whereas for cen-turies the primary beneficiary of development was at the same time its ag-ent, in the nineteenth century, agents of development, starting with the Eu-ropean colonizers, began to act for others, even though those actions were at the same time self-interested. This change occurred slowly and partially.

In the nineteenth century colonialism bloomed, very much a product of a firming up of the idea of progress that had begun in the eighteenth century. Nineteenth-century European colonialism, particularly in Africa and Asia, marked a subtle departure in the idea of progress, which began to be exported outside the homeland. The "mission civilisatrice" of France, though never pure and though subsumed under a political and profit mo-tive, initiated the idea that progress-cum-development is also a grand mis-sion, something to be brought to others, for their benefit. Here is what Hu-bert Lyautey, the military governor of Madagascar in 1898, saw as his job: "Lyautey . . . describes his daily duties as waging war against disease and il-literacy, planting trees, building roads, founding schools . . . with Lyautey, the army's colonial vocation was born."[4]

Yet despite this mission, the material welfare of the majority of the "na-

---

4. Sanche de Gramont, *The French: Portrait of a People* (New York: G. P. Putnam's Sons, 1969), 182.

tives" did not necessarily improve much. The real beneficiary of such development was still largely the colonial power, which naturally enough saw its colonies as extensions of the mother country. In many cases they — and the French are the best examples of this — were therefore really developing themselves.

While there had always been notions about poverty, the concept needed to become generalized and associated with underdevelopment before the modern endeavor could begin. The fourth antecedent is the shift to seeing poverty as a deplorable condition. This occurred gradually.

J. K. Galbraith makes the distinction between "mass poverty" and "case poverty." "Mass poverty" is where almost everyone is poor. Thus, all things being relative, if we are part of that mass, we do not see it, and if we are not part of that mass, we see it either as "natural" or, when it gets too close, as a condition to be feared rather than deplored. In the time of famine in sixteenth-century France, for example, life's precariousness made poverty so ubiquitous and close by at times that the poor often constituted a threat. Thus, when famine and poverty increased, "the towns soon had to protect themselves against these regular invasions, which were not purely by beggars from the surrounding areas but by positive armies of the poor, sometimes from very far afield. Beggars from distant provinces appeared in . . . the town of Troye in 1573, starving. . . . They were authorized to stay there for only 24 hours. But the rich citizens of the town soon began to fear that 'sedition' might be spread among the poor inside the town . . . and . . . in order to make them leave . . . an ample amount of bread was baked, to be distributed amongst the aforesaid poor. . . . After the gift the dismayed poor were driven from the town of Troye."[5]

"Case poverty" is different; it refers to instances of poverty in the midst of well-being. It is chronic rather than intermittent (as in the case of famine). Rather than evoking fear, it evokes pity and sometimes moral outrage.

Generally well into the early part of the twentieth century, most people in Europe and America lived off the land and, though they owned little, did not see themselves as poor. With urbanization and industrialization, case poverty — something to be deplored — began to be "seen." But if and when it was, it was generally seen in the West as a condition, a state of being that at times had an almost tautological cast — you were poor because you were poor. If poverty for certain social observers was the result of something, it was an institution (slavery, for example) or a new phenomenon (factories and urbanization) that had as many stakeholders as critics.

Seeing poverty as deplorable also meant a change in the consciousness of wealthy people. As wealth became a function of capitalism rather than

5. Fernand Braudel, *The Structures of Everyday Life*, vol. 1 of *Civilization and Capitalism, Fifteenth–Eighteenth Centuries*, trans. Siân Reynolds (New York: Harper and Row, 1982–84), 75.

inheritance or feudal landholding, and as it became more widespread, so did a degree of self-consciousness about it.

Still, people in the nineteenth century did not generally deplore poverty. And when they tried to respond to poverty, it was with charity. The many organized charities were in a sense an indication of how prepared people were to live with poverty, rather than eliminate it. And as for the underdeveloped nations, they were then not yet nations, not yet "underdeveloped," but exotic "lands," faraway places, which, though destitute by any material scale, were characterized not so much as poor as they were seen as primitive and their people as savages. To a degree this state was romanticized as "natural," or at the least a subject of curiosity (see *National Geographic* well into the 1950s). If the occasional traveler with a sensitive eye (e.g., Mark Twain in India in the 1890s) "saw" poverty, it was nonetheless a remote phenomenon, not one that created any resolve to do much about it. A genuine change in public consciousness about poverty as a deplorable condition, one found in most of the underdeveloped world, indeed its chief characteristic, did not occur until the mid — twentieth century.

The fifth important antecedent to come along was the idea that governments had a role to play in development. Until the first third of the twentieth century, the main actors in development (with a small *d*) were those who represented private interests. In nineteenth-century colonialism the flow of goods and services between rich and poor countries was substantial, but it was largely through trade and private investment, either directly, on a business-to-business basis, or facilitated by the major colonial powers (France, Britain, Germany, Holland, and so on) as they pursued their own geopolitical interests. Throughout most of the colonial period, which really did not end until after the Second World War, the colonial power governments were the handmaidens of private capital, not the prime movers of capital themselves.

With the Great Depression of the 1930s, the flow of private capital to the underdeveloped world was stanched. In the United States, to some extent, this coincided with a nascent view in government that the nation had interests in the underdeveloped world which it ought to promote more directly, especially in Latin America.

In the 1930s a few American and international institutions financed by the public sector began providing early versions of development assistance. The League of Nations supplied experts to China. In 1934 the Export–Import Bank, set up earlier to finance trade with Russia, began making loans also to Argentina, Brazil, and China. And in other ways, the U.S. government began extending "help" to developing nations in limited fashion. The U.S. Department of Agriculture had experimental stations in Latin America to develop improved crops. In 1939, President Roosevelt set up the Interdepartmental Committee on Scientific and Cultural Cooperation.

There were also some development projects in Latin America in agriculture, health, and education, which were begun by executive branch agreements outside the official framework of the committee.

Before the Second World War, some private charities, largely religious organizations, also gave to the underdeveloped world. Such giving and the work it spawned was a natural extension of the missionary approach that had begun in the latter half of the nineteenth century. And so schools, hospitals, demonstration farms, and the like continued to be built and experts sent by these charitable organizations, the precursors of today's NGOs.

A Tour d'Horizon of the Modern Development Idea: A Chronic Inability to Come to Terms with Complexity

World War II

World War II was a turning point not just for the world in general but also for development. With the stage set by the above five antecedents, Development with a capital *D* came into being. Development was now a deliberate goal, a public policy objective — which governments would take on. It became something nations in the West believed they could do for others, without being 100 percent self-interested (though self-interest remained and still does). Governments for the first time took an active role in development in areas where they had no direct responsibilities. In the heady days right after the war, progress was seen as a right that no country should be denied. H. W. Arndt, a historian of economic development, puts it this way: "[The] new departure was an almost universal acceptance of the view that the countries that had hitherto been left behind in this process should seek to participate in it and be assisted in doing so."[6]

And the confidence to take on the task of assisting others to catch up, exemplified in the almost embarrassingly self-satisfied tone of C. P. Snow's sentiments, came from the experience of the war. The Allied victory showed the enormous organizational power of the modern industrial nation. And the conduct of the war itself, by both the Allies and the Axis, palpably demonstrated not just the strengths of modern military strategic planning and the dazzling mobility of modern armies but more fundamentally the capacity to mobilize economic resources as well.

Having escaped direct suffering within its own borders, the United States experienced even greater confidence. As the boom of the 1950s came to be accepted, so too did the idea that anything could be accomplished — that

6. H. W. Arndt, *Economic Development — the History of an Idea* (Chicago: University of Chicago Press, 1987), 9.

there was no earthly reason why the benefits Americans enjoyed at home could not be enjoyed anywhere in the world.

To be sure, political reasons underlying the founding of the development endeavor were just as powerful as this newfound confidence, and perhaps more urgent. The balance of power had changed. The great colonial powers (especially Great Britain and France) were weakened. The independence movement in Africa and Asia had begun in earnest. And the spread of communism gave the underdeveloped nations the status of a "third world" situated between the West and communism and thus some bargaining power. The cold war, of course, was to become a major driver of the development establishment, especially the institutions created by Americans.

Still, while political imperatives may have been urgent, they could not alone have justified the development endeavor. There had to be the humanitarian and liberal goals expressed by Snow — to raise the standard of living of the poor countries. And both politics and caring got their support from the new confidence to take on development.

The institutional infrastructure for the new endeavor began to grow. The Bretton Woods Conference in 1944 set up the World Bank, recognizing that the flow of private capital had stopped and that the need for capital transfers from the public sector would become great as soon as the war ended. In March 1947, Truman announced what came to be called the Truman Doctrine, designating assistance to Greece and Turkey, and in June 1947 the Marshall Plan, aimed at the reconstruction of Europe, came into effect. The reconstruction effort itself was a testing ground for many of the new organizations and agencies that by the 1950s had shifted their focus to the underdeveloped world.

President Truman, in his 1949 inaugural, announced Point Four, which became formalized as national policy in the 1950 Act for International Development. Point Four is a landmark in the history of development because for the first time development was seen as a "program," a notion that has had far-reaching consequences. Point Four was also the explicit beginning of the modern U.S. foreign aid establishment and included the first use of the term "underdeveloped": "It is declared to be the policy of the United States to aid the efforts of economically underdeveloped areas to develop their resources and improve their working and living conditions by encouraging the exchange of technical knowledge and skills and the flow of investment capital."[7] For the first time, the notion of material growth coincided with economic development. The accepted measure of development, certainly then and even to some extent today, was per capita income.

7. Harry S. Truman, *Years of Trial and Hope*, vol. 2 of *Memoirs* (Garden City, N.Y.: Doubleday, 1956).

By the end of the 1950s most of the public institutions were in existence which still today account for the bulk of the official moneys directed to development. On the private voluntary side, big NGOs such as the Cooperative for Assistance and Relief Everywhere (CARE), Catholic Relief Services, and Save the Children were already entering their second decade of operation. The confidence to undertake the task (for it was seen as a task) was abundant, bolstered in part by the evidence that Europe's reconstruction was well on its way.

In the history of an idea such as development, denoting the beginning and end of a phase has to be arbitrary. There are always institutional laggards and leaders, critics, and cheerleaders, some of whom influence ideas early, others late. One has to talk in terms of a bell curve — when does a development notion reach its peak and become embraced by the largest number of people in the profession? I therefore mark the phases and their "beginning" and "ending" by looking at the bell curve of rhetoric, the content of development publications, and the use of terminology.[8]

The Age of Confidence: 1945–1960

In these first years of the formal development endeavor, various cultural and economic threads began to interweave. The most enduring was perhaps the merging — embodied in the notion of a "program" — of the engineering model with the notion of planning. (As we will see, these modes remain current in development assistance today, albeit with less vigor.)

Had there been an accepted metaphor for the late 1940s and early 1950s period it would have been the machine. For development was an engineered, mechanical process of imitation and replication: "As we did in the West in our rise to riches, so you should do." It was also a grand purpose, almost godlike in its scope and ambition. Thus, inject industrial capital; build basic industries so you will not have to rely on outsiders for your essentials (import substitution); send your people to our universities to learn how to run them; set up government planning agencies to plan, to "command," and to control; and so on. The machine of development was also well designed, well oiled, and smooth running. There was much discussion of "internally balanced growth," as if the machine, once designed and built, could be hermetically sealed and would run on its own.

Not only was the process mechanical, but in a sense real-life machines were also the objective, for what is industrialization about if not machinery? Indeed, the phrase "the process of industrialization" was used early on as a

8. There have been several attempts to delineate development history. I found K. Griffin's paper "Thinking about Development: The Longer View" particularly useful (SID Nineteenth World Conference, New Delhi, March 25–28, 1988).

synonym for development, as if development meant only that. The imposition of our way of life was evident.

To be sure, critics emerged right away. Isolationism in the United States still had its proponents, and sharing our wealth did not make sense to many. But critics who were *for* foreign aid were upset that some of it was being wasted, and if anything they reinforced the mechanical metaphor. Here is Eugene W. Castle in 1957: "The history of foreign aid has been littered with the wreckage and rubble of incompetent and wasteful administration. The task of shoring up sick economies or planning vast development projects is a task for the highest order of engineering brains. But we have assigned such tasks largely to civil service routineers and irresponsible political headline–hunters."[9]

Castle and others were also becoming aware that much aid does not end up where it should. He refers to the foreign aid "merry-go-round," the one-hand-washing-the-other phenomenon that still goes on in the industry. For example, he notes that of the $30.4 billion spent on foreign aid between 1948 and the midfifties, 77 percent went to suppliers in the United States.[10]

The metaphor of the machine would also have been apt because machines are fast, and an underlying conception was that a nation could relatively quickly catch up with us. The whole endeavor was dominated by engineers and economists, with economists the dominant theorists and engineers the primary designers and executors. A mark of their supremacy was the amazingly one-dimensional way in which they had cast the process being talked about and practiced. The nature of the political system, the maturity of the political system, the literacy level of the populace, the nature of culture, religion, ethnicity, geography, and a host of other factors that explained our own complex development history were basically left out of the equation being applied to others.

Most important, people were left out. It was nations that were poor, not people. And if people were poor, which we knew, then the solution was to make the nation rich; the benefits would "trickle down" to the poor. The faith in our way of life was so strong that there was almost a tacit acknowledgment that you could jump into industrial status, skipping steps along the way. The essential message being sent to the underdeveloped world was: "We got here the hard way, over hundreds of years, but that was because we were the first ones, the pioneers. Now that we know the way, here are some shortcuts you can take." The sense of speed was exemplified in the terms that some economists used in the 1950s, the idea of a "big-push" strategy of multiple development, which would put nations on the runway poised for "takeoff." And this sense of speed did not come only from our side of the

9. Eugene W. Castle, *The Great Giveaway* (Chicago: Henry Regnery Company, 1957), 37.
10. Ibid., 47.

fence dividing rich and poor. It was shared by many of the poor nations themselves, who had their own hopes and illusions. W. W. Rostow, one of the main proponents of the takeoff idea in the early 1960s, said that a good part of the motivation of many nations to develop was "reactive nationalism"—a result of contact, some of which occurred through the war.[11] Simply put, reactive nationalism meant that "if we don't catch up to what they have, we'll be left behind."

And finally there was an implicit imitation of our "character" in the term "self-sufficiency," which began to be used in the 1950s. The term was applied to nations, not so much to people. We had the illusion that we did not depend on others, and so we naturally projected that illusion on the underdeveloped world.

The values of much of the West were implicit: those of an idealized, manly, protestant-ethic, stand-tall-on-your-own-two-feet, there's-no-free–lunch, robust, chest-thumping Americanism. This American version of self-sufficiency found interesting parallels in the third world itself, where the term "self-reliance" began to be used, especially by Julius Nyerere of Tanzania in the 1960s. For him, the first postcolonial leader of his country, "self-reliance" was a way of fending off a feared dependency on the West.

The day-to-day business of the development "program" soon got further reduced to "projects," planned, budgeted, and managed in the same way that a skyscraper was a building project. With the project as the main mechanism and central government the main actor, financial aid itself was a mere tool in the process. Decidedly not a giveaway, aid was a pump primer—an additive that when put in the fuel tank of the engine of development would cause the nation to lift off the runway and "take off," climbing to cruising altitude on its own.

Once our experts and practitioners began going out to do this heady kind of development work, "mucking in" to build airports, roads, factories, to help governments organize ministries and agencies, and so on, reality began to alter expectations. And while the core idea of development as an engineered process remained, some seeds of doubt begin to be planted about how we were going about things, some directly by critics of this mode of development and a few indirectly via literature and even movies. In 1958, for example, *The Ugly American* was published, and while it did not deal with development per se, it became a spur for a new, more sensitive, less impositional approach to the underdeveloped world. Disappointment with industrialization based on import substitution also began to set in, as professionals began acknowledging how hard and long the process ap-

11. Walt Whitman Rostow, *The Stages of Economic Growth: A Non-Communist Manifesto* (London: Cambridge University Press, 1960), 34.

peared to be and to a lesser extent as it became clear how much of the under-developed world was rural and agricultural and likely to remain so.

The term "economic development" began replacing the term "industrial-ization" toward the end of the 1950s, and with that came a renewed belief in trade as the engine of economic growth. Human capital gained greater at-tention, as did education, manpower planning, and "technology transfer."

A Transition: 1960–1965

The 1960s was the first self-conscious development decade. Indeed, the United Nations declared it the "Decade of Development." The 1960s also coincided with the time when most of the world's new nations came into be-ing (in the 1940s only 15 new nations were born; in the 1950s, only 7; but the 1960s saw 44 newly independent nations). By the middle of the decade, these 66 new countries accounted for 40 percent of the world's population. The 1960s also saw the establishment and growth of the United States Agency for International Development (USAID), under the 1961 Foreign Assistance Act; the Peace Corps (1961); and the United Nations Develop-ment Programme (UNDP) in 1965. The demand for technical assistance and foreign aid grew rapidly as new nations came into being. In Europe, the reconstruction process had produced enough economic strength for Euro-pean nations to begin foreign aid programs of their own. The Development Assistance Committee (DAC) of the OECD was formed in 1961, its mem-bers signing the "Resolution on the Common Aid Effort": "To secure an ex-pansion of the aggregate volume of resources made available to less devel-oped countries and to improve their effectiveness."

If the fifties concentrated on infrastructure, the sixties combined eco-nomic infrastructure (factories, ports, and so on) with social infrastruc-ture such as schools and universities, raising knowledge transfer to a more formal and prominent level. Transferring knowledge became "technical assistance."

The number of ingredients for development had increased and to some extent changed. Physical and financial capital remained important, but without knowledge and skills — that is, the capacity to create growth — they counted for far less. Underlying this was the same sense which had existed in the 1940s and 1950s that development was about something we had and "they" did not.

Development theory held that we in what is still called "the West" (Japan was not yet in the club, and political correctness had not yet made us self–conscious about the term) intuitively understood modern life. There was an element of cross-cultural sensitivity (however misused) in the idea we then had that an African child who has never played with an erector set cannot understand nuts and bolts. In contrast, we grew up with these things. We understand the importance of lubricating an engine. But "they" have to be taught. When that transfer takes place, the theory held, development would kick in. C. P. Snow's vision of men who will "muck in" and "pass on what they know" was thus activated repeatedly. Advisers, teachers, and other experts went "out" everywhere into the underdeveloped world.

But things began to get still more complicated. Practitioners noticed that development efforts had unintended consequences. With increasing emphasis on education, and especially with funding for higher education and even university training in the West for bright young people from the third world, we also began to notice what came to be called the "brain drain." How do you stop educated people from leaving the poor nations their education was intended to serve?

As other problems showed themselves, we can see now, in retrospect, that the arrows were all pointing to yet other ingredients for development — institutions, culture, and the policy conditions for growth, which all came to be considered important as time went on. The development endeavor, as our awareness of its complexity began to grow, took on components and emphases without ever really letting go fully of old ones. We did not eliminate infrastructure, planning, and engineering but added to it a much larger dose of knowledge transfer and technical assistance.

Debate on trade, still viewed as a major component and engine of development, continued in the 1960s. But the debate centered on who got hurt and who won in trade. The idea of protectionism remained at the center of the debate — if a small new country starts an infant industry, shouldn't it be protected until it gets on its feet? Again, in retrospect, we see how parochial this debate too was, premised on a yours/mine framework that did not acknowledge interdependency and certainly did not foresee globalization.

It is also during this phase that "Development" as a discrete field of study arose. It began to be offered fairly widely on academic campuses and in specialist schools (such as the School for International Training in Brattleboro, Vermont). While for years there had been such institutions as the Fletcher School of Law and Diplomacy at Tufts, Columbia's School of International Public Administration, Johns Hopkins's School of Advanced International Studies, and the Woodrow Wilson School at Princeton, their role had traditionally been to prepare diplomats and public administrators. Now, for the first time, one could earn a degree in international development. And true to this pattern of adding on, economists were soon joined by sociologists in the pantheon of development theorists.

But the 1960s was largely a one-dimensional time. We still believed we knew something that the underdeveloped world did not and we could teach it to them. What began to change, however, was style. The West's style (particularly that of Americans) changed to be less "ugly" and more culturally sensitive. The Peace Corps was one exemplar of the new style. It's underlying stylistic emblem was the friendly smile. But our confidence remained what it had been in the fifties. Nothing better illustrates the faith of our vision than the Peace Corps's belief that several hundred twenty-two–year-old liberal arts graduates, with no experience or particular skills, sent abroad for two years, could make a difference in a country's development.

But the Peace Corps was a radical change nonetheless, one that previewed other changes to come in development. First, Peace Corps volunteers would interact not with machines and governments but with real people, poor people. Second, they would learn the language of the people with whom they worked. Third, they would work alongside them and live with them. Fourth, their actions would be local actions, on the spot, at the level of the village and rural hamlet. Later, the term for such a locus of development work became the "grass roots."

The Peace Corps was not the only volunteer-sending agency. Others included those of Ireland, Canada, Great Britain, and the United Nations. And it is this voluntarism, in the sixties still a characteristic of many NGOs and formalized in such agencies as the Peace Corps, that helps us recall that for all the self-confidence and hubris of the time, many who worked in development felt a sense of calling, if not mission. In important ways, the field had not yet become a profession, not yet an industry.

During the sixties, in development just as in the broad culture, these more populist influences did not quite reach the players in the mainstream of development. The big institutions, such as the World Bank, and some of the major bilateral agencies continued along in their macro modes, emphasizing capital formation, export-led growth, and large projects. Without anyone intending it, a polarization in the development endeavor had come into existence. At one end were the big players, doing their thing. At the other end were the Peace Corps types and many NGOs, some just founded, who began a more grassroots-oriented kind of work. The two parts of the development endeavor ignored each other and rarely came into contact. World Bank staff stayed in the capital cities, to which they traveled in the first-class compartment of the plane. Peace Corps volunteers stayed in the villages, and when they moved about by plane, they were in row 45, cramped in the middle seat.

But while this new brand of development assistance appeared to be the polar opposite of the older branch, the overall culture of development was still broadly shared by all. Peace Corps volunteers (PCVs) and NGO types were younger, more idealistic, and certainly more "hip" than World Bank types. But they shared the idea of self-sufficiency and of technical assistance as a means to achieving it. Out of this time came the term "self-help," which is another way of saying that you cannot really give something for nothing. Of course, this idea also served an illusion. By calling our actions at the grass roots "self-help," we were able to deny to ourselves that we were giving some-

thing for nothing and especially that we were merely providing symptomatic relief. For liberal as we were, the idea of dependency was not one with
which we were happy. It was during this period that the catchy phrase "Give
a man a fish and you feed him for a day; teach him to fish and you feed him
for life" came into use.

It was day-to-day reality — the complexity of *doing* development — that
caused things to change. At the least, the old one-dimensionality of development was beginning to break down. The end of the 1960s brought the realization that development is a total process, an explicit recognition of its inherent complexity and multidimensionality.

The Golden Age of Development and Era of Great Debates: 1965–1980

If the first phase was unitary in its faith and motivated by a combination of
calling and the thrill of ersatz military planning and execution, the second
phase was a time of organizational expansion, consequent bureaucratiza-
tion, and debate. The debate was about ends and means, to some extent
about ideology, and about who should benefit. But no one, even the biggest
critics, disagreed with the broad goal: the fostering of development as a deliberate intervention. Rather, they were critical of foreign aid and how it was
undertaken. Looking back from 1971, Willard Thorp writes in *The Reality of
Foreign Aid*: "[In 1968] the aid program was described as a wasteful and futile effort to buy the friendship of other nations; as supporting dictatorships;
as not making any real contribution to the less-developed countries; as subject to mismanagement, lacking in competence and zeal; as a give-away program tending to reduce the sense of responsibility on the part of the recipient; as serving the interest of the recipient rather than the United States; as
failing to use multilateral channels; as containing too large a grant element;
and as contrary to the principle that 'charity should begin at home.'"[12]

All in all, the call was for more action, not less. And more action there was.

During this period, the development industry experienced extensive
growth, which continued into the 1980s. NGOs proliferated. Peace Corps
volunteers returned home and went into NGOs and into USAID. Academics became interested in development and themselves became staff or advisers on projects. The big players began talking regularly to the small players. The literature on development increased.

For the first time, we had some data about the results of earlier work.
Oddly enough, the years to date had shown impressive economic growth, at
roughly 5 percent worldwide. But it was becoming evident that that growth
was not reaching very deep into societies; indeed, the gap between rich and
poor appeared to be growing. Led by the Left, questions arose about whether
equating growth with development was a correct view of the process. If

12. Willard L. Thorp, *Reality of Foreign Aid* (New York: Praeger, 1971), 11.

growth did not promote poverty reduction, then what was it for? As the data came in and as thousands of young Western people witnessed poverty in the third world, a sense of urgency about poverty began to build. The sentiment was: "Maybe trickle-down works, and maybe it doesn't, but how can we let people wait? They have basic needs, and these have to be met."

Adding to the urgency was a growing pessimism about world resource trends, particularly in relation to population growth. A Malthusian wave of fear arose in the early 1970s, a fear that we would run out of essentials, from food to oil. And finally, the high hopes the newly independent nations had in the first few years after independence began to come up against some very unpleasant realities, not the least of which was the challenge of simply holding themselves together. Nationhood itself was soon seen as something requiring more than the founding of an airline and the designing of a flag. Pakistan began to split apart. Nigeria entered a state of civil war as Biafra tried to become independent. Zaire and other nations began to feel the rumblings of ethnic, religious, or language-based unrest. In other areas, food was running out. Resources were indeed a problem.

New responses and new concepts were not long in coming. In 1973, US-AID promulgated its New Directions, an explicit emphasis on basic human needs. In 1975 the Hammarskjöld Foundation report "What Now?" focused on poverty and brought forward the idea of a "redistribution" of resources. Scientific research on new disease-resistant high-productivity seeds accelerated and led to the "green revolution." The World Health Organization accelerated the war on smallpox, the result of which was the elimination of this disease from the planet in 1979.

No one really stopped doing capital formation or physical infrastructure. But the ends of growth became widely questioned. Simply put, poverty had been rediscovered, placed at the center of things, and made more poignant, more human, and more urgent. New keys to development were brought forth under the basic human needs banner, in particular, nutrition and health to join with education, and employment generation to join with industrialization. Because most poor people were in rural areas, agriculture took on greater importance. In some quarters, particularly among the NGOs, the trickle-down idea became an enemy and bogeyman.

The goal of development by the mid-1970s was as much the eradication of poverty and the redressing of an imbalance of opportunities as it was economic growth. As I noted above, very little in the development tool kit has ever been given up, just added to. This characteristic is exemplified in the widely used slogan "growth with equity," which continued well into the 1980s. Both the softhearted, poverty-obsessed former PCVs and the hard-nosed, growth-obsessed economists at the World Bank could use the phrase and feel more or less comfortable. Robert McNamara entitled his annual address to the World Bank in 1972 "Social Equity and Economic Growth."

Basic human needs and social equity seemed to mesh well with the frustration felt by a few earlier practitioners that doing one thing was not enough. As we began to see that development is a total process, the notion of integration came into prominence, and for a time, Integrated Rural Development (IRD) was all the rage. At its core, the idea was this: We had to tackle everything at once — teaching new cultivation techniques, bringing in new technology, promoting primary education, local institution building, health, nutrition, roads, water systems, dams. The list was almost infinite. The idea was theoretically sound; for the first time we explicitly acknowledged the inherent complexity of development, making a nod to our own past when all these things needed to exist before we ourselves became developed. But there were two problems. First, however integrated the planners and practitioners thought they were being, it is almost axiomatic that something critical would get left out or forgotten (e.g., the complex arena of property rights or land reform were not things a project at the local level could do much about). Second, while the idea of integration seemed sound, applied on the ground it was a managerial nightmare. We forgot that our own complex development was not the result of a "program." It had not been engineered, planned, or managed. On the ground, as a project, particularly a project with a three-year funding "time frame" (as many of the projects had and do have), Integrated Rural Development was systems thinking run amok — good idea, impossible to make it work.

Also in the early 1970s, GNP and GNP per capita as *the* measures of progress were dethroned. Quality of life and the fulfillment of basic human needs (food, water, health, nutrition, legal rights), as I pointed out in chapter 1, now took their place alongside GNP as a way to measure development progress.

All these changes took place, not surprisingly, at a time of general societal self-questioning in the West. Recall the cultural revolutions of the 1960s — the broad onslaught on the part of many educated young people against Western industrial society, against cities, against materialism, against inequality. Inevitably, aspects of the revolution carried over into the development mix, including prominently the Women in Development (WID) movement, which paralleled the feminist movement, and the Appropriate Technology (AT) movement, which paralleled the movement of the back-to-the-land set.

Windmill and solar power, biogas, yurts, hand-operated oilseed mills, more efficient bicycles, and a host of other innovations became grist for the development assistance mill. USAID and others funded projects involving appropriate technology, buying into the notion that if rural life could be made more efficient and productive at low cost and without machines requiring energy, then the people in the third world would stay on the farm and their basic needs would be met.

It is fascinating in retrospect to realize that these essentially utopian and romantic idealists made the same arrogant mistake that their precursors, the engineers, had made. They thought, "We know what's good for you." The difference was simply that we were now talking about a different "we" and a different "what." Because the poor of the third world were farmers and peasants on the land, many Western back-to-the-landers projected on them the same desires they had.

No one seemed to notice that third world people were not buying it. Sophisticated third worlders noticed early on that this was a put-down, a way of saying "let them eat cake." To them, especially those who had benefited directly from previous growth, basic human needs and appropriate technology were threats — ways for the West to fulfill its own dreams on their backs, ways to keep the poor of the third world in the bush. Clearly the mix of ends, means, solutions, and players was getting thicker and more spicy.

The last prominent addition to the development soup of the 1970s was the resurgence of the humanitarian relief organization. Large NGOs such as CARE, for example, had begun years before as relief organizations — they delivered "CARE packages" of food and other essentials. They existed originally to respond to emergencies and disasters and help people recover from war. It was later, in the 1960s and 1970s, that the CAREs of the development field became diversified and more oriented to long-term development, though many continued to deliver food aid. What changed in the 1970s was the arrival of humanitarianism as a political movement. The accepted beginning of this was the founding of Médecins sans Frontières (MSF) in 1971 and its role in promulgating the right to intervene with humanitarian aid in situations of natural and political disaster. It would not sit around and wait to be formally asked by governments to help, as was the policy of the International Red Cross, but would come to help people in need, even if the government had not asked for help, and especially if government itself was one of the perpetrators of the disaster. From then on emergency relief work took on a life of its own within the formal development industry and has carried forward until today as a major wing of the industry (there is a good argument to be made that emergency relief and refugee-oriented agencies are indeed the last growth area in the industry).

From about 1975 on, grassroots organizations, relief organizations, and development assistance NGOs began to have some legitimacy in the eyes of the big players (the World Bank, the UN agencies, and others). And interestingly, anthropologists began to be in demand as the economists and sociologists needed help in dealing with the new emphases of the time.

As the ideological mix grew in this lively period between 1965 and 1980, several new strands began to fly about somewhat loosely, waiting to come together. With the movement of "people" to the center of development thinking, the growing attention paid to their way of life, and more genuine respect for them, a degree of humility entered the field, even in some quarters a mea culpa attitude. This, to be sure, occurred at the periphery of the development field and did not creep toward the mainstream until well into the 1980s. But some field practitioners had noticed how problematic IRD had been, and even more had realized that many efforts, all so well meaning, had not worked. We began to think: "We are not the experts, they are! They know how to do things, they are not idiots! We must learn from them, listen to them. They know the nature of their problems a lot better than we do. Who are we to impose solutions? We — development professionals — must become partners with the poor. They must participate in the planning and design of projects. They must have a stake, and to do so they must 'own' the project from the beginning." "Participation" began to enter the development debate not just as a new concept but as a new paradigm as well.

The years between the midsixties and the early eighties saw a loss of consensus on what development was all about and its practice. No longer evidencing even a loosely unified approach, development had become a large basket of diverse and much argued approaches, with new and diverse constituencies for each.

And for the first time the voice of the third world itself became louder and strident. People in the developing countries wanted modernity, wealth, and power, but not on our terms. In Latin America, where a hundred years of independence had not solved poverty, leftish liberation ideologies held sway. The significant buzzwords were freedom from economic dominance and exploitation and the call for a New International Economic Order (NIEO), a movement that rippled through much of the "south," a term both we and the third world now began using to describe the underdeveloped world.

The NIEO had support in the "north." In his *Vast Majority: A Journey to the World's Poor*, Michael Harrington warned that the West, and especially America, was taking a morally unsupportable position in relying on capitalism and growth to solve the problem of poverty. It was plainly unfair that the West controlled such a large percentage of the world's wealth. Like Snow, Harrington adamantly declared that poverty was "not on," but his solution (and that of the NIEO) was redistribution. One way to put forth and justify such arguments was to imply a threat. If the rich do not voluntarily give up some of their wealth, the world's poor would rise up and "wars of redistribution" would begin to occur.[13]

Finally, as if to remind everyone that, after all, growth really does work, the end of the 1970s saw the arrival of the Asian Tigers, or newly industrialized countries (NICs): Taiwan, Singapore, Hong Kong, and South Korea. These were, ironically, tributes to 1950s thinking about economic develop-

13. Michael Harrington, *The Vast Majority: A Journey to the World's Poor* (New York: Simon and Schuster, 1977).

ment as growth (or so it was thought). But the lessons to be drawn from the Tigers were hotly debated and not at all conclusive. And the south itself experienced segmentation, as some parts of it began to do better than others and some countries began to go backward. Underdevelopment, which had never been homogeneous, was now palpably and undeniably varied. Complexity would not go away.

A Wake-up Call: 1980–1990

The 1980s was as much a transition between phases in development assistance as it was a phase in its own right. Many of the threads of the 1970s and even the 1960s continued through the decade. New ideas and new answers were introduced. But the big influences in this period came from outside. The external world became a more important and forceful context for development than it had been in the previous periods, when the development field, for all its internal burblings, was relatively free to carry out in its own good time what it thought needed doing. The worldwide benefit of the doubt given to the field was coming to an end.

One of the primary contextual influences during this period was the beginning of a profound change in the dimensions and to some extent the dynamics of the world economy. Propelled by the increased speed of transactions enabled by communications and computer technology, capital markets became much more international. Indeed, the era of globalization was under way in the commercial arena. When times were good in the 1980s, they were so good that wealth grew by unprecedented amounts. And when times were bad, as they most often were in some places, they were so bad that they took whole countries backward in time.

It is revealing that during this period, when development was threatened by much larger and bolder forces than ever before, the reaction of the development field was not defensiveness and retrenchment. There was a loss of confidence and in some quarters, particularly among NGOs, a new element of self-consciousness, but overall it was a time of a more intense search for financial resources and an even more arrogant presumption that if "we" did not have all the answers before, we were now on the verge of having them.

Despite the brusque awakening caused by the recognition of much more powerful forces at work in the movement of the world's future than the role of development assistance, along with the mounting evidence of mistakes and failures, the development assistance business enjoyed continued growth. The 1980s saw a growing legitimacy for NGOs and, for the first time, recognition of the rise of the southern NGO as a force to be harnessed in the fight against poverty. In 1987 a landmark conference in London brought together 120 northern and southern NGOs from forty-two countries. The meeting was not as humble as its title — "Development Alternatives: The

Challenge for NGOs"—made it seem. What occurred was both a flexing of newfound muscle and an acknowledgment of a need to catch up with the "can-do" image of NGOs as antipoverty foot soldiers that they themselves had promoted.

Development itself began to come under more serious attack from both inside and outside. A host of new book titles used the word "rethinking" or "reconsidering," as in John Lewis and Valeriana Kallab's *Development Strategies Reconsidered* (1986), which began by acknowledging "those observers who assert that the whole development promotion effort, past and prospective, is a waste of time."[14]

Indeed, the record did not look so good. The Asian Tigers' success, we recognized (though we did not really acknowledge this publicly), was not so much the product of *our* interventions but of decisions made internally about policy, which helped attract private investment and enabled its efficient use. When outsiders did influence key reforms (as in land reform in Taiwan, which in turn paved the way for the country's success), they came from other governments or academia, rather than the development community. And where formal development interventions had been the dominant "input," as in sub-Saharan Africa, the record was very poor. Quite a few of the grand international resolutions about clean water, healthcare for all, and the elimination of hunger were beginning to ring hollow. While we all knew that healthcare for all by the year 2000 (a date that seemed so comfortably far away in 1978 when that commitment was made) was more of a hope than a promise, we did not, quite honestly, believe that our timing was off by much. After all, some enormously dramatic problems had been successfully solved by development intervention — the most cited example being the victory over smallpox, which took just about a decade.

It is humbling to consider all the "International Years of. . . ," "Decades of. . . ," and "Declarations on . . ." that were promulgated under the auspices of the UN between 1960 and the mid-1980s — there were at least thirty. Looking back at these good intentions from the vantage point of the late 1980s should have caused some embarrassment if not severe cognitive dissonance among development professionals, though no evidence exists that they did. Here is a sample:

1960–1965   Freedom from Hunger Campaign
1960–1970   UN Development Decade (Resolved: Increase economic growth by 5 percent by end of decade)
1968   Declaration on the Human Environment

14. John P. Lewis and Valeriana Kallab, eds., *Development Strategies Reconsidered* (New Brunswick, N.J.: Transaction Books, 1986), 5.

1970–1980 Second UN Development Decade (Resolved: Create a just world order and 6 percent economic growth)

1974   Universal Declaration on the Eradication of Hunger and Malnutrition

1975   Lima Declaration and Plan of Action on Industrialisation (Resolved: To have the less developed countries' share of production go from 7 percent to 25 percent by year 2000)

1976–1985 International Decade for Women

1978   Alma Ata International Conference on Primary Health Care (Resolved: Health for all by the year 2000)

1980–1990 International Drinking Water and Sanitation Decade (Resolved: Clean water for all by 1990)[15]

Of course, we were always ready to cite extraordinary events as excuses for the various delays in the fulfillment of these hopes. In Africa the 1984 widespread famine was a particular jolt to the continent and to the development community. And while the publicity about it had its silver lining (more private funding for NGOs engaged in relief), it was a major setback. War and strife also continued, and whole projects that had looked as if they were moving forward were in effect ground to dust by these traumas. A World Bank–sponsored health project, a Dutch-sponsored education project, or an NGO-operated agricultural extension project that had taken painstaking planning to get off the ground would disappear quickly once instability took hold. Nothing is worse for development than instability, especially the kind development practitioners were becoming accustomed to — that prompted by famine, flood, economic disaster and capital flight, or religious and ethnic wars. Much of Africa began to be a thorn in the side of development professionals because during the 1980s many countries lost economic ground steadily. Dependence on foreign aid for quite a few African countries began to look permanent.

Finally, in some quarters the development community during this period began to face the negative consequences of some of its own past work. Not only had tremendous outside forces complicated development significantly, but internally in many poor countries development work itself had raised expectations that could not be met, sometimes creating incentives for corruption and theft and in the main adding a heavy debt burden to countries with no resources.

The first of these consequences — expectations — is difficult to measure, but we began to notice a very large movement of people from country to country, not only from south to north but also from south to south. The

15. *Everyone's United Nations: A Handbook on the Work of the UN* (New York: United Nations, 1979).

effect of better communication and globalization began to merge with rising expectations, thus refugees from strife on the move were joined by people who simply could not wait for things to get better at home. Labor migration became a major phenomenon, with its own complex and difficult–to-measure side effects.

As for corruption, almost everyone who works in development on the ground had become aware of it, and the siphoning off of a certain percentage of development funding began to be inevitable, a price of doing business. But it was not talked about publicly.

It was growing debt that led the World Bank to institute a massive program of what was called "structural adjustment," a get-tough attempt to make countries face up to their fiscal laxity and tighten their belts. As the effects of structural adjustment on the poor began to be felt, development faced yet another unintended by-product of its tinkering: more poverty and of a more dramatic sort.

Meanwhile, the public in the Western countries grew tired of and cynical about foreign aid — even those who were staunch supporters had doubts. Though philanthropic giving in general had never been greater, the public, which supports foreign aid for development, was experiencing what came to be called "aid fatigue." The money did not stop. But it was not as easy to obtain.

Many NGOs, and not a few large official public sector agencies, began a period of navel gazing and self-doubt, holding retreats, hiring management consultants, and thinking about their role and their inner meaning. Ironically, this occurred at a time when NGOs were being given much more credit for effectiveness than ever by their larger, more powerful peers. Almost as if the attention made them self-conscious, they began professionalizing, particularly in the marketing and fund-raising area. In not a few instances the fund-raising personnel began to come from outside the development profession, earning salaries out of line with those of their development colleagues. Even the big institutions were not saved from a gnawing questioning and a degree of doubt. The World Bank itself began a series of restructurings and reengineerings that continued through the 1990s.

Throughout the period, the thread of participation and people-centered development became stronger. The once polarized grassroots-oriented agenda of the NGOs and the World Bank–led agenda of economic growth — the "softhearts" and the "hardheads" — began to move toward each other. A centrism evolved. Neither "side" stopped doing its thing, but they began to speak to each other with more comprehension, if not yet full respect.

Across the board, we saw a growing tendency to "unpack" key ideas and reach for more refined levels of explanation. Political scientists took their turn sitting at the theoretical podium, joining the economists, sociologists, and anthropologists in dissecting the dynamics of free enterprise. Much more work took place in the area of markets and enterprise development; those interested in financial institution building and the dynamics of international capital flows gained influence. At the elite end of development work—the interaction with governments and large institutions—the discourse was now about the role of incentives and the "policy environment" in promoting growth. Policy reform and "getting the prices right" became buzzwords.

At the ruder end of things, where the NGOs meet the people in the villages and slums, there was for the first time a borrowing of free enterprise rhetoric. The idea of business, not to mention capitalism itself, had been anathema to most NGOs. But NGOs now discovered that when the "little people" are engaged in it, then business is OK. The "informal sector" was discovered and a growing sexiness attached to NGOs that worked with microenterprises. Microcredit became the new magic bullet. In effect, while public works infrastructure projects were no longer in vogue, the desire to engineer things remained.

Moreover, the 1970s appropriate technology theme of the rural romantics joined forces with the environmentalists. Now the environmental movement entered the development debate. Widespread use of the term "sustainable development" came about, and the development industry began to employ much more sophisticated language about doing things that would not destroy the earth, that would have lasting effects.

It is as if, in this trying and mixed-up time, development took on aspects of a religion under siege. Syncretism was one way of reacting to this—a knee-jerk, uncritical grabbing at strands from many other fields and trying to make them fit the development endeavor. The strongest and strangest influence from 1980 to 1990 was the growing, still hesitant reaching out for the language and concepts of the for-profit business world. Talk was of "niches," of development as "product," of beneficiaries as "customers." The implicit organizational model became that of the bottom line–oriented, cost-effective, productivity-obsessed commercial world. Sensing the larger outside forces and the incipient threat of the southern indigenous NGO movement, those in the practice of development assistance prepared to enter a newly rough-and-tumble, much more competitive, far less gentle world.

Among U.S. NGOs, for example, competition for money grew, especially for public money. Between 1973 and 1986, USAID assistance to U.S. NGOs increased from $39 million to $450 million, almost a twelvefold increase, while NGOs' private source income went from $673 million to $1.86 billion, an increase in volume of huge proportions but, in percentages, less dramatic than that of public source income. Many NGOs came to prefer public money, hard as it is to get, because it comes in larger chunks generally than private contributions and can be used in part for overhead. Public money represented over 20 percent of the budget of U.S. NGOs in this period, up from about 5 percent, and these organizations wanted more. The number of American NGOs registering with USAID to make themselves eligible for public funding increased significantly in the 1980s (from 205 in 1988 to 439 in 1996).

And a new threat was rising—the local, indigenous NGO. From 1987 on, the proportion of USAID funding given to local NGOs in the category of child survival, health, and AIDs prevention grew steadily. In 1987, U.S. NGOs received $41.3 million, while local indigenous NGOs received $8.9 million (82.1 percent versus 17.9 percent). The U.S. proportion dropped in the following years: In 1988, $43.9 (81.2 percent) to $9.8 (18.8 percent); in 1989, $57 million (77.5 percent) to $16.6 million (22.5 percent); and in 1990, $68.5 million (72.1 percent) to $26.4 (27.9 percent).

Feeling all these forces and changes, however inchoately, the development field seemingly began to corral the horses and draw the wagons in close. Despite the differences among the various players, a kind of rallying around the flag began to occur. For all the diversity and healthy debate, for all the doubt cast by critics on development assistance (and which here and there some practitioners began privately to have as well), the development assistance community now completed the long process of transforming itself into an "industry." Increasingly, just as in the world of commerce where firms exist to make a profit for themselves, development and all the organizations within it began to live by a new imperative — our own survival. It was as if, in subconscious denial of our growing collective irrelevance and ineffectiveness, we needed to hype what we do, not only to funders (we can accept that as natural) but to ourselves.

Full Industrialization of the Development Business: 1990–2000

More than earlier phases, this most recent decade saw the effect of big changes in the global context for development. And they were (and continue to be) large indeed. The very early 1990s witnessed the defeat of communism and the apparently definitive triumph of capitalism. With that, both the U.S. economy and American culture entered a period of seemingly unstoppable dominance. The globalization of the world marketplace became far more evident. The idea of each country making the things that it needs and being "self-reliant," the idea of protectionism, began to seem not only obsolete but downright quaint. As computer technology raced ahead and the possibilities of the World Wide Web began to astound, even the concept of a "new industrial revolution" sounded like a slightly old-fashioned way of signaling a new era.

The rules, the playing field, and the stakes in the game of development changed. The implicit understanding was that if a country did not have stable and democratic institutions and a threshold of educated people, it could still develop, but it was likely to be doomed, in the medium term at least, to dependent, second-class status in the new world order.

Let's imagine that a poor country (call it "Sisyphustia") had made real progress using all the resources and technical assistance of the previous four decades of development. It had rooted out corruption, become politically stable, built a port, maintained its roads, improved the productivity of its largely small-scale agriculture, and put up factories. But Sisyphustia is small, has few natural resources, is not an attractive tourist destination, is not a democracy, and has fallen significantly short on the secondary and higher education front. Despite its relatively high marks in the old development subjects, these are no longer very important. The game has changed faster than Sisyphustia did. Small-scale agriculture is simply not where it's at, unless you produce boutique-style high-value crops such as orchids or goat cheese, exportable by air. Manufacturing, which Sisyphustia now does some of (shirts, pants, baseballs, wicker furniture), is now suddenly not the road to wealth. Indeed, the north, which touted industrialization back in the 1950s, does not do much of it anymore. Most of what we buy is made in the third world, in such countries as Sisyphustia where the wages are low. To be sure, Sisyphustia, having played by most of the rules, now has more low-paying (but steadily so) jobs than ever and has eliminated famine and abject poverty. All this progress is good, but what has happened is that once it began to catch up, we leaped ahead. Sisyphustia is again way behind, and even its progress to date does not guarantee future progress, for now a new brain drain is beginning to take place, at a time when brains are the new world currency. The country's few young, brightly educated people are not about to wait for opportunities at home, even if the prospects look good over the long term. They want to leave, and they do. Sisyphustia, which once had hopes of being a star, is increasingly a satellite, an adjunct of our dominant, now global, system.

But why is this all bad? It is not bad in the sense that what we will begin seeing is more trickle-down. The digital age will, ironically, be the main promoter of bricks-and-mortar industrialization in the once "backward" third world. And as that happens there are likely to be more wage jobs and more people will have greater purchasing power, and *over time* (and it may be quite some time), they too may find a toehold on the great wheel of capitalism.

Moral judgments about capitalism aside, the only field for which this scenario is immediately "bad" is the development assistance field. As capitalism's steamroller moves on, it makes much if not most of what the development field does irrelevant (as I will show in the next chapter).

P. T. Bauer, one of the few economists who has criticized development, has admitted plainly that the problems of underdevelopment are not "readily rectifiable": "The potentialities of development economics for the promotion of material progress have been oversold to a credulous public. . . . Economic development is a major aspect of the historical process of entire societies, and is therefore not susceptible to general theories."[16]

The formal development assistance field has never really been able to deal with the inherent complexity of the work it chose to take on. Now, the pace of globalization seems to have multiplied the complexities of the development challenge.

Yet, Sisyphus-like, development thinking continues to try to find the right answers. The last decade saw much greater recognition of the importance of governance and especially the crucial role in growth of policy incentives. Serious attention was paid to human rights. And the informal internal dialogue that has always existed began to address some long-felt discomforts. NGOs seemed to come to terms more with their traditional distaste for the private sector. Practitioners appeared ready to talk more openly about the problematic nub of all direct projects — dependency. The word "corruption" was used more openly in development assistance circles, and the issue of corruption is now directly addressed by initiatives of the World Bank.

Despite all the changes in the idea of development that have taken place over fifty years, some of it quite explicitly directed at coming to terms with complexity, and despite yet another round of attempts to "get it right," development practice has not really changed. If new ideas get added on, few of the old ones are let go. As at the beginning, we are still wedded to the daily project and program work of our organizations. And the built-in tendency to "do" things has been reinforced by the organizational imperatives for survival that the development assistance industry has come to represent.

16. P. T. Bauer, *Dissent on Development* (Cambridge: Harvard University Press, 1976), 20.

Warm Bodies

Washington, 1984

"YES?" Ben said as he answered the phone.

"Hi, Ben, I'm John Becker from ProjectSuccess International in Washington. We're about to respond to an RFP for a two-and-a-half-year integrated health project in the Philippines. Your name came up in our database, and we'd like to put you forward as the Chief of Party."

Thirty months in the Philippines! Ben had been thinking it would be fun to go overseas again. The expat life is a good one, and few opportunities like this come up anymore for Americans. And to go as COP (Chief of Party) might even be therapeutic — Ben had often felt that a repressed "cop" existed within him — perhaps this would be his last chance to be a boss. Besides, his recent work had become routine. He's ready, no, anxious for a change. But Ben knows he should play it cool.

"Well, can you tell me a little more about it? Like, how long is the assignment, where in the Philippines is it, how big a project is it? Like that."

"Sure. I can send you a copy of the USAID PID. But basically, it will be located in the northern part of Luzon, a town called Baguio about a hundred miles from Manila, and involves working with a very poor rural district to set up health clinics and the like. It would involve setting up an office in the town of Baguio and running the project with about twelve local-hire staff. Plus you'd have two other expats."

"Sounds good. I look forward to receiving the PID."

It was January, and Becker assured Ben that the whole process would be over by summer. If ProjectSuccess won the contract, Ben would have an answer in time to go by September.

Ben didn't waste much time thinking about the scheduling because he knew that the chances of this call developing into a real overseas job were remote. He knew how the system worked.

In a memo from USAID's Washington headquarters to the field offices, the agency administrator indicates that AID must begin implementing the spirit of a new law passed in Congress which states that all U.S. official aid must provide for "basic health needs" to be met in all "relevant projects." The memo provides guidelines and instructions.

A review of the projects in the health sector is therefore requested from the health project officers at all USAID missions. The cable adds that the Alma Ata declaration (an international health protocol dating from 1978) should be used as a benchmark. Do programs focus on the availability of basic drugs at the community level? Do they focus on maternal and child healthcare, particularly preventive care? Are they implementing a nutrition education component and a weight monitoring system for newborns? Is there coordination with local primary schools? Are mothers being encouraged to come to local clinics? What is the governance structure of local clinics?

In Manila the USAID mission director sees the cable and requests his chief health project officer to deal with it. The project officer, who has been in the country for twenty-eight months and is, by USAID standards, well seasoned, knows the key players at the Ministry of Health and the Ministry of Planning, her counterparts in the other bilateral aid agencies (they meet monthly to discuss the health sector), and the representatives of the various multilateral agencies, such as UNICEF, the UNDP, and WHO, with whom, increasingly, projects have been shared.

At the USAID mission, meetings are held to discuss what the new mandate means. Some staff argue that they are already doing what is required and protest the way Washington imposes new hassles on them. They will, however, soon get to work. An analysis of the current health project portfolio will be done. Meetings will be held with the Ministry of Health and others.

It emerges that there *is* something new that can be done. One of the poorest areas of the country, an area with no government services, a high level of infant mortality, poor water, a low level of female education, has no significant presence in the health sector on USAID's part. There is, however, a Dutch-sponsored project in the area, as well as an immunization project under WHO auspices, which uses volunteers from several international and bilateral volunteer-sending agencies, including the Irish volunteers and the United Nations volunteers.

Mindful of the possibilities of treading on others' turf and recognizing that it is often difficult to create a coordinated multidonor project, the USAID team tentatively proposes to the mission director that USAID launch a new separate project in one district. It would be a five-year project (an initial thirty months with a renewal of an additional thirty). The first stage would be the construction of clinics at the village cluster level. Then there would be training of nurse practitioners and midwives, followed by the initiation of a village-based pharmacy program and a children's education program component. The team plots the different components of the project on a board. (They use the word "package" for some of the components, as in the "drug package," the "training package." This makes it easier to connect up with the expected outcomes on the "log frame," the "logical" framework that for some years has been USAID's main tool to ensure that objectives are met in a measurable way. Thus when the training "package" has been "delivered," the objective for that component of the project design has been met.)

These tentative plans are debated back and forth by cable with counterparts at USAID in Washington. Eventually, Washington hires a consultant to go to the Philippines and assist the health officer do a feasibility report and prepare a draft concept paper, called a PID (Project Identification Document).

As the reports and papers go back and forth, meetings are held in both Washington and Manila. Eight months after the original cable, approval of the PID comes through. Several of the Washington people who had been working on this project have since moved to other positions, but those who replace them take up the project's supervision.

The staff in Manila now guide this process under the lead of the health officer, who now has twenty months to go on her forty-eight-month assignment to this post. She wants to make this new project happen before she leaves. (She has considered extending for a second tour, but she's been told confidentially by a friend in USAID/Washington that if she does not take advantage of a slot opening in Latin America in a year, one she has an excellent chance of getting, she will be jeopardizing a promising career. Now thirty-four years old, she knows that if she takes the right assignments in the right places, under the right mission directors, she will be in line for a deputy mission director slot within four or five years and by about age forty-two ready for a mission director's position.)

It is understood by USAID that a project of this type will require either a nongovernmental organization (NGO) or a private contractor to run it, one with experience in grassroots work, with a record of achievement in getting things up and running quickly and recruiting good people from both the United States and the host country.

Informally, only three NGOs are being discussed — Save the Children, Catholic Relief Services, and CARE — along with two of the oldest private contractors in Washington. All five organizations are large. Their directors are well known to key Washington USAID staff. They have their own informal network of lobbyists, and they are visible. But this will be no inside job. There are rules, indeed finely wrought rules, about the contracting process.

The PID leads to production of the project paper (PP), and now a request for proposal (RFP) must be written. The RFP is a lengthy document, often running to a hundred pages or more; it is this proposal to which the NGOs and contractors will respond. It will specify the concept of the project and the details and background of the setting in which it is to be run. The RFP will ask the applicant to say how it intends to accomplish the goals, which people it would recruit (complete with detailed résumés), and how it would budget the project. It will ask for benchmarks, guidelines, and accountability documents; for demonstrations of the capability to undertake such a contract; and for statements of financial probity. Finally, it will ask for a proposed budget with line-by-line justifications.

Though the RFP is made available to anyone who reads the government-published *Commerce and Business Daily* and looks to see what's being shopped around for bid, AID project officers in Washington who know people in various NGOs and contracting companies will make informal phone calls to encourage them to apply.

A typical contract in the mid-1980s would be a four- or five-year project; it would have two or three expatriate personnel full-time including a Chief of Party. The COP is the head of the project and the legal representative of the contracting party. There will be one or two specialists in technical fields. A contract usually will call for short-term technical assistance (TA)—measured in person months of TA—positions that consultants will typically fill.

Though designed to be an efficient way of delegating to the private sector what the U.S. government wants to do in the development assistance realm, the contracting process in reality is, in bureaucratic fashion, about checking off a series of politically important boxes. The number of different boxes grows as the American democratic process becomes more sophisticated. In the United States by the 1980s, so many different concerns and sensibilities about development were being effectively voiced to Congress that USAID has to make sure that these myriad "thou shalts" and "thou shalt nots" are built into each RFP and consequently each overseas project. Inevitably, the realities of the time frame and the urgency to comply with many different congressional mandates begin to reduce the overarching goals of the project to line items on a chart. Often the only one of the original large goals that remains intact is that of completion — delivering the "packages" and closing the project.

ProjectSuccess is one of the older contractors in Washington. It has a reputation for running things tightly and getting the job done. But it is, like all the others, a "body shop." Its database contains thousands of names of consultants such as Ben, with key words linked to the kinds of development projects that are likely to be put up for bid (primary heath, microcredit, agricultural extension, refugee rehabilitation, nutrition education, and so on). Ben's name is in the databases of several of these contractors, and he receives four or five calls a year, usually for short-term consultancies. If you have twenty years of experience in the business as Ben does and you want even more calls, you need only design your curriculum vitae (CV) so the clerk inputting your information to the database will link your name to more specialties and geographic areas.

Willard Thorne Jr. runs ProjectSuccess and is known as a tightwad. He has to be. Making a profit when you do win a contract with the U.S. government is tough, and if you don't watch the dimes on your cost side, the pennies you hope to make in profit disappear fast. The process of getting the contract in the first place is only for the hearty of spirit, so daunting is the paperwork and the details that USAID requires. Those people who are able to lead a team through such an ordeal are green eyeshade types who get a kick out of "dotting i's." So when Willard Thorne Jr. gets hold of one of these, someone like John Becker, he makes sure to pay him well.

Ben recalled meeting Willard Thorne once at a cocktail party given by the president of one of ProjectSuccess's chief competitors, New Applications Inc., for which Ben had worked briefly in the early 1980s. That was not long before Ben quit after he made it known at a retreat being held to focus on the company's competitive advantage that he was not going to be a "team player." The president had stood before the senior executives of the company and had led a discussion of how the company was different because it stood for something. And that something was "excellence." Excellence was its advantage. Excellence was its niche. Excellence was its specialty. Everyone had nodded. Ben remembered raising his hand, knowing he was about to can himself. "Excellence in what?" he asked. When the president asked Ben what he meant by that, that was Ben's chance to say, "Oh, nothing." But he hadn't. He had continued. "Well, excellence is not a stance or a moral position. It's about means. You can be excellent at cheating, lying, saving lives, building bridges. We're saying New Applications stands for something. But we still haven't heard what that is." Ben quit three weeks later, when it became apparent that the other executives' sudden coolness toward him was not going to be temporary.

Ben recalled Willard Thorne as a tall patrician man in his midforties, with an icy demeanor. He'd gone to Ivy League schools and belonged to a horsey set in Virginia. He came from family money and had married more family money. He had a law degree but had never practiced. Ben couldn't figure him. Willard didn't need to make money. He could have gone into politics. He could have done any number of things, including running a business. Why of all things was he in government contracting for USAID? Maybe he liked to travel to the third world. Maybe he liked the image of himself as a do-gooder who also made a living at it. Or maybe he truly wanted to do good.

But still, the contractors' game is a hard one to play, year after year.

When one of these organizations decides to respond to an RFP, they have to be prepared to commit considerable time and money to the effort. If it is a for-profit company such as ProjectSuccess making the bid, then putting in the time and money is simply a business decision: Is this something we've got a good shot at? But if it is a nonprofit, an NGO, then the decision is more complicated because the organization will have to use its reserves in the process of bidding — that is, money it collected from those rare donors who did not ask that it be used for a specific purpose. These "unrestricted" funds are hard to come by. What donor is disinterested enough to say, "Look, we trust you, use this money as you see fit?" An unrestricted dollar is worth far more than a restricted one. It is rainy-day money, and for a nonprofit to spend it bidding on a government contract is therefore risky. But many NGOs do it. Oddly, they have to play things the same way the for-profits do. They will need to fly to Washington on their own dime; they'll need to take a few folks out to dinner—a bit of "representational entertainment"—and sometimes they'll need to fly to the country where the proposed project is to be located and do a little quiet reconnaissance work. They may even need to hire consultants to help them draft particular parts of the proposal.

And to make matters more complicated, if the requested proposal is for a complex project, then both private for-profits and NGOs will jockey to align themselves with each other. They do this, first, to ward off competition and, second, to make sure they have all the requisite skills that might form the criteria for judging the winner.

Ben had seen when he worked for New Applications that the organization making the bid has no real say in the project agenda, and more than likely, neither did the supposed beneficiaries. Ben used to think how apt the phrase "supply side" was becoming in development work— these were the Reagan years. Almost no one was asking about the "demand side": Was the project necessary from the beneficiaries' point of view?

USAID decides what the project's overall parameters will be. And that initial shape can come from many different sources, some of which may have little interest in development. The originating idea can be the AID mission in a country, where the new mission director might want to make a mark for career reasons, or the AID mission can be influenced by a political concern put forward by the ambassador. Just as often the initial idea will come from a congressional mandate that requires US-AID to do something in the third world that satisfies a basket of particularly American interests; it may thus be inappropriate for the country in which the project will be undertaken. Finally, it may also derive some of its initial push from some new perception of the state-of-the-art in development, a bandwagon that picks up momentum as a new buzzword travels around the industry. In the fullest sense, all these pushes are on the supply side of the house.

So the prospective contractor has little choice about the grand design of the project and goes into the bidding process knowing that it is a hired gun and little else. But once won, USAID development project contracts are attractive sources of money for any organization in the nonprofit world that believes its survival depends on building its capacity or its track record or on positioning itself for geographic expansion by tacking new flags onto the map it publishes in its annual report. And for a for-profit, of course, winning contracts is its lifeblood.

So the job of the bidder is not to convince USAID of what it believes makes sense in developmental terms but simply that it is the best-positioned organization to carry out the project effectively. It must demonstrate "capability," and the first task is putting together the capability statement — a kind of CV of the organization. The more one wins contracts, the more likely it is that one will have a longer and more impressive capability statement.

Ben had pretty much forgotten about the whole thing as the summer passed, taking on short five- and six-week consulting assignments. The rhythm of his year was again like the ones before it: a three-week trip to somewhere, two to three weeks writing his report, a few weeks off, and then another assignment. So he had to dig a bit into his memory when John Becker called him the Monday after Thanksgiving to say that ProjectSuccess had heard through the grapevine that it was "Best and Final" for the project. (Best and Final is a tentative declaration of the winner, pending certain verifications, some more dotting and crossing of i's and t's, and a few to-be-negotiated adjustments in the budget.)

At first, Ben was not clear who Becker was. His initial reaction was surprise. These things so rarely come through that Ben was not used to thinking about the reality of a position he never expected to get. But Becker tells Ben that it's going to be another month or so because there is a possible conflict-of-interest question that needs to be sorted out. John is not at liberty to tell Ben what this is about, but some congressman has been put on ProjectSuccess's case, possibly at the behest of a competing organization.

So, first pumped up and then quickly let down again, Ben did not bother noting to John that, under these still iffy circumstances, he was not going to be holding his breath. Nor was he going to turn down any future assignment. In the end, Ben put the thirty months in the Philippines back where it had been, on the dusty fantasy shelf of his mind.

Of course nothing happened through all of December. Finally, in mid-January ProjectSuccess received formal confirmation from USAID of the contract win. But because the start-up of the project had been de-layed by seven months, ProjectSuccess now found that all the original prospective staff but Ben have taken full-time or long-term positions elsewhere. Like Ben, they too had not put their lives on hold. After all, it had been over a year since they had given their names, and everyone knows these are not binding commitments.

Becker calls Ben, desperate for help. How can ProjectSuccess now move forward? Having for months been all dressed up with no place to go, the contractor now finds itself with a firm place to go, with its dress clothes all lost at the dry cleaners. Ben feels a little embarrassed and not a tiny bit insecure. If he's so good, why is he still available? Ben knows ra-tionally that he is available only because he is an independent consult-ant and has deliberately not been looking for full-time work. But is that how Becker and the others at ProjectSuccess will see it? Is Ben going to be subject to a reverse of the Groucho Marx rule — in this case, Project-Success not wanting anyone who would want to work for it?

But Becker does not see things this way. He is happy to have Ben and calls him daily to ask him, please, to recommend others to replace the people who are no longer available. This is what "body shop" means, Ben thinks. Of course, any body will do. And, usually, any one does. Ben himself has gotten about half his assignments because someone else originally chosen to do the work took on another job while waiting for the inevitable delays to be worked through. It doesn't mean Ben was sec-ond best. There is no second best because there was really never a first best. We're all interchangeable. The organization, in this case Project-Success, has to do exactly what all its competitors do. The USAID parameters and rules are the same for all. They all have the same data-base of names. The names and the bodies move from one body shop to another.

So what exactly is it that the contractor is selling? Basically two things: Assuming all reputable contractors will make similar proposals about how they plan to carry out the work, the first distinguishing feature will be how they cost the project, and this is where the tightwads such as Willard Thorne Jr. have an edge. They manage their operation tightly and squeeze more out of less. The second thing is name and reputation. But that name is somewhat fictional. It is tied to success in a way similar to what has happened in baseball, where the illusion of the Baltimore team or the Cleveland team is only in the eyes of the fans, when in real-ity the players move around from team to team, year to year, wearing one uniform one year, another the next. But at least in baseball, the trading around of the players is based on some degree of real talent. In most contracted development projects the outcome is similar whether one contractor or NGO or another wins the bid. There is no World Series.

It's now late January, time for Ben to get down to cases and ask about fees and perks. Ben knew going into this that ProjectSuccess was going to claim that it had little leeway as to daily rate equivalents, for this is where, ProjectSuccess would have him believe, the USAID system is most rigid — it may not offer any overseas person a base salary greater than the scale specifies. And Ben knows that Willard Thorne's habit is, as is that of other contracting companies, to try to squeeze his profit out of salaries and the daily rate for project consultants. Salaries and personnel costs are where the money is to be made, because as much as 50 percent of a typical contract will consist of salaries and related costs. So ProjectSuccess will offer to pay Ben a salary of X (which is, hopefully for Thorne, lower than the allowable AID maximum for the qualifications and experience of the person) and then mark it up, charging AID X + Y percent, a function of the all-important negotiated overhead rate, which might go as high as 250 percent. Ben knows the principles behind the formulas, even if he doesn't know the numbers. And he knows what to push for. First, he has to get to or very close to the AID "max," the highest consulting rate allowable. Even though this is about one-half to one-third of a basic rate in the for-profit commercial world, it's an OK salary for the development industry, but *only if one goes overseas*. After a short exchange of calls, ProjectSuccess reluctantly accepts Ben's demand, obviously calculating that they still can make a profit.

But for Ben, getting the AID "max" is in the end more about his own sense of self-worth than about money. The real financial incentives lie in the rest of the package. It's the freebies that make the difference. Most important is the free housing, complete with U.S. government–issued Drexel Heritage furniture and all utilities paid for. Then there is the travel, baggage, and shipping allowance. Ben has decided to rent out his home for the two and a half years he and his family will be away, thus the household effects he is not taking with him (75 percent of them) have to be put into storage. This too is paid for. His wife and son will be with him, of course, so all three will have round-trip airfare. Ben has already suspected, given where the project will be located (far from Manila), that the schooling at the "post" is likely to be inadequate. He knows he will have to demonstrate this through a bit of paperwork, but the likelihood is that he can do so, as he did the last two times he was overseas, in which case the project will pass the cost of private boarding school back in the United States on to USAID. In that case, Ben's son will go back to the States to school. One trick is to pick a post where good schools are hard to find, and Ben knows some people who routinely do just that.

Then Ben wants to be sure that a home leave will be paid for halfway through the project, if he decides to apply for a second two and a half year tour as COP. Normally, AID will send you on home leave every two years. As this too is a standard added cost that will simply be passed straight to USAID, ProjectSuccess agrees.

Ben will have a project vehicle. This will be strictly controlled and not really usable for private purposes, but how that is defined is always a bit open.

But the thing Ben counts on most is the hardship differential. This could go as high as 25 percent of his base salary. Ben guessed from the project's location that this would be forthcoming, which Becker confirms. The first time Ben gave this curious artifact some thought, he realized that "hardship" is fundamentally a product of American chauvinism. It presumes that if you are an American, you are a Norman Rockwell American — white, small-town, and Christian. It follows that if you are posted overseas in anyplace other than a Paris or a London, life will be hard to bear, but not because the material things you need won't be provided for you. One of the ironies about "hardship" posts, all of which are in the third world, is the protean effort made to make up for those hardships (clean water, decent housing, and electricity will be provided free even when they are not available to the "natives," and almost every other material thing one could possibly be used to, from Thanksgiving turkeys to Budweiser and Jack Daniels, to hot dogs on the Fourth of July, are all likely to be available for sale at U.S. prices through some arrangement made by the local U.S. embassy). No, the real hardship you suffer is because of what you might miss in American social and cultural life and how you might feel about being "uprooted." So the definition in the first instance is a reciprocal; it is defined in terms of what is missing in the ephemeral realm — your hometown "community" or going to a football game or the mall — not in terms of the reality of what you actually have to endure. The hardship allowance is the product of a myth, the loss of which is translated into dollars.

When Ben had been the Peace Corps director in Yemen some years earlier, his colleagues at USAID received not only a hardship allowance because of the post's remoteness, as well as a "hazardous duty differential" because of the dangers in the country — there was a civil war going on the time — but also a "Sunday differential." The Sunday differential is the oddest of all the derivatives of the assumption that official overseas Americans are unwilling outcasts from a Norman Rockwell magazine cover. At the time (1979) it was apparently assumed that all Americans working in the Muslim Middle East were practicing Christians. Since in Muslim countries Friday is the holy day, the normal work week of the U.S. agencies adapted to that of local government by beginning the week on Saturday and ending it on Wednesday night. The weekend for U.S. government employees was therefore Thursday and Friday. So even though you had Thursday and Friday off and were free to pray with fellow communicants on either of those days, you were still deprived of "Sunday." To make up for this loss, an additional percentage of one's base salary was added to total pay.

Ben thinks back to some of the other ways that the insularity of the "expat" is assured. The first time he was sent to a developing country under the official aegis of the U.S. government, he was struck by the realization that he never bought local postage stamps. When he wrote letters home, he would pick up a roll of U.S. stamps at the embassy, address his letters to friends and family in the States without adding "USA" in the address, and take them over to the embassy mailbox. From there they would be combined with all the other mail of U.S. employees and put in the diplomatic pouch to Washington, where they would be sent all over the country as if that were where they had originated. It worked in reverse too. It was especially thrilling, for example, to place an order with L.L. Bean from a remote part of the developing world and a month later receive the package through the embassy pouch.

He remembers how much some of his friends who had lifetime careers at USAID used to complain when the time came for them to do a stint in Washington (most USAID employees who are overseas will be obliged at least twice in a twenty-five-year-long career to work back home). Back in Washington, they'll live in an apartment or a house with a high mortgage, pay their own utilities and schooling, have to maintain their own car, and deal with the plumbing when it needs fixing. They'll be living, in short, like other Americans, free to go to the mall on Saturday and to church on Sunday.

They lose not only the freebies but also the various differentials to their salary. A person making a mere forty-five thousand dollars in an overseas hardship post could end up with one hundred thousand dollars saved or invested at the end of a three-year assignment. The catch in the arrangement is the real material "hardship" incurred upon coming home, for which there is no special "allowance."

These perks seem to say something about the third world itself and the work of development assistance. It is a tacit but real message — as real as money — that the third world is not worth living in and that no real compensatory satisfaction exists in the work itself.

Ben has some qualms about all this, as do others in the industry. But most of those who do still take the money and run. And so will he.

By the middle of February, Becker has managed to find other people to replace those originally named for the project. ProjectSuccess will submit these names to USAID, which will approve the new people after asking some perfunctory questions, even though the bid was won, presumably, on the basis of an almost entirely different "team."

Finally, work begins in earnest. Part of what ProjectSuccess received in its contract is money to orient and build the "team." Ben and the two other expats are to spend a total of four weeks in Washington, in two separate visits. They will use one week at ProjectSuccess to fill in forms and become acquainted with the ProjectSuccess accounting system. During the rest of the time, they will meet with the USAID project officers to get the "face time" needed so that USAID can directly convey its objectives for the project.

As Ben gets ready for the first of the two trips to D.C., he recalls the first time he encountered an angry and skeptical African who, contrary to what Ben had been used to, was not happy and grateful for his country to receive development assistance. This man, a husky Kenyan with whom Ben was having a beer at a Nairobi hotel, worked for USAID (he was what is called a "local hire") and had spent a number of years in the bowels of the accounting department for AID's Nairobi-based regional office for East and Southern Africa. He was therefore in a position to see the detailed paperwork on projects in a number of countries. He ranted on about how small a percentage of the money actually came to these countries, most of it having been reabsorbed into the U.S. economy. As the details of the next few months of preparation and the thirty months of his "stint" in the Philippines began to become clear, Ben could put his finger on the ways in which his Kenyan friend was correct. He made a mental list of just a few of those in the United States who would benefit directly and indirectly from USAID's contract to ProjectSuccess for the Philippine project: there was the telephone company; the office equipment supplier; the travel agency; the airline; the hotels and restaurants in Washington where Ben and his colleagues spent their orientation weeks; the U.S. government itself, which would get income taxes from Ben; and so on.

In Washington in late February, Ben finally meets John Becker, with whom he's had countless phone conversations. Becker is young, maybe twenty-seven or twenty-eight. He was in the Peace Corps after college and then went to the Woodrow Wilson School at Princeton for two years to get his master's degree in public administration, from where he was recruited to ProjectSuccess. This is a new route to a career in international development work — a more direct path than the one Ben took a generation earlier.

One of the new skills much in demand in the 1980s is proposal writing, an ability that an NGO or private contractor must develop to be competitive. NGOs traditionally have not put a premium on staff intellectual or verbal skills, looking instead for commitment, ideology, and interpersonal skills or, in other cases, technical ability. The contacting game has meant a shift to careers in proposal writing. For the money-making organizations such as ProjectSuccess, the competition has increased and the need for more polished proposals along with it. Young people like Becker will work hard and stay late in the office. They'll take a low starting salary if they see a career path. Becker's degree made him attractive, and Thorne actually pays him slightly more than he would get elsewhere in the industry. Nonetheless, all John Becker does is write proposals.

As Ben chats with him, it becomes clear how unselfconsciously ambitious John is. The first evening after work that the two go out for a drink, Becker begins pumping Ben about contacts in other agencies. He thinks he'll stay with ProjectSuccess for a couple of years but ultimately wants to go overseas "to do real development work — that's the fun part."

Becker is now part of a team that Willard Thorne has put together to seek new contracts. In fact he is working on three different bids at once. Thorne has said he wants to position ProjectSuccess for the 1990s — they are going to have to become larger and more diversified in order to compete.

For Becker, Ben's project is already "over." The energy of the company has moved on to new battles. Once the contract is won, all ProjectSuccess has to do with a project is maintenance. Ben will go out to the Philippines with his two expats, hire some "locals," set up a project office, and do the work specified in the contract. No one will check on progress until the "midterm evaluation" required in the contract at the two-year mark (that will be followed at the end of the project by a termination evaluation). Becker, if he is still with the company, will be setting up the Scope of Work (SOW) for that evaluation in about twelve months and begin recruiting the short-term consultants for it. That's probably the next time Ben will have an intense series of communications with the company. In the meantime, assuming nothing goes haywire, he'll be left alone to be the COP.

Someone once said to Ben that however much the profit motive may in some moral sense "mar" the dignity of work in the world of commerce, one can at least cull some consistent meaning from the fact that the work in that world is "demanded" by the marketplace — someone buys it and pays money for it. Development assistance is different; work is often created, conjured up, and invented for spurious purposes, few of which have to do with real demand or need.

But as he boards the shuttle to Washington in March, Ben isn't thinking about such matters. He is wondering how much a maid and a gardener might cost in northern Luzon.

Sliding toward Dependency

Ada Foa, Ghana, 1985

Ben had an hour to kill before John Dogbe would take him to meet the management staff of the Rabbit Project at the Chinese restaurant in Ada Foa. Because the coastal town had no hotel deemed good enough for a foreigner, Ben was to spend the night at the old guest quarters of a defunct road construction project a few kilometers away.

After the bumpy three-hour drive from Accra, Ben needed to stretch. He took a walk through the abandoned construction camp, a concrete graveyard of rusted earthmoving equipment. The massive machines — Caterpillar front loaders, Kumatsu road graders, bulldozers — looked as if they had died young; some still had all their "teeth." The trail of derelict equipment went on for hundreds of yards, down to the edge of the Atlantic. The machinery, paid for by various aid donors, took on a sad presence as dusk fell. These hulks had not expired from overuse or hard work but from lack of parts and maintenance. Mute orphans of development, they had long been forgotten, "written off" by their donors' accountants in Washington or London.

Dinner at the Chinese restaurant was a rare treat for the Ghanaians with Ben. For five years Ghana had been in a state of economic free fall. A few months back, on Ben's last trip, he had had to bring canned food into the country. The Continental Hotel in Accra (once a proud member of the Intercontinental chain) had had nothing to offer in its restaurant except rice and beer. But things were slowly beginning to pick up. Food was more available. The edges of Ghana's endemic corruption were being nibbled at. Government was liberalizing the economy. People were hopeful. In Ada Foa the Chinese restaurant was new. It was packed with a mixture of aid workers and local merchants.

After dinner, back at the camp, Ben arranged his jacket as a pillow cover, the pillow itself being encrusted with dirt. His jacket wasn't too clean either, but at least his head would be on familiar dirt. He thought about the Rabbit Project.

In 1974 the Ministry of Agriculture had been successful in obtaining USAID funding for the National Rabbit Project (the NRP), and in early 1975 the commissioner of agriculture had asked WorldServe (WS), the American NGO for which Ben worked, to help put the NRP on a more business-like basis. Ben's NGO specialized in helping to develop what the founder of WS called "community-based enterprises" in rural areas of the third world. Since he had first visited Africa in the early 1960s, the founder of WS had maintained that rural Africans did not need handouts but advice and assistance in getting themselves organized into businesses that could profitably sell what they grew or, even better, process what they grew and then sell it. If this could be done, he fervently believed, then Africa could move forward. WorldServe did a study on rabbit production for the government's NRP project and sent off its recommendations. There they sat.

Meanwhile, WS went on about its other work. Then, in 1980, a group of farmers from the Ada Foa area asked WS for advice. This group was just the sort WS liked to work with: a community-based farmers group which the farmers themselves had formed without outside influence and which had never received (nor was it now asking for) any kind of handout. The farmers wanted to start a business and had several ideas, including constructing a cannery for their excess tomato production or possibly raising rabbits. Some of the farmers had heard the government media promoting rabbits in Ghana since the NRP days as a cheap source of meat, with the potential for cash income from both the meat and the pelts. WorldServe jumped at the prospect. Here was a chance to apply its knowledge of rabbits from five years earlier.

Since its beginnings in the late 1960s, WS had been trying hard to find ways out of the dependency dilemma that it thought was the central problem in most development assistance efforts. In theory, WS leadership had long concluded, giving things directly to poor farmers, or even doing things for them, put both the organization and the farmers on the slippery slope to dependency.

To avoid this, WS at first tried to help farmers raise their income by offering them only advice. The advice was free, but nothing else was given to the farmers or done for them. The problem was that the farmers usually listened politely, but if they followed the advice, it was not for long. WorldServe knew the farmers faced other constraints besides lack of good advice — they needed things they did not have and could not afford. But providing the farmers fertilizer, machinery, or seeds was giving things away and would not work because the farmers would have no sense of "ownership" (a similar lack of "ownership" might explain the rusting bulldozers at Ada Foa). WorldServe tried to resolve the dilemma by learning to be more careful about assessing the character and intentions of those it was prepared to help. If the group was serious, sometimes WS might choose to get some momentum going by subsidizing certain small things. But if larger, more costly inputs were needed, WS would direct the farmers to a bank or some other agency that might provide a loan.

By the early 1980s, when it looked as if WS had learned to limit dependency, WS began to see that even if a group of farmers *was* able to start a commercial venture without too much help, they were not necessarily good at managing the business. Improving production was one thing, managing a business was another. WorldServe concluded that this was something these farmer groups would have to be taught and thus began teaching farmers management. But because modern management cannot be taught in a day, WS quickly discovered, these little agricultural businesses risked going under while the farmers were learning.

WorldServe therefore began taking over the management of its clients' community-based enterprises directly and picked a few farmers (usually young men) to train as managers. These "counterparts" worked alongside WS's managers so that way the business could be kept going. Though WS worried that in this fashion it risked coming, if not full circle, at least partway back to dependency creation, it held on to the hope that its tough initial screening of the groups it agreed to help would prove the right antidote.

The first step in the WorldServe screening process was to make several visits to interested groups, to make sure they understood what WS would and would not offer. WorldServe's founder had years before formulated a "rule of five." People, he said, needed to be told things at least five times before they really heard what you were saying. These visits, therefore, were ways to make sure people heard. Then WS would raise the ante: It would work out with the group what initial capital the venture required and insist that the group not only pledge its own share equity but also actually put it in a bank before WS would begin its work. And WS would insist on this even if the groups (and they always did) said they didn't have a penny to spare. In the Ada Foa group's case, thirty-five hundred dollars had been agreed on as the initial share holding, and that amount had been deposited in a local bank by August 1981.

The second kind of test, a Preliminary Project Report (PPR), was internal to WS. In the Ada Foa case, the PPR was a ten-page document packed with questions, projections, and worst- and best-case scenarios. It was an attempt to create a complete picture of the project's fit with WS's own purposes and, more important, its own capabilities. The document asked, "Is the project in response to local need and request?" "Is there a demand for the product?" "Will there be any negative impact on the area's ecology?" "Does the project discriminate in favor of any group or gender?" And it ended with specific questions about rabbit production: "Is breeding stock available?" "Will disease prevention be possible?" and so forth.

The PPR had concluded that "WS has deliberately kept a low profile in the development of this project, wanting to see if the people really meant business, and whether or not they could come up with the required equity. Their enthusiasm in meetings and the payment of their equity share prove they are serious." WorldServe's vice president for Africa had written, "Good fit for Ghana . . . however, management and organizational skills will be severely tested in the current economic environment." One of the Africa program officers had noted that "the main problem will be feed [for the rabbits]."

And so the project had been approved. In the fall of 1982, using US-AID grant money, WS took ten weeks to develop a careful business plan that called for it to work with the group for two years to get things off the ground. The first thing needed was seed capital; WS introduced the Ada Foa group to Barclays Bank, which had a branch nearby. A loan was arranged, but the bank had one condition: It would grant the loan only if WS agreed to manage the project for a full five years. In effect, the bank wanted WS as the informal loan guarantor.

In mid-1983 WS placed a full-time manager on the site and construction began. Fifty rabbit hutches were completed, and a hammer mill (to be used to process feed) was ordered from an agricultural machinery importer. Over the next few months WS Ghana staff immersed themselves in the details of rabbitry, procuring supplies, feed, pumps, tattoo boxes (used to "brand" the rabbits), freezers, generators, and so on. The economy was still in bad shape, and most materials needed were hard to obtain in Ghana. The options for import were all expensive (Does one get chicken wire from the United States, Europe, or Togo?). Telexes flew back and forth to the WS home office in the States, which pretty soon could not help getting involved. Inexorably, an "in-for-a-penny, in-for-a-pound" attitude developed. The Ada Foa group trainees were on hand as management counterparts, but it is unclear how much they were able to learn. Once having committed to the project, WS wanted to get it going at all costs. The specified time frame of the USAID grant hovered over the project. So did the deteriorating economy.

The first rabbits were finally installed in the hutches in mid-1984. But six months later it was clear that the project costs had been seriously underestimated. Disease (and mortality) rates mounted. Rabbits began to die — well, like rabbits. The first real sales had not begun until this summer, four years after the project began. In June, forty-six rabbits were sold. In July, fifty-eight. Ben had been sent to Ghana this time to look at all aspects of the Ada Foa project and to report back to WS headquarters in the United States about the project's future.

That morning in Accra he'd made the rounds with John Dogbe, WS's chief Ghanaian agronomist assigned to the project. Their first stop was at the loading dock of a major brewery. John was in Accra for the weekly pickup of wet spent brewers malt, which, after some cajoling, the brewery had agreed to let WS take away. The brewers malt would be dried and later mixed with dried cassava chip, blood meal, and other mostly recycled local by-products to become feed for the rabbits, a system WS had developed after the first year's high costs meant local feed substitutes had to be found. After loading the WS pickup truck with a couple of cubic yards of wet malt, John and Ben went on to the next stop, Chez Mammie, a small restaurant in Accra, to deliver four rabbits.

This was the first time that a restaurant had ordered rabbits from the Ada Foa group. John had proudly pulled the rabbits from the box behind his seat. They were black with soot from the traditional smoking process used to burn off the fur. Most Ghanaians who eat bush rabbit, when they can get one, like to smoke the meat in this way. But the restaurant owner was not pleased. He had been intrigued with the thought of offering his clientele fresh rabbit. That was why he said yes when he was first approached by the project. He had had in mind a cleanly skinned animal, with the flesh still pink. There had been poor communication. John offered to bring the next batch the way the owner wanted them.

After one other stop John and Ben began the seventy-mile drive out to Ada Foa from Accra. They had lots of time to chat as they drove. Fifteen years earlier the trip would have taken about an hour and a half; now it took three hours. The reason was clear as the pickup threaded its way around potholes and jagged bits of broken asphalt. This road had been built using some of the machines at Ada Foa, but like them it was never maintained. Alongside the road Ben saw telephone lines cut and dangling from every third pole, birds' nests and bits of straw here and there among the tangled wires. The phone lines had not been maintained either.

Ben thought about the broken road and the dangling wires. Was WorldServe, about as well-meaning and sincere a development assistance organization as they come, falling into the same trap as had other organizations twenty years before? Here we were, Ben thought, doing things for the people, accepting the Barclays Bank condition that WS run the Ada Foa project for five years. In the 1960s, the engineers and the technicians who came to Ghana to build roads and put in the phone lines did not know that building things was not enough — that one had to transfer knowledge, train people, create institutions, find ways to support such a system financially, and, hardest of all, somehow get people to think of all that stuff given them for free as really theirs. But we knew better, so what was our excuse? Ben wondered.

When Ben arrived with John at the Ada Foa group's office that afternoon, he asked to look at the account books. Nelson, WS's full-time project manager, was completing the entries for the month. Ben saw that twenty-four of the thirty-five rabbits sold in Accra that month were sold for breeding, while all but two of the twenty-three sold locally were sold for the table. Ben asked if this was significant, but Nelson didn't know. He and John are agronomists, not marketing specialists, Ben remembered. Their main qualification to run the Ada Foa project under the management contract is that they are honest and bright and above all single and willing to live on-site, rather than in Accra.

Ben looked at the balance sheet. The project had been losing money since its beginning. Were Ben to add to the liabilities column the actual cost of WS's donated management time, the years of indirect, informal (and uncosted) time of the U.S.-based staff who had intervened in solving chicken wire types of problems, and the use of WS's pickup to get brewers malt from Accra and deliver rabbits to Chez Mammie, the balance sheet would look insane, not just ridiculous. He made a rough calculation. The total cost to WS to achieve, finally, the sale of 104 rabbits in the last two months — in the fourth year of this enterprise — was between $150,000 and $200,000, or between $1,440 and $1,920 per rabbit sold.

Of course, WS had begun telling itself, its goals included more than a viable rabbit business. WorldServe is not a for-profit consulting firm but an NGO and had always sought to achieve social benefits. Among them was an anticipated improvement in nutrition among the local people. Since the government was promoting family rabbit production for home consumption, some of the money in WS's USAID grant was earmarked to construct a model family backyard rabbit hutch. The design of this impressive hutch was in sharp contrast to the wattle and daub structures in which the people lived. When Ben learned from Nelson that the project's model hutch was now occupied not by rabbits but by the family on whose land it had been built, he rolled his eyes. The rabbit hutch had turned out to be nicer than the farmer's own house!

Ben wrestled with the ironies. The period in Ghanaian economic history during which WS got involved in the Ada Foa project saw a convergence of political, economic, and environmental disasters in Ghana. The years 1982–84 had been particularly rough. One of the worst droughts in Africa's history had by 1982 begun to affect Ghana heavily. In 1983 widespread bush fires destroyed over 150,000 acres of cocoa trees (cocoa having been one of Ghana's few remaining foreign exchange earners). A drop in Lake Volta's water level (Lake Volta is one of the largest man-made lakes in the world) resulted in a 40 percent decrease in electrical capacity and widespread power shortages. A massive expulsion of Ghanaian migrant workers from Nigeria had also occurred in this same period. Inflation between 1978 and 1984 never fell below 100 percent and at one point reached 140 percent. Declining exports, inadequate producer prices, scarcity of foreign exchange with which to bring in imports, mounting deficits — everything that could go wrong had gone wrong.

Shortages were felt by everyone, including the staff of WS. World-

Serve's home office in New England had begun shipping food to its Ghanaian staff. Projects could not be visited regularly because of fuel shortages. Ironically, one of the reasons WS had justified the Ada Foa venture in this high-risk economy was because of its promise of addressing a long-standing food problem in Ghana, a shortage of meat protein. Yet here it was struggling to help raise rabbit meat for folks seventy miles from Accra when its own staff was being shipped canned food from its U.S. headquarters, and building housing for rabbits that farmers could not afford to build for their own families.

Ben could see that five years earlier, WS had asked the right questions. The PPR showed that it had gone into the Ada Foa project with its eyes open, more so than most NGOs he knew would have. Was it right to have ignored the larger economy? Should it have pulled out? Should it drop the ball now? Ben had come out to Ghana because the home office was now stymied. WorldServe, Ben knew, had an emotional tie to Ghana because this was the first country it had begun working in, almost twenty years earlier. Now, even though WS had operations in nine countries on two continents, Ghana held a soft spot in the organization's memory and culture. The rabbit project was its biggest in Ghana, and much money and effort had gone into it. But lately, even though small signs of progress were being made, pressures at WS were mounting and were reflected in some queries coming from USAID. A few senior staff at the WS home office were realizing that, at best, WS was keeping the Ada Foa group from dissolving.

Alone in the abandoned camp, uneasy about what to put in his report, Ben slipped into sleep while the dumb rusty machines stood guard.

CHAPTER THREE

Development Assistance as an Industry (the "Dev Biz")

*Among the ladies who were most distinguished for this rapacious
benevolence (if I may use the expression), was a Mrs. Pardiggle, who
seemed, as I judged from the number of her letters to Mr. Jarndyce, to be
almost as powerful a correspondent as Mrs. Jellyby herself. We observed
that the wind always changed, when Mrs. Pardiggle became the subject
of conversation; and that it invariably interrupted Mr. Jarndyce, and
prevented his going any farther, when he had remarked that there were
two classes of charitable people: one, the people who did a little and made
a great deal of noise, the other, the people who did a great deal and made
no noise at all.* —CHARLES DICKENS, *Bleak House*

At a September 1984 conference on NGOs held at the United Nations in
New York, one of the speakers used the term "dev biz." He meant to dis-
tinguish between a relatively innocent past when development work was
more of a calling, and an image-conscious present, when the same work has
become more of an industry, like "showbiz." Many since have come to use
the term "industry" quite routinely to refer to the development establishment. Most use it without irony.

Industry used to mean simply a branch of manufacture or trade: "steel
industry," "automobile industry." These terms roll off our tongues, no more
loaded than the words "dog" or "cat." And without too much trouble we
quickly get used to neologisms such as the "hospitality industry."

But implicit today in the term "industry" is the concept of a community
of interested parties, the interest they share being the good of the industry
itself. Thus today industries create their own research or trade associations,
whose work, including lobbying the government for favorable treatment, is
meant to benefit all the companies in an industry. And industries periodically hold meetings or conferences to exchange information, share and
solve problems, and praise accomplishments.

The organizational realm has become so well wrought in the last half century that we are no longer surprised to see that virtually every industry has a

magazine of some sort (e.g., *Hotel and Motel News*, *Do-It-Yourself Retailing*, or the magazine of the electric motor industry, *Motion Systems Distribution*). An anthropologist, observing them as if from Mars, might notice that industries also have distinguishing cultural and linguistic characteristics. There is usually a shared jargon, shared values, and shared delusions, such as the notion that the hotel industry is in the business of "hospitality."

Sometime in the last few decades the American public became used to other industries beyond the once strict limits of manufacturing and trade. We do not blink now if a pundit speaks of sports as an industry or of punditry itself as one, for that matter. But is there a subtle line that gets crossed here, at least conceptually if not morally? Well, so far, no. If at the core of the concept of industry is the notion of interested parties, the "interest" being the good of the industry and the "good" being (in the end) money and profit, then there is a seamless logic to putting professional sports under the same lexical umbrella as steel or hamburgers. We accept that all share the same ultimate goal — making money.

But development assistance as an industry? If so, what "business" is it in? Development is not really about products or services. It is also not about the self-interest of the organizations that came into existence to promote development. Moreover, given its own hopes to bring development to underdeveloped countries, to cast itself as a self-perpetuating industry should at the least be an embarrassment.

Capitalism, however, is different. It is legitimate, indeed "natural" that industries which exist to make money must find new markets, create new wants, and invent new products. Sports, leisure, recreation, and entertainment are grist for that mill. And as capitalism's underlying imperatives continue to break through the surface of our lives and reveal their full selves, we see how easily some lines become blurred and other fields become "industries" too.

Healthcare has become an industry in the full sense of the term. So has information, and now education too is becoming an industry. It would not be surprising if even such nonprofit entities as museums soon became industries. This would suggest that a common denominator broader than money is evolving — that is, self-perpetuation. Like the flip motto of the gold digger that "you can't be too rich or too thin," our society as a whole is now saying, "You can't have too much information, too much health, or too many (good) museums." To seek new demand and supply in those arenas, as well as in the steel and hamburger business, has by now become natural and expected. Even the institution of religion, by definition the most sacred of all, is "industrializing" in this way. Churches join in multiple associations, vie for members, have campaigns, produce newsletters, engage in commerce, and generally promote themselves. But people do not mind if the church too shows its instinct for self-preservation so blatantly, because the needs of the soul are infinite, or at least unknowable. The soul too, as an economist might put it, is demand-elastic.

Because these blurrings have snuck up on us, we in the "dev biz" have not noticed how significant it is that an endeavor whose ultimate goal is not money, profit, or *self-perpetuation* should take on virtually all the characteristics of an industry with just such goals. A brief description of the industry's dimensions and members will serve not only to orient the reader to just who and what I am talking about but also to illustrate some of the characteristics that make development assistance the "dev biz."

Players in the Development Industry

Generally, the industry is divided into three groups of institutional players: The multilateral donor institutions are financed in whole or part by the member countries, which in turn get money from their citizens in the form of taxes or in the form of bond purchases. The multilaterals include the World Bank; the United Nations Development Program; the regional development banks (the Inter-American Development Bank in Washington; the African Development Bank in Abidjan, Ivory Coast; the Asian Development Bank in Manila); the International Fund for Agricultural Development (IFAD); and the United Nations Children's Fund (UNICEF), based in New York.

Bilateral donors are departments or ministries of national governments whose mandate it is to grant or loan money for development on a nation-to-nation basis. Until recently the bilateral donors have been a distinct group: twenty-two members of the Development Assistance Committee (DAC) of the Paris-based Organization for Economic Cooperation and Development (OECD), which is a combination trade and research institution supported by its advanced-economy members. Examples of these bilateral aid agencies are the United States Agency for International Development, the Department for International Development (DFID) in the United Kingdom, the Swedish International Development Cooperation Agency (Sida), and France's Caisse Française pour la Cooperation.

Groupings of private (and for the most part nonprofit) institutions are larger in number and have more varied characteristics.

Universities and University-Affiliated Institutes

Off to the side, in the sense that they are not usually "practitioners," are university departments and university-affiliated institutes, such as the School of International and Public Affairs at Columbia (SIPA), the Woodrow Wilson School at Princeton, the Kennedy School of Government at Harvard, the Institute for Development Anthropology at the State University of New York at Binghamton, and, in the United Kingdom, the International Development Centre of the University of Reading. These academic institutions have contributed to the "professionalization" of development assistance. Some, besides doing research and offering courses and degrees in development-related subjects, also take on contracts for Western governments to train development workers from the developing countries themselves.

The advanced-economy countries, along with more and more developing countries, have such institutions. There are easily hundreds. And to complicate matters further, consortia of institutions also exist, in which several universities get together and bid on contracts to manage or design development projects. Lines increasingly cross here as persons in these institutes become consultants or work on advisory committees and task forces, while practitioners from the bilateral or multilateral agencies take time off for fellowships or become adjunct professors at university-affiliated institutes.

Needless to say, as the "dev biz" has "industrialized," an intertwining of all these institutions has occurred. Taking a degree in "development studies" at one of the above institutes or publishing an article in one of the development journals becomes part of the career path within the industry and ensures that the industry develops a shared specialized vocabulary, not easily available to or understandable by outsiders.

Foundations, Think Tanks, and Policy Institutes

Hundreds of foundations work in international development exclusively and hundreds more devote only part of their grant giving to international development. Examples of the prominent ones are the Ford, MacArthur, Andrew W. Mellon, Soros, and Rockefeller Foundations. But there are also hundreds of small family foundations that are increasingly involved in international development assistance work, as well as corporations that give money to development assistance through their own foundations, such as Aetna, United Airlines, Liz Claiborne, Pfizer, and Xerox.

Finally, some development policy institutes and think tanks run projects, some do research, and some are advocacy bodies. Examples are the International Food Policy Research Institute (IFPRI) and the sixteen international laboratories that make up the Consultative Group on International Agricultural Research (CGIAR), which includes the International Center for Maize and Wheat Improvement, based in Mexico, responsible for the drought- and disease-resistant grains that made the "green revolution" possible.

Contractors and "Beltway Bandits"

During the 1960s the U.S. government began increasing the amount of its international development business put out for bid. New private for-profit companies were founded to capture those contracts. These have been called "development contractors"; privately, many know them as "beltway bandits" because almost all are located inside the beltway that surrounds Washington, D.C. A few of the older and better known among these are Chemonics International, Robert R. Nathan Associates, and Development Alternatives Inc. These firms operate with a core staff who develop proposals and manage the contracts they win. For the most part, the personnel who will run the projects once the contracts have been won are found from large databases of consultants maintained by each of these firms.

As these contractors exist for profit (though the people who staff them are often the same people who used to be in the nonprofit side), they depend on marketing themselves as viable recipients of contracts. Thus a few companies have developed that specialize in helping contractors write proposals. Here, for example, is the text of a 1988 flyer from a company in North Carolina:

> The international development contracting industry becomes more competitive every day. HOW CAN YOU GAIN AN ADVANTAGE? . . .
>
> A crisis occurs in a third world country where you have a team stationed. Phone calls are not going through and it's Sunday at 7 AM. How can you quickly find out if your team is safe?
>
> You didn't link up with a firm with minority status on the last proposal because you didn't know of any who had appropriate experience in the region. What you don't realize is that over 50 minority owned forms were managing USAID contracts during 1987. . . .
>
> A subscription to the . . . 1988 Profiles of International Development Contractors and Grantees will provide all this information and more.

Nongovernmental Organizations

The term "nongovernmental organization" (NGO) was first used by the United Nations in the early 1950s. Though there are many other kinds of NGOs in the world, the term as used here refers to nonprofit organizations engaged in international development assistance or humanitarian work. As I discussed in chapter 2, NGOs began to be taken much more seriously as part of the development industry in the 1980s.

One distinction is useful to keep in mind with respect to NGOs — that between voluntary membership organizations and intermediate organizations: The former include "grassroots" organizations, in which members are linked by community or some other affiliation (e.g., a registered village women's group in Kenya). The common characteristic of voluntary membership organizations is that they work for the members' own interests. Intermediate organizations are neither membership based nor fully voluntary. They have part-time or full-time staff, seek funding, and deliver programs and services to people, communities, and/or voluntary membership organizations themselves. Internationally, there are two basic types of intermediate organizations: charitable welfare and relief organizations, and development organizations.

Though many now include voluntary membership organizations in the broad term "nongovernmental organization," it is the intermediate organizations that are more formally part of the development industry. The largest of these, while not exactly household words, are fairly well known to the public and are most often thought of when "NGO" is used: Save the Children, CARE, Amnesty International, Oxfam, Catholic Relief Services, ActionAid, and World Vision are examples. The oldest of these NGOs generally began as relief and welfare organizations and later evolved into "development" organizations concerned with poverty alleviation, primary health care, the environment, education, legal rights for women, human rights, and so forth.

Partly because the terminology around NGOs continues to change, there are no reliable statistics about how many NGOs currently exist. The OECD in the late 1980s listed about four thousand NGOs among its advanced-economy members. But the growth of NGOs of the intermediate type has been in the developing countries, about which there is only speculation. It is safe to say, however, that the combined total of NGOs in the advanced economies and the developing countries is at least in the tens of thousands.

NGOs have always relied on fund-raising. As development assistance evolved and the organizations doing it became an industry, more and more NGOs began to mix private and public funding. For example, in 1998 over 50 percent of Save the Children's income came from grants and contracts from government, with only 20 percent coming from direct sponsorship of children. Large NGOs' fund-raising operations have also become highly professional and sophisticated. Some make use of major celebrities including Hollywood stars, sports figures, and even former White House aides who have become celebrities (George Stephanopoulus is on Save the Children's board of directors).

How Big Is the Dev Biz?

In round numbers the development business is about $55 to $60 billion annually and has hovered in that range for a decade. The sum is the aggregate of moneys from many different rich countries, either directly from citizens to the many private nonprofits that assist the developing countries, or indirectly from citizens through their government's foreign aid programs.

That $55 to $60 billion needs to be seen relative to other sums. Here's an odd assortment, but it should make the point.

- In the late 1990s, the U.S. auto repair, auto services, and parking industry was also about $60 billion.
- Individual charitable giving just in the United States topped $105 billion in 1994 (only 2 percent of which went to international development).
- The annual cost of U.S. advertising in the late 1990s was over $120 billion.
- Annual figures on U.S. betting and gambling in the same period hovered around $700 billion.
- Americans in 1999 had over $1,300 billion tied up in consumer debt (almost 22 times as much money as represented by the development industry) and almost 10 times the annual dev biz total in credit card and other revolving debt.
- And just for fun, note that in 1996 Americans spent $8 billion on pornography alone.

Even within the development industry, some costs dwarf others in surprising ways. The 1997 staff costs of the World Bank (which then had about fifty-five hundred full-time regular staff) was $810 million, equivalent to 1.3 percent of that $60 billion. Just the airline travel of World Bank staff in 1997 cost $125 million, which represents 57 percent of the annual budget of Chad. And depending on which day you look at the stock market, Bill Gates could underwrite the whole of the $60 billion annual expenditure of the "dev biz" and still not drop down more than a single place in the ranking of the world's richest people.

On the other hand, $60 billion is still real money. The entire GDP of the countries of Haiti, Chad, Benin, Burkina Faso, Central African Republic, Eritrea, Cambodia, and Laos put together just equals $60 billion. The 1997–98 combined military expenditure of Italy, Canada, Brazil, Israel, and Spain did not quite reach $60 billion.

What Makes Up the $55 to $60 Billion in the Development Industry?

Multilateral Aid

As noted above the money distributed in loans and grants by the multilateral agencies comes ultimately from the member nations. It is usually counted in the aggregate aid statistics, in addition to the overall amount devoted to bilateral assistance.

Bilateral Aid

The bulk of the industry's annual funding is "official development assistance" (ODA), which is the money that the governments of twenty-two advanced economies designate for foreign aid programs of different kinds.

In 1999, these twenty-two countries were ranked in order of the percentage of their GNP they give each year for foreign aid, as follows: Denmark, Norway, Netherlands, Sweden, Luxembourg, France, Japan, Switzerland, Finland, Ireland, Belgium, Canada, Germany, Australia, Austria, New Zealand, Portugal, United Kingdom, Spain, Italy, Greece, and the United States.[1]

The reason the statistics begin with ranking countries by the percentage of GNP they give to poor countries is because of a pledge made in the 1960s: seven-tenths of a percent (0.70 percent) of each country's GNP would be donated to assisting the developing countries. This "tithe" has consistently been met or exceeded by the Scandinavians and the Dutch but almost never reached by the other countries. So, for example, the 1999 average "burden-sharing" figures show Denmark ranked number one, with 1.01 percent of its GNP committed to the poor countries, and the United States ranked last, at 0.10 percent.

The picture is different, of course, in terms of absolute amounts given. From 1950 to 1977 the three big donors were always the United States, Germany, and France. Japan joined the big three in 1978. And in 1989 for the first time, Japan became the largest aid giver, then dropping behind the United States for the next three years. But for the period from 1993 through 1999, Japan again became the number one giver, with U.S. aid, which peaked in 1992, declining ever since. In 1995, for the first time, the United States dropped from the big three, ranking fourth after Japan, France, and Germany, though it moved back to second place in 1996 and again in 1999. In the period 1950–97 the contributing member countries of the OECD gave a total of $982 billion in bilateral aid. Of that amount, the U.S. total represented 25 percent.

The twenty-two countries are all members of the DAC, formed in 1961. In all, twenty-nine nations belong to the OECD; the seven nations that are not in the DAC are Turkey, Iceland, Mexico, the Czech Republic, Hungary, Poland, and Korea (the last five of which joined the OECD since 1993).

It is revealing how these donors divide up the recipient pie. Every donor country, especially the small ones, seemed to have realized early on that giving a little bit of money to one hundred different nations was not a wise strategy. Each donor wants to have impact, if not a degree of recognition and clout. So most concentrate on a small set of priority poor countries. For example, Italy, which gave out $2.54 billion in 1986–87 and $1.98 billion in 1996–97, has had longtime aid relationships with Ethiopia and Egypt,

1. OECD online <http://www.oecd.org>, August 2001. Note that Japan and Switzerland both ranked seventh; Australia, Austria, New Zealand, and Portugal all ranked thirteenth; and Italy and Greece both ranked sixteenth.

but also (though less faithfully) with Somalia, Malta, Libya, Tunisia, and Argentina.

The United States, which generally donates to more countries than do other DAC members, also has had its favorites over the last quarter century, with only three being on its top-fifteen list for twenty-five years in a row: Israel, Egypt, and the Philippines. In 1976–77, Israel and Egypt represented 21.4 percent of U.S. foreign aid; in 1986–87 these two countries represented 26.9 percent, and in 1996–97, 19.9 percent.[2]

There are some obvious patterns here, especially in donor countries with a past as a colonial power (France, the United Kingdom, Italy, Spain, Portugal, the Netherlands), where former ties are related to economic interests, such as trade. With others, such as Norway and Austria, comparative visibility is a consideration ("Let's aim where others are not so present"), but trade plays a role too. Probably the only donor country for which trade is less a factor than other considerations is the United States. The U.S. pattern for its top recipients is related to historical, quasi-colonial ties in the case of the Philippines (where the former U.S. military bases were part of a quid pro quo) and to a mixture of politics that involves strategic, constituency, or diplomatic deal-making considerations in the case of others, especially Israel and Egypt.

During the last fifty years of bilateral aid, there were two great leaps in development assistance. The first was from the early to the late 1970s, while the second was more intense and shorter, from about 1985 to about 1991. The reasons for the two jumps in bilateral aid were different (as I indicated in the previous chapter). The first was connected to a period of new ideas and considerable hope. The second leap occurred during a time of crisis in which aid was seen as part of a rescue effort. But except for a small dip between 1979 and 1981, bilateral official development assistance had steadily risen for well over forty years. That rise essentially stopped in the early 1990s, as I will discuss below.

NGOs

Finally, we have the grants of NGOs from the advanced industrial nations. These are mostly moneys from private citizens. In 1999, there were 439 American NGOs (private voluntary nonprofit organizations) involved in overseas relief and development that were registered with the U.S. Agency for International Development (they register with USAID so as to be eligible for some U.S. bilateral money to flow through them as implementing organizations). Seventy-six percent of their overall support came from

2. In the case of Israel and to some extent Egypt, not all the foreign aid the United States provides is for "development assistance," strictly speaking. A large proportion of the money is for government support.

private sources. The total support (income) of these organizations was $12.32 billion, of which $9.38 billion was private support. Of the $12.32 billion the organizations spent, $5.93 billion (54 percent) went to overseas programs; the rest went to domestic programs.[3]

The top thirty agencies alone accounted for $3.4 billion of overseas expenditures, or 58 percent of the total for overseas programs of all 439 agencies. Those top thirty include CARE with $375.9 million in overseas program expenditures; World Vision with $279.8; Catholic Relief Services with $244.45; Americares with $189.5; Christian Children's Fund with $93.3; and SCF with $79.1.[4]

An OECD estimate for 1993 is that $5.7 billion passed through NGOs worldwide;[5] the World Bank estimates that in 1998 over $10 billion went to developing countries through NGOs (half of which came from official development assistance).[6] Roughly, then, between 10 percent and 20 percent of all official development assistance is provided through NGOs.

Since 1960 a total of over $1.7 trillion from all development assistance sources has gone from rich countries to poor.

The Shift to Private Capital and Development as an Industry

Money — having it, getting it, keeping it — is a great motivator. For most of the formal history of development assistance, money was largely taken for granted. It always required some work to get it, but many if not most of the organizations in development assistance could count on a steady flow: if there was going to be development assistance to the third world, the "dev biz" was the only medium there was, and the money followed that conviction.

But in the 1990s the flow of money changed. A huge shift occurred in the magnitude and relative weight of private capital flows to the developing world. These, for the first time in the history of development, began to overwhelm official and multilateral flows. Though not acknowledging it openly, the development industry is under siege, and that condition has reinforced all the characteristics of a traditional self-serving, self-perpetuating industry — it wants, above all, to survive.[7]

In the period 1983–88, net private capital flows to the developing coun-

3. USAID, 2001 *Report of Voluntary Agencies Engaged in Overseas Relief and Development Registered with the U.S. Agency for International Development* (Washington: USAID, 2001).

4. Ibid.

5. OECD, *Development Assistance Committee Report* (Paris: OECD, 1994).

6. World Bank, *World Development Report, 2000–2001* (New York: Oxford University Press for the World Bank, 2001), 200.

7. After September 11, 2001, many prominent development agencies called for large in-

tries amounted to $15.1 billion, while net official flows (the development field's grants and loans less the debt repayment and other reverse flows) were $29 billion.[8] The ratio was 1.92 official/private. In the period 1989–95 the situation reversed. Net private capital flows were $107.6 billion, with net official flows at $21.4 billion, for a ratio in favor of private flows of 5.03. In 1996 net private capital flows were $200.7 billion, with net official flows a negative $3.8 billion; by 1998, net private capital flows had reached $268 billion.[9] And while these data were heavily skewed by the dominance of Asia as the major recipient of private capital flows, the situation in Africa suggests that this trend might have been dominant everywhere. In Africa for the period 1983–88, net private capital flows were $3.5 billion with net official flows $5.0 billion. But there too the tide turned from 1989 to 1995, with net private capital flows totaling $7.2 billion, while net official flows were $6.0 billion.[10]

It could reasonably be argued that a few years of data are by themselves insufficient to declare a definitive sea change, and indeed the Asian crisis of the later 1990s did result in a decline of net private capital flows to developing countries in the region. But what these data really reflect is the coming of age of globalization, and about that trend there is no doubt. Despite short-term ups and downs in the late 1990s, the long-term trend toward private capital's growing dominance over official development assistance seems assured.

In other words, private capital is becoming the main fuel for development, surpassing official flows. Read large, it is capitalism — the for-profit sector — that is now driving development in an area where heretofore the public and the nonprofit sector (NGOs), relatively recently allied with governments, had been in the driver's seat.

Finally, and maybe not surprisingly, we have seen a strong tendency of advanced-economy governments to pull back on their bilateral support of developing countries. Net disbursements of official development assistance by the OECD countries to all "less-developed countries" (or LDCs, OECD's term for developing countries, which do not include the former Eastern bloc countries) peaked at $43.3 billion in 1991. In 1992 they were $43.1 billion; in 1993, $39.3 billion; and in 1994, $42.18, a small move up, but clearly, for the first time in history, bilateral development assistance began heading downward in terms of real dollars.[11] The totals to all recipients and for all

creases in foreign aid money. My conversations with colleagues left the impression that many agencies were feeling relief that the world again saw us as useful.

8. "Net private capital flows" include foreign direct investment as well as bonds, portfolio equity investment, and commercial bank lending.

9. World Bank, *World Development Report, 2000–2001,* 190.

10. International Monetary Fund, *World Economic Outlook* (Washington, D.C.: International Monetary Fund, May 1997).

sources (including the multilaterals) show that the trend continues downward, with 1996 dropping 6 percent from 1995,[12] and 1997 dropping by 14 percent from 1996.[13] And even though the majority of DAC members reported increases in their ODA for 2000, the drop from 1999 to 2000 was still 1.6 percent in constant prices (whereas the full total of ODA [the DAC members plus the multilaterals] dropped even further, having gone from $56.4 billion in 1999 to $53.1 billion in 2000).[14]

In addition to private capital flows from outside investors, there has been a major shift, hardly noticed in all the statistics on "flows," in "remittance credits," the term for money sent home by people working outside their country of birth or citizenship. At the end of 2000, many of the more than 150 million people living outside their country of origin were supplying remittance credits (note that the total number of "people on the move," including internal migrants, is estimated to be 1 billion).[15] In 1980 the World Bank estimated that remittance credits which went through formal (and thus measurable) channels amounted to about $43 billion. By 1990 this had increased by 65 percent to $71 billion, by itself greater than the $60 billion total for the "dev biz." Obviously, many workers send money home through informal channels, which if added in would increase the totals.

The Many Jobs at Stake in the Development Industry

No figures exist on how many people make their living in this industry. But some illustrative numbers will give us an idea. The World Bank, which provides about $20 billion annually in loans, employs about 6,000 full-time regular staff, plus another 3,000 to 4,000 long-term consultants. A U.S. NGO with a budget of about $7 million annually might employ about 100 persons full-time. A very large NGO with an annual budget of $100 million and programs in 20 to 30 countries might easily have 3,000 to 4,000 full-time employees worldwide. A conservative global estimate would be roughly a half million people whose livelihood depends on the industry. And while most are employed as staff of the many agencies and institutions, many people in this industry make their livings as independent consultants.

The World Bank database of consultants includes some hundreds of job classification categories. The May 1991 World Bank listing shows fifty-two specializations, such as AGR: Agriculture/Rural Development (Agriculture

11. OECD, *Development Assistance Committee Report* (Paris: OECD, 1996).

12. International Council of Voluntary Agencies (ICVA), *The Reality of Aid, 1997–1998* (Geneva, Switzerland: ICVA, 1998).

13. World Bank, *World Development Report, 2000–2001*, 190.

14. OECD, *Development Assistance Committee Report*, OECD online, August 2001 <http://www.oecd.org>.

15. Worldwatch Institute, *Vital Signs, 2001* (New York: W. W. Norton, 2001), 142.

[Crops]); TRP: Transportation (Air, Port, Rail, Road); BAN: Banking and Credit; LEG: Law; HPE: Health/Nutrition; PPN: Population/Demography; and PRO: Procurement.

The list is further broken down into over one thousand skills, so each specialty code has subgroups. Under Agriculture/Rural Development, for example, there is the subgroup Pulses (BDF), under which there are four skills: BDFA: Chickpeas; BDFB: Pigeon Peas; BDFC: Field Beans; and BDFD: Phaseolus Beans.

This categorization of skills and specialities shows how organizations such as the World Bank think or are increasingly forced to think. For it must create these categories partly to address the thousands of projects and the subsequent need for experts to staff them. When a project is in the planning stage, the computer will be asked to spill forth the names of consultants according to the skills deemed necessary. The very extensive range of specializations reveals how much the industry has become just that — a domain for which tailor-made expertise is deemed to exist.

The forces that have been at work to make development assistance a lasting industry are stronger than ever and are in direct contradiction to the sort of "less-is-more" lessons we should have learned. Just as no commercial industry will voluntarily go out of business, so too has the "dev biz" taken on the self-perpetuating persona of the commercial corporate world. We still seek relevance and effectiveness. What has changed is why we do. We want to survive as an industry. More than ever we want market share. And to do that we will, just as industries in the commercial world do, sell what we do as if it were a commodity. We will make compromises, and more and more of them, to remain alive. We will put our own survival ahead of our mission. This attitude is profoundly different from that in the for-profit commercial world, where "one's own survival" is "the mission," and legitimately so. The speed with which resources shifted from development assistance in truly needy areas such as Africa to the newly independent states of Eastern Europe in the early 1990s is a sign of how market oriented, rather than need oriented, we have become. We too want to be where the action is. We want to keep our jobs, continue to develop our own institutions, and to the extent possible publicize and justify what we do.

Development was not always this way. As I discussed in chapter 2, it did not begin with its own special jargon, institutions, and careers. It did not begin by seeking self-perpetuation and coveting contracts. Yet, more and more, as development became, in my view inevitably, an "industry," it got to be like Dickens's reference to the people who "did a little and made a great deal of noise."

Dedication

Rift Valley Province,
Kenya, 1988

MR. MWONGE CLIMBS the makeshift steps to the office of the Aberdare Water Society and timidly knocks on the door. He is stocky and strong, about forty years old, and has the hands of a laborer, which he is. Today, though, he is wearing his Sunday best, a threadbare pinstriped suit coat, second- or, more probably, thirdhand. It is an early afternoon in March. The weather is cold and cloudy, typical for this mountainous part of the country on the edge of the Rift Valley. Most people are inside their huts. There is no activity in the village square other than a few scrounging chickens.

Alex Abuya and John Kirui are inside the society's office, bent over their desks. A kerosene stove hisses in the center of the square room, but even with it the men wear sweaters. They are both full-time employees of Water for Health International (WHI), an American NGO. Alex is preparing the project quarterly progress report that he must send to the WHI office in Nairobi at the end of the month. John is putting the finishing touches on the form that will be used as the society's monthly water bill. Next to him is Peter Gichiru, age eighteen, who comes from the village. Peter is nearing the end of two years of training under Alex and John's tutelage. When the project is finished and Alex and John leave, Peter will be the accounts clerk for the society. It's a big job, crucial to the success of the society. Peter will manage all the bookkeeping and accounting for the twelve hundred families who own shares in the society and whose houses will be connected to the system. If he fails to keep the accounts properly, the project will go the way of hundreds of other water projects that collapsed in Kenya over the last twenty years. But John and Alex constantly reassure Peter that he is prepared to do it.

Alex looks up. "Come in!" he shouts. Mr. Mwonge enters. He has a sheepish look on his face. Mwonge pulls a tattered square of paper from his coat pocket and hands it to Alex. He clears his throat. "Sah, I am membah number A46, registered with the society in October 1986, you will see my name in the ledger. But I have not been a good membah — I have not paid up my shares and I have not done my part of the labor and I have come now to put this right."

Alex looks for Mr. Mwonge's name in his shareholder ledger and sees right away that he not only has not paid his shares or contributed his share of the labor for the project but also has not shown his face at meetings in the two and a half years since he joined, not once. He closes the ledger.

"You are welcome, Mr. Mwonge." Alex then points to John and introduces him. "This is John Kirui, who works with me. We are both from Nairobi. You may know Peter Gichiru, since he is a villager. Please take a seat."

Alex puts his quarterly report aside and over the next hour and a half concentrates on Mr. Mwonge. He takes great pains as he explains to Mr. Mwonge what has been going on since 1986. He has never seen Mr. Mwonge before, and after nearly three years Alex knows almost everyone. But he knows that Mwonge's lack of participation in the society has two sides. He guesses that Mwonge works outside the village, probably in Nairobi itself, and sends what money he can to his family here. But so do quite a few of the other men, and their participation in the project has not been as limited. The other side is that people like Mwonge are skeptical. They're old enough to recall past projects in the area and how they've been burned by unkept promises.

The village, Murwanga, rests at an altitude of six thousand feet on the Aberdare escarpment. The area is partly forested, with patches of rough and stony open land, suitable for grazing a few cows here and there. And that is what most of the villagers do. There is a bit of surplus milk, but as it usually comes from the evening milking, it would spoil before making it to a market. People have only small amounts of cash. With just over 1,200 families (about 4,000 people), Murwanga lies on a dirt road about eighteen miles from the nearest macadam road. But that eighteen miles is a long way. It has kept Murwanga isolated from markets, jobs, and the few benefits the government might, if one happened to be in the right political camp, bestow.

About a decade after independence, Murwanga thought its turn had come. Engineers from the Ministry of Water Development (MOWD), funded by UNICEF, arrived in the area to begin laying out a water distribution project. That was sixteen years ago, in 1973, when running water was unheard of. And while the concept was no longer new after that, it has remained a concept. In all these sixteen years, water did not flow. Every day, women and children still made the long uphill climb through the forest to the nearest stream and walked back down again with full buckets on their heads.

There is usually no sensible sequence in third world rural development, even if there may have been in the history of the "first" world. It is not inconceivable that electricity, paved roads, or even television might arrive before running water. Each of these changes would bring other changes in tow, but the coming of clean running water to a village will have an immediate and palpable impact, followed by some very subtle ones. The big change is in people's health. If the system is properly built and maintained, they will have, for the first time in their lives, clean drinking water. They will also be able to wash more often. Since dirt and bacteria debilitate and kill in Africa in ways Westerners have long forgotten, people will live longer and be sick less. Women and children will save the time they once used to fetch water. Altogether, people would have more time to be more productive, to invest more in what we now call "social capital," or, if they are children, to focus on schooling.

Of course, there will be other changes and some challenges as well. Women with more free time might behave differently with their husbands and or each other. The stream in the forest would no longer be a meeting place. The increases in production as the result of healthier farmers might end up being superfluous if there is still no way to convert those gains to cash by getting products to a market at a good price. The savings in work time by having piped water will be offset by the need to

pay for water, difficult in a still limited local economy. But project planners usually do not spend much time thinking about these more complex ramifications. Running water is important, and that's that.

The earliest water projects in the Kenyan countryside were simple.
They involved wells, boreholes, and hand pumps. A foreign donor
would come in with a contractor, drill the well, pour the concrete slab,
bolt on the pump, and leave. With the 1970s came the idea of "self-help"
and "community-based water schemes." These were going to cost more
because they would be whole water systems, with storage tanks, dams,
pipes, and in some cases even household connections. Once built, the
communities would run and maintain them. In this way one of the most
taken-for-granted attributes of modern life — running water — would
come to rural Kenya. Both the government and the international development assistance community were excited about these projects, and it
was expected that from 40 percent to 50 percent of the cost would come
from development assistance financing. Donors big and small were interested and included the Dutch bilateral aid program, UNICEF, US-
AID, and, later on, the European Economic Community (EEC).

In the 1970s, the Dutch government alone spent $12 million on water
projects in Kenya. A decade later, no one even *tried* to deny that the
Dutch-backed effort had been a total failure, as were most of the others.
Hundreds of village water systems were affected. The reasons were corruption and mismanagement of funds, shoddy and incomplete construction, lack of maintenance, poor or no financial control systems, and
no systems for long-term operation, such as having water meters and
billing users for consumption. The idea that water systems, once built,
would have "recurrent costs" had slipped through the cracks. "People
forgot that water is a commodity, not a 'right,'" as Alex put it in explaining the past to Ben.

Alex used to work for the MOWD. Water is his business. He could
have become rich from bribes like many of his colleagues in those days.
He quit instead. Alex knows far better than Mr. Mwonge what usually
happened. He saw it over and over again. When you mix valuable commodities such as pipe, cement, valves, and steel tanks with middlemen
and poorly paid government personnel, there are rake-offs, payoffs, mid-
night thievery, and fake bills to donors for materials not delivered. At
least 50 percent of water project funds were lost up front in this way. But
the tipping point for Alex came as he saw what happened to the communities themselves in the early days of the community-based water sys-

tems concept. The promoters of self-help would come into a village, get the villagers together under a tree, lay out a blueprint of the water system, and tell them that if this was going to be "their" project, they would have to own it—they would have to put up the first moneys for inputs. Having no reason then not to think the government wouldn't fulfill its promises, people paid. These were significant sums in a local economy where cash is hard to come by: three hundred shillings, five hundred shillings (in those days perhaps twelve dollars).

After the rip-offs and the squandering were over, people realized what had happened. But besides the fact that there was no water, there were no records, receipts, or contracts and thus no recourse. The money was gone, and so were the MOWD engineers.

A few communities actually got finished projects, but these soon deteriorated. In most cases the pipes were laid above ground to save money, and thus people who were not members of the community water user groups (economists call them "free riders") simply cut the pipes at night and made crude connections by wrapping the joints in strips of rubber from old tires, bits of cloth, and wire. Leakage soared, and then cows and donkeys stepped on the pipes and made the leaks into floods. Valve handles were stolen. Storage tanks became contaminated. No one took responsibility for repairs. The water user groups disbanded. It didn't take long for the water to stop.

In Murwanga between 1973 and 1986, if there was no progress at all on water, there *was* a great leap in wisdom. People became wary of development projects and especially about self-help and how they were all going to benefit from Kenya's modernization. By the late 1980s, Kenya's independence honeymoon was over. Jomo Kenyatta had come and gone. The Mzee (old man) had caught the attention of the world for a brief time and made most Kenyans proud enough to forgive his indiscretions. Daniel Arap Moi, his successor, was to raise official corruption to levels never before imagined.

Now, in 1989, such men as Mr. Mwonge were not going to be fooled anymore. Despite the apparent sheepishness on his face when he stepped inside the Aberdare Water Society office this March afternoon, Mwonge was demanding something: like the folks from Missouri, "show me." Alex understood.

"There *has* been a dragging of the feet due to the past, there's no doubt," Alex told Ben that night in the staff hut. "That's why we have to spend so much time with the members. You have to be visibly present day in and day out. You can't say 'I'm busy now'; you have to take the time. When they come in, they are really asking *you* to help *them* have confidence in the project."

And so Alex had showed Mr. Mwonge the detailed map on the wall of the society's office tracing the fifty of fifty-six kilometers of pipe that had already been laid, all of it underground. All but one of the main twenty-thousand-gallon storage tanks had been completed. Two of the three main branches of the system had been tested and leaks and problems fixed. These branch lines all had concrete valve chambers with locks on the covers. Alex showed Mr. Mwonge the books. First the inventory ledger, listing the spare parts and remaining inputs, all accounted for and stored under lock and key in the society's new shed, including all the half-inch pipe needed for the household connections and every single one of the meters ready for installation.

"Come, Mwonge, let's have a look." Alex got the key from his desk and they went out to the shed next door. Mwonge walked in first. Everything was there, on the shelves, labeled and numbered.

Back inside the society office, Alex motioned for Peter to come over. "Show Mr. Mwonge the billing form." Peter puts it in front of Mwonge and explains how they had tested several versions before settling on this design. With the enthusiasm of an eager student, Peter tells Mwonge how they had learned that the first thing the member wants to know is "how much must I pay," and so the "sum total" line was moved from the bottom of the form where mathematical logic would suggest it should be, to the top. "Thank you, Peter," Alex says and turns to Mr. Mwonge.

"Now, Mwonge," he shouts with mock sternness and puts his hand on Mwonge's arm. "Are you ready to pay?"

But Mwonge isn't ready to be humored. He is a formal and serious man. He is worried about how at this late date he will be able to pay for his participation. Alex pulls another form from his desk and shows it to Mr. Mwonge. "This is the application for domestic connections. As you can see, you must pay a meter deposit, a pipe deposit, and the first four months' base rate for the water itself."

The water deposit (four months times the base rate of twenty-five shillings per month) is designed to get the members used to paying for their water. Alex and John know from experience that new users tend to go a bit wild when they first have running water; as consumption goes up, so will the rates. In the water business, discounts come for conservation, not for volume consumption.

Mr. Mwonge seems slightly relieved looking at these items, but as he gets to the bottom of the form that Alex has been explaining, he sees six boxes to be checked. The form asks if the member has fully paid the shares, the labor contribution, any penalties for missed labor or late share payment, and the pipe, water, and meter deposits.

Mwonge swallows hard. What about the late penalty and what about the labor? he asks unhappily. Alex explains that there is a now a fine of five hundred shillings for late share payment, recently voted by the members. Then he picks up the labor ledger. Next to Mwonge's name is the required number of labor days decided on by the section commit-tee for construction in Mwonge's area of the village. All the days are marked "o."

As Alex explains to Ben that night, the initial plan for the project was worked out with the members through the sectional meetings and through the elected management committee of the society. The most contentious area by far had been what to do about labor. The manage-ment committee wanted to charge each member fifty shillings for each day of missed labor. But WHI had cautioned against this as too high. The two-year construction plan would involve one day a week of labor for each member, so missing all one hundred days would mean a fine of five thousand shillings, a huge amount of money. But the management com-mittee was adamant. They knew this was a sensitive area, but precisely because of it, they had voted to impose tough penalties.

The general membership clearly needed to feel that the labor was equally shared, but WHI had tried to argue that there were legitimate reasons not to participate — sickness, absence, old age, and so forth. But soon John and Alex began to accept that management committee mem-bers, who after all represented the village, were intent on overcoming past injustices and nothing would dissuade them. The majority of the members felt that many people, particular the few who were better off (the salaried schoolteachers, for example) were staying away from the project and not showing up for labor days just because they did not want to get their hands dirty. The leadership was going to be tough. Either dig or pay the fine. Finally, after weeks of discussion, John and Alex, on be-half of WHI, agreed with the management committee, and the rule was written into the society bylaws: no work or no paid-up fine, then no do-mestic connection.

Mr. Mwonge is visibly vexed. He wants very much to participate. His neighbors will have domestic connections. He sees that this water proj-ect, unlike those in the past, is being carefully and honestly managed, and the moneys, carefully spent. He was particularly impressed when

Alex had shown Mwonge the receipts for the trunk line pipes, which WHI had purchased directly from the factory, thus saving the society forty thousand shillings by not going through a middleman.

"I can pay you the late shares and the deposits. I'll have to dig deep to do it, but I will. But what can I do about the five thousand shillings for the missed labor? I don't have this money. Will the management and the members ever consider changing the structure of the fines?"

Alex says he doubts it and tries to smile as if to offer Mr. Mwonge some reassurance, but he is in fact worried, and Mwonge's dilemma is just the tip of his concerns. To say that the project has been carefully husbanded and guided by Alex and John over the last two and a half years is an understatement. The work is now almost completed. Alex and John have been living on-site since the beginning. And while they used to go back to Nairobi on weekends to be with their families, there has been so much detail to cover in the last six months that they have chosen to go down only once a month. Fourteen- and sixteen-hour days have been routine. They have spent countless patient hours building the confidence of individual members, resolving disputes, supervising construction, recruiting and training the six people from the village who will be the paid employees of the society, but above all making sure that all tendencies to cheat or steal or compromise on quality were nipped in the bud. And now, as the final days are in sight, the dozen or so outliers like Mr. Mwonge are trying to come back into the fold, but it seems like they will not be able to. And while they seem a small number compared with the general membership, Alex knows how vulnerable the society really is. Just as the pipes can spring a leak, cracks in the structure of the society itself could easily widen into fatal breaks.

Despite his confident assurances to Peter Gichiru, privately he is also worried about whether the society will be able to manage itself once WHI leaves. And he remembers feeling the same thing when thirty months earlier WHI had gotten roped in, against its better judgment, to placing him and John — two senior employees — on-site full-time. The recollection of the bind that WHI has got itself into makes Alex shudder. He had been so used to immersing himself in the day-to-day frenzy of work in the last few months that he had mercifully avoided thinking much about it.

Ben's visit gave Alex the opportunity to go back in his own mind and recall the history of the project. Ben was visiting for a week, on behalf of an institute that was studying water projects in Africa. Because of Ben's presence, Alex, who normally would have spent the evening in the office, had come back early to the hut and over the next few hours filled Ben in on the last thirty months.

Back in 1986 there had been fierce competition among several NGOs to get the model water systems grant of which this project was part. Water for Health International was determined to win. It needed to win. Once known in Kenya by government and donors alike for its high-quality work in irrigation and the organization of agricultural co-ops, WHI had had a couple of bad years in Kenya. Donors can be fickle, and irrigation had gone out of favor, as had co-ops. Seeing this, the U.S. headquarters (HQ) of WHI had put its Kenya operation on the back burner while it opened two new country programs elsewhere in Africa. By the mid-1980s, Kenya had been neglected in WHI fund-raising efforts for some time. People in the Nairobi office had been let go.

At the end of 1985 word came that a U.S. consortium of small private foundations was ready to put up $250,000 dollars for a two-year model community water systems project. The operative word was "model": the consortium wanted to have a project so successful that it could and would be replicated elsewhere in Kenya and in other countries in the region.

Two other NGOs with experience in water in Kenya had been bidding for the grant. Under the principle of community involvement, the area communities themselves were to have a say in which NGO was picked. Alex remembers coming out here to Murwanga and meeting with the village headman, Duncan Makilya, a tough old former Mau Mau general. Makilya was clear that he intended to be the new chairman of the society and that he was determined to ensure that his village not get burned the way it had been in the 1970s. When he learned that WHI was proposing to manage the project from Nairobi, sending one or two staff members out to Murwanga every few weeks or so, Makilya had been eloquent in his appeal: "This 'normal advisory' approach," he had said, "is like having a wife and going away to engage in relations with other women. It leads to no good, especially if you want to have a child. You must stay at home with your wife. If you don't, trouble is bound to begin."

It was when WHI agreed to put two of its top men on-site that it was selected for the contract by the community. And though WHI had serious internal qualms about the extra costs involved, it brushed them aside, figuring they'd work everything out later—first get the grant. In the summer of 1986, WHI got the nod from the consortium and agreed to begin work on October 1.

Alex's appointment as project supervisor had struck him as a mixed blessing at the time. He'd been with WHI for ten years, valued because of his honesty and his talents as a field man. He was good at developing rapport with any community easily and was a natural teacher. He knew how important this project would be to WHI and appreciated the trust placed in him, but he was getting older, and as a Kenyan he felt that the time was soon coming when he should be in an executive position with WHI in Nairobi, beginning the process of replacing the expatriate Americans whom WHI had always put in the two top positions since its entry into Kenya in 1972.

But at the end of the day, Alex was not just a dedicated development worker and an optimist who wanted to see his country move forward. He was also a frontline soldier who knew that you had to make personal sacrifices.

Alex and John both knew what mistakes to avoid. They worked closely with the engineers during the survey and design. This was going to be a gravity feed system, use a large mountain spring as a source, simple in its design and technology, but challenging in its construction. The system would supply 1.2 million liters of water per day, with a storage capacity of half that amount. The challenges lay in the little things. Every pipe joint would be vulnerable, so Alex and John knew they would be doing a lot of labor-intensive and repetitive work. Just installing the valves would require double work. Once installed they would need to be covered with earth to protect them temporarily while the rest of the branch line was laid. Even leaving them exposed for a day would risk breakage. The valve chambers would have to come later. Once each branch line is finished the valves are dug up again and tested. Leaks are repaired by the maintenance crew as part of their training. Only then would the valve chambers be constructed and the finishing touches put on. Sabotage is a major night-and-day fear: people, animals, leaves, brush, and mosquitoes are threats. The storage tanks are covered, the ventilation vents are covered with mosquito netting, and the tanks are lined with waterproof cement. Every phase must be closely supervised. Even the mixing of the cement was vulnerable to cheating or just inexperience. If the proportions were not correct, if the curing was not timed properly, the valve chambers and the tank slabs would crumble within a few years.

Because Alex and John knew all this, in their hearts they had agreed with Duncan Makilya about being there full-time. It was the twin costs that they couldn't reconcile: the cost in money and the cost in dependency.

By Christmas of 1986, Alex had decided to take a stand. He wrote a stern memo to Nairobi to be passed on to WHI's New York HQ outlining a number of unavoidable realities. First, Alex strongly argued that WHI was in danger of being caught on the horns of an impossible dilemma: If the Aberdare Water Society project was to be a model, it had to be successful. To be successful, it would have to avoid the pitfalls of past projects. To avoid those pitfalls, impeccably honest construction supervision had to assured. The job of teaching the six villagers to run the operation was, however, going to take second place no matter how dedicated he and John were. And because of that and because two outsiders living there for thirty months would provide the overall supervision, the chances were high that the society, no matter how well the six team members were trained, would have severe problems with adjusting to autonomy once the WHI people left. To avoid the danger of dependency, Alex argued, a three-year plan of postcompletion monitoring would be crucial. This would be a weaning period during which one WHI person would monitor initially for three days per month, winding down to one day per month in the third year. With this monitoring phase the society might have a chance of sustaining itself.

But more money would be needed. He then presented a revised budget based on these "necessary realities," taking the full real cost of WHI into account, including the backup office costs in Nairobi, the detailed material costs over and above the community contribution in shares and labor, and even a guess at the fund-raising costs to the New York office. Alex came up with a budget that was twice the size of the original consortium grant.

He urged WHI's New York HQ to get going immediately on a second round of supplemental fund-raising. Without this the project would fail and WHI could kiss its Kenya operations good-bye. As it was, he pointed out, they would still have to face the possible final irony of having a successful project that would seem to other donors considerably less than replicable because of its high cost. The model, however valid, would likely be rejected. But even so they had no choice except to proceed and do things right.

To his surprise, a month later WHI's president came out to Kenya and visited Murwanga. After a long evening of discussion, he promised a major effort to raise the additional moneys.

Over the next twenty-two months, from January 1987 to March 1989, WHI wrote proposals for various sums they thought different donors might be able to fund and entered into talks with USAID, Danida, Sida, Norway's Norad, Rotary Club International, Lutheran World Relief, and two small independent foundations. The proposals ranged from $10,000 to $160,000. Sure enough, the replicability argument was always the Achilles' heel. People saw the value in the WHI approach, but the high cost turned them off. If water system development was going to be such a labor-intensive, custom-tailored kind of work, it would cost too much to be spread around. From where, the donors asked, would any economies of scale come? Where and when would a learning curve "kick in"? When WHI's fund-raiser would retort that if you want something that works, you have to pay for it, he'd get an answer of "Yes, but still . . ." and a polite brush-off.

At the end of the first summer, in August 1987, Alex and John were called into Nairobi and told that WHI was thinking of pulling out.

"My God, " Alex had said. "After all the effort we've made to restore these people's confidence, you would pull us out and leave them in the lurch again!"

The struggle between the finance vice president in New York whose job it was to look at the bottom line and the field people who had invested their hearts in the project did not last long. Alex and John won, and WHI agreed to stretch itself to carry things a few more months.

Finally, with WHI reaching into its unrestricted reserves — its crucial rainy day money — to carry the project, the fund-raiser in New York struck gold. The Seventh Day Adventists accepted a proposal to grant $175,000 to the project. But this eleventh-hour reprieve would only bring the project to completion. It would not cover the three-year monitoring phase.

Ben had said very little during the course of the evening. When Alex finished telling the story, however, Ben decided to broach something that had been bothering him from his first day. Where was the government of Kenya in all this? Where was the private sector? In most countries a water system was either the province of the government, built with tax moneys and then run as a utility paid for by the users, or it was an outright private sector venture. Water systems run and owned by the community are very rare. Because foreign donors paid for the bulk of the project through the work of a nonprofit (Ben noted that people like Alex and John work for less than employees in the private sector do), were there not just several layers of subsidy here but also several concentric circles of dependency reaching far beyond Murwanga? Wasn't the government itself getting a hidden incentive *not* to take on its proper role? Ben was bothered as he asked Alex and John these questions, not the least because he had been so impressed by their seriousness and dedication.

Now it was John who spoke. He pointed at Ben angrily: "You are being unrealistic, Ben." "It's not like in your country. We are a poor third world country. Our government, even if it wasn't corrupt, would still not have enough moneys to fund such public works. The economy isn't developed enough to have a tax base that would provide the funds, and we don't have a civil administration capable of running such projects. If the people are to have water, this is the only way."

Alex looked at Ben and nodded his agreement with what John had said. But his heart wasn't in it. Ben was right and so was John, and that made him, for the first time since his initial doubts, begin to lose his optimism. For all his zeal to cover every angle and prevent every possible slipup, to make sure this project would be done right and succeed, Alex now saw clearly that this great effort would not, could not be replicated — no donor would want to pick it up and do it this way again. And, with the dam holding back Alex's deeper worries now breached, he began to doubt for the first time whether in ten years' time, even the people of Murwanga would still have running water.

Trying Simply to Help

Eastern Europe, 1990

IN THE LATE 1980s, a couple who had made so much money that it was a slight moral embarrassment to them decided to start a private foundation. They had lived part of their childhood in Africa and loved the continent. They believed in education. They also believed in simplicity and had made their money by acting on one of those time-honored, commonsense business fundamentals: They made their business moves on the basis of trust in individual people rather than sophisticated analyses of markets or economic trends (though they did not skirt these entirely). Most of the time their instincts about people were right, and they established wide-ranging and intricate but always personal cum business relationships that helped their business prosper enormously. When luck brought large opportunities for multiplying their investment, they were in position to take advantage.

Thus, when they began their development assistance foundation, they did not bother to study the field, get to know how the World Bank does it or how other foundations do it. They simply surmised that these institutions and organizations, however much expertise resided in them, were not relevant to them, if only because they were just that — institutions and organizations. They did not, above all, want their foundation to be an organization.

They wanted to give away about $1 million per year, directly to people involved in education in Africa who they felt could and would do good with the money. They did not demand much paperwork, lengthy proposals, or revisions to the proposals but simply a sense that the person knew where he or she wanted to go and that this end goal (building a new school, repairing a classroom, extending primary education to an underreached group) made sense and was reasonably achievable.

Above all, they did not want their help diluted along the way — if a grant was to be for ten thousand dollars, they did not want to spend more to get the money to its "target" than the cost of wiring the money. Of course, they needed some sort of agency, in the pure sense of the term. They had their own lives to lead and could not spend months in Africa getting to know such individuals or searching them out. Thus some of their decisions were made on the basis of recommendations from those they knew and trusted already. That this once-removed stance might make some of their grants more risky, they were more than willing to accept. For their other basic principle was that if you were not prepared for the possibility of failure, even total failure, you simply had no business giving away money to help others. Development, intended to be of help, is in the end a gamble — you *could* lose it all; the money could indeed go down a black hole, leaving nothing behind, not even the final defense against the abjectness of such an egregious loss: the illusion of having "learned a lesson." In the end, they knew it was their money and they had to answer for it only to themselves.

On one of their visits to Africa they met a white man who had gone there to seek a more meaningful life. He was working with schools. They liked him. Around that time they had been thinking it would perhaps be more efficient if they had someone managing things on a day-to-day basis, that perhaps they could accomplish more if they had a full-time person, for they were beginning to learn that it is not that easy to give away $1 million per year.

They also had a geographic expansion of sorts in mind. With the fall of the Berlin Wall, Eastern Europe began to seek development help from Western institutions. It so happened that the husband of the couple who established the foundation, during his many years in business, had often had dealings in Eastern Europe and had felt frustrated with how much talent and resources were being wasted there. He had a strong feeling that if examples could be given to Eastern Europeans about how differently the economy could work, that two generations of communist mentality would begin to erode. He knew also that Eastern Europe was not Africa and that providing assistance by doing things directly in the schools was not going to be the way to help.

Not knowing exactly what approach to take but wanting to do something, the couple offered the young man a job back in their country to run the foundation. They would set up an office with a computer and fax and copier. The young man would be the foundation's manager. He would do all the work himself, with the couple acting as the board of directors.

Pretty soon, after a few reconnaissance trips, the young man discovered that a lot was going on in Eastern Europe. Many aid agencies had begun work; hundreds of projects were already "in the pipeline" and quite a few up and running. What could usefully be done by the foundation he was being paid to administer?

A reflective person, he began asking himself, the more he discovered, whether his foundation had any particular advantage in Eastern Europe — anything to offer that others did not have. And if it did, what sort of a difference could his foundation make? A discomforting conclusion began to form. After his third visit to the one country in the region that seemed a possible base, he had by now met many government officials, many NGOs, many Western aid officials, and several aid contractors. He was struck by how professional and organized they seemed. Yet they were very interested in meeting him and offered him their time freely, even though his foundation was neither well known nor well organized. Were they interested in his foundation only because they sensed there might be money available to them?

At the same time, he was beginning to wonder whether it made any sense to try to help in this country. First, much was being done. Second, he had noticed that the field was becoming saturated; in some of the towns he had visited, several development assistance agencies had already visited before he came along, and the local officials were becoming confused. There seemed to be considerable project overlap. Third, he also noted that much was happening spontaneously, outside the development agencies' efforts. There were entrepreneurs everywhere, new shops, street stalls, much activity. The people were educated people, after all; there was electricity, land, cheap fuel (however much it polluted the air), and roads. These advantages made this Eastern European country seem light years ahead of the African country from which he had just arrived. Would not this country manage to do just fine without his foundation? Would not any effort they tried to make be the merest drop in the bucket? Might it even slow certain things down?

These doubts, however, remained private. As a professional, the manager of the foundation, he had a job to do. He was being paid by the founders. They wanted something to happen in Eastern Europe. To do his job, to merit his pay, he felt, it would be necessary to fulfill their wishes. And so he hired a consultant he had come to know in his years in Africa, Ben Rymaker. Ben made a three-day visit with the foundation manager to try to help determine what could be done.

It is conceivable that Ben would have been able to say publicly what the director had thought privately: "What's the point?" But Ben was a professional. He understood that he was being paid to produce something, a map or strategy of what *to do*, not a recommendation to do nothing. He also believed that there was something that could be done. But, being a professional, before he was ready to outline what that might be and how it might work, he recommended caution and further study.

All the while, the founders were becoming somewhat more uncomfortable with the approach. But their discomfort was tempered by their investment (and clear commitment) to the young man they had brought from Africa with his wife and children. While he was their employee, he was also now their responsibility. The same moral sense about people that led them to want to help in the first place was an extension of their history of recognizing that their employees, whether house servants or workers in the man's former business, were human beings with lives and problems. The couple had always been slow to release people, even when they were not doing their jobs. So they also became invested in having their director do a job, which in some inchoate way they too sensed may not now need doing. Too, having worked in Europe they appreciated the value of being organized and professional. The young man's efforts in this direction appealed to them at one level. And though they felt a conflict between that appeal and their instinct to do things in a light-handed and informal way, they decided not to interfere. After ten more months of visits, some of which involved Ben, and after several plans and revisions, a pilot project was launched in one of the countries. The project was planned to last four years, after which, if it was successful, the founders and the foundation director hoped to look for other places in which to replicate it.

CHAPTER FOUR

Avoiding History

> *Large scale development takes place in many parts of the world without foreign aid, and did so long before this policy was invented some forty years ago. . . .*
>
> *. . . Since its inception in the early postwar years, the central argument for foreign aid has been that without it Third World countries could not progress at a tolerable rate, if at all. In fact external donations have never been necessary for the development of any society anywhere. . . . Economic achievement depends on personal, cultural, social, and political factors, that is people's own faculties, motivations, and mores, their institutions, and the policies of their rulers. In short, economic achievement depends on the conduct of people and that of their governments. . . .*
>
> *. . . The argument for aid as necessary for development rests on the belief that possession of capital is critical for economic advance. If this were so, how is it that large numbers of very poor people could have become prosperous within a few years without donations, as they have done the world over? . . . To have capital is the result of economic achievement, not its precondition.* —P. T. BAUER, *The Development Frontier*

Although the past is never an accurate guide to the future, there are broad patterns from the past that provide valid lessons which ought to inform our expectations of what development assistance can accomplish. In this chapter I look at several lessons about which the development assistance industry appears consistently to avoid thinking.

Mixing Up Cause and Effect

From its beginnings the development industry has focused narrowly on doing and measuring things. It has avoided facing the historical evidence that Bauer refers to above: economic achievement depends on the conduct of people and their governments. Determining what that conduct means is, of course, not so simple — a great deal of explication is required to clarify and understand the interplay of specific behaviors and policies that would result in sustained and *widespread* economic achievement. But two things seem evident nonetheless. First, the keys to development are mainly in the hands of the developing nations themselves and far less in the hands of outsiders, and second, development is not the same thing as its outcomes. To make that second point more clear, consider a set of typical development projects over the last four decades.

- In the 1960s, a factory to produce rope is planned and built in a poor third world country; external donors provide the funding and expertise. Everyone involved in the project is focused on the task. They are getting paid and evaluated according to whether it is built and functioning by a particular date. It is expected that this factory will contribute to the country's development.
- In the 1970s, an international NGO undertakes a community development project in ten villages in Country X to deal with basic human needs (wells, clinics, agricultural implements). Everyone involved is focused on the task. The work is challenging, hard, and fraught with problems. All the NGO staff work long hours and are dedicated. The donor behind the project expects to see certain line items in the budget justified by the end of thirty-six months. The "expected output targets," such as eighteen wells, three clinics, distribution of four hundred agricultural implements, and so on, are met. In its annual report the NGO notes the progress it has made in promoting development in Country X.
- In the 1980s, a biogas project funded by an international agency and implemented by a local NGO in India is under way. NGO staff set up shop in several villages. They enlist twenty-two farm families to participate in the project. The biogas plants are built and the families trained to operate them. The plants are expected to be demonstration projects that the rest of the villagers will copy. All the staff work hard and focus on the tasks at hand. The project is completed on time and considered a development success.
- In the early 1990s, a large for-profit development contractor receives a USAID contract for a women's legal rights project in two North African countries. The design of the project calls for legal rights information centers to be built and staffed and a community awareness campaign to be mounted by the end of the first year. By the end of the second year, the plan calls for twenty seminars and classes to be given and two thousand local women to have been made aware of their legal rights. The contractor accomplishes all this in the allotted time and is applauded by USAID.

These projects, typical of much development assistance over the years, rest on the belief that we must respond to poverty by putting in place the things that people in the wealthy nations have. In other words, poverty is seen as a condition of not having, and thus to change it is to make it into a condition of having.

But not having is not a cause of poverty but the condition of poverty itself. If we or anybody were to be successful in addressing that condition, the outcome would be long-term, aggregate positive material change, a formal economics-sounding term for the desired outcome of development, which in the end is about tangible economic improvements in the day-to-day life of average people (the root of the word "economy" in Greek is *oikonomos*, meaning the management of the house). Real development success is about having enough material security not to suffer all life's vicissitudes. It is about being beyond mere subsistence, about having surplus *for long enough* to give one the possibility to make choices. And it is finally about increasing the number of people who have this possibility. To be meaningful, development must build wealth for long enough to be a sustainable condition for enough people to be widespread throughout the society.

And the question that remains unanswered in a great many development projects is precisely that: Does it make any difference in long-term aggregate positive material change? In more than a few cases we know within five years that the particular development effort did *not* make this kind of difference. Most projects make little lasting difference of any kind. In the four actual cases cited above, the rope factory stopped operating, half the wells went dry or the pumps broke, the clinics and the biogas plant stopped working, and after a while women stopped coming to the legal rights information center.

Why? The benefits of projects like these were not sustained for many reasons. Such projects as the rope factory failed either because there were no roads to get the product to the market, no reliable transport, government officials ripped it off, the manager, who was a brother of the local prefect, had no training, or perhaps the color of the rope offended local people. The well pumps broke because the people did not maintain them, did not know how to maintain them, or did not have the parts to maintain them. The clinics failed because the government stopped paying the nurses or the local traditional healers drove them out of town. The biogas plant stopped working because the farmers found the process too time consuming, and women stopped coming to the legal rights information center because their husbands were threatened by it.

A shorthand way of summing up these reasons is to refer back to Bauer's reading of history — it is the conduct of people and their government that matters. But whose job or responsibility is it to change that conduct, and just as pertinent, how can it be changed? International development assistance has concentrated for so long on short-term effects — the "trees" of individual project and program interventions — that it has avoided the realities of what matters — the "forest" represented by the question above.

The production/engineering model, the foundation of the day-to-day workings of development assistance, is the perfect complement to our misguided direct action agenda and reinforces it. By dividing up development into tasks that can be planned, budgeted, staffed, and implemented by experts, the production/engineering model makes it easy for almost everyone in the industry to lose sight of the forest and stay focused on the trees.

There Is No "Model": Development Is Not Technique

When we try to unravel the complex interweave of threads that accounted for development in the past, we find again and again phenomena which are particular to place and time and which thus cannot be generalized. As the great French historian Fernand Braudel points out:[1] "Every culture has its own distinctive features: Chinese windmills turn horizontally; in Istanbul, the scissors have hollow blades, and the luxury spoons are made from wood from the pepper plant; Japanese and Chinese anvils are different from ours; not one nail was used to build the boats on the Red Sea and the Persian Gulf, and so on. And each has its own plants, domestic animals (or at any rate its own way of treating them), its characteristic houses, its own foods. The mere smell of cooking can evoke a whole civilisation."[2]

The planning and engineering model of development has led quite naturally to hope for the efficiencies that come from economies of scale whenever something occurs that appears to "work." We continue to look, therefore, for development "models," and when we think we have one, we want to "replicate," to do the same thing again somewhere else, as if the first instance was a prototype that now needs to "go into production." This rarely succeeds because we forget how much the factors that appeared to work were particular to time and place.

Braudel also makes it clear that development can be slower or faster in different places, cultures, and times. In France, for example, economic development was almost glacial until perhaps 1945. And while trade, shipping, France's geography, and the very size of its land mass were all advantages, developmentally speaking, compared with other countries nearby, France's development was slower, and it remained more "backward" for longer than its neighbors. It is humbling to recall that not until the three decades from 1945 to 1975 did France leap into economic modernity.[3]

1. This book is not meant to be a scholarly thesis on the large forces of historical development. Still, I have read much history trying to understand development, and there are many possible sources one could cite. I concentrate on Braudel in this chapter because he is one of the few historians to deal with the daily life of real people and relate that life to the large sweep of history.

2. Fernand Braudel, *The Structures of Everyday Life*, vol. 1 of *Civilization and Capitalism, Fiteenth–Eighteenth Centuries*, trans. Siân Reynolds (New York: Harper and Row, 1982–84), 64.

3. Fernand Braudel, *People and Production*, vol. 2 of *The Identity of France*, trans. Siân Reynolds (New York: Harper and Row, 1990).

History shows that in accounting for development, no one thing works by itself. Braudel notes, for example, that technology alone is not enough to account for progress; it has, and has had, value only in relation "to the social pressure which maintains and imposes it."[4]

History should also be a reminder that development, once begun, is never guaranteed to continue. Some societies dropped out of a pattern that originally showed developmental promise. For example, China, Braudel points out, remains a great anomaly. It had technological advances early on and had resources similar to those of the West. The Chinese invented gunpowder, firearms, and carbon steel in the early middle ages, and yet by the seventeenth century their mastery of the techniques related to these inventions was inferior to that of the West. While the particulars of the interactions between resources and other factors may begin to explain development in individual cases, it is hard enough to try to get a hold on the intricate details of those interactions, let alone seek patterns that could be deliberately replicated elsewhere.

Avoiding the Power and Complexity of Large Forces

In many developing countries, the condition of people who are poor has to do as much with their position in society as with the lack of roads, the presence of corruption, holes in the rule of law, or misguided or missing policies. Where there is slavery, a caste system, or the predominance of a feudal type of landownership, these large forces have tremendous power over millions of people. It is not only that those who are poor are put in an inferior position in society vis-à-vis others but also that it is close to impossible for them to leave that position. And those forces are complex and have much to do with a nation's, a people's, or a civilization's past. It is hard enough to face how little the conditions of poverty can change unless the *positions* of poor people in those societies change. But because the large forces (and stakes) behind a feudal landownership system or behind a caste system are so intertwined, it is close to impossible for outside agencies to do much to change them. While the poor who are kept in their "positions" by those forces can be helped temporarily, they remain where they were.

Again we are reminded that development has always involved interacting forces too complex to be planned or engineered. It has always involved transactions and interactions between and among culture (tastes, preferences, values, identities, religious ideals); human psychology (motivations, self-interest, habits, inertia, security needs, superstitions, and so on); climactic changes; differences in climactic zones; new technologies; external in-

---

4. Braudel, *Structures*, 431.

fluences through trade and wars; kinds and patterns of crops; markets; roads; epidemics that affect crops and people; changes in prices; and more.

The development endeavor ought to be more humbled by history than it is. If it were, it would be loathe to say that this or that process, structure, or institution is *the* key to a change.

Avoiding the Importance of Time

The history lesson that the development assistance industry avoids most is that development takes time. It is axiomatic that development will always take more time than that "available" in any standard planning and engineering model.

And let us not be tempted to think that the rule of time no longer applies because of the speed that computer technology brings to the world. Yes, we feel the acceleration caused by computers, but the critical question to ask is how much time is needed for others to catch up. For example, in the past, while inventions often appeared suddenly, the spread of these new technologies was slow. In the fifteenth to eighteenth centuries, technological innovation did not give anyone much of a permanent edge because it eventually was adopted elsewhere. One of the keys to that adoption was the slowness with which innovations were communicated; it gave people time to learn: "No innovation remained for long at the service of one group, one state or one civilization," notes Braudel. "Or if it did, it was because other groups did not really need it. The new techniques were established so slowly in their place of origin that neighboring groups had time to learn about them."[5]

There was an oscillation, if not quite a natural rhythm, to change. Things changed slowly as techniques were adopted and as more people learned about them. And then as some sort of critical mass was reached, another technique might come along that would be more truly revolutionary, though never wholly revolutionary in the sense that it alone captured the future. One of these was the coming of steam power, after which the pace of technological change began to accelerate rapidly. In effect, there was a kind of preparation of the ground for such a change.[6] Yet the development assistance industry does not tend to think about the time needed to prepare the ground for change.

Bauer sums up this issue in a pertinent way: "The time dimension of historical processes is widely neglected in contemporary discourse. . . . Income and living standards in the West are the outcome of many centuries of cultural and economic progress; they have not come about in one or two

5. Ibid., 385.
6. Ibid., 372.

generations. It is therefore not surprising, abnormal or reprehensible that many Third World countries . . . which do not have centuries of progress behind them should have much lower incomes than the twentieth-century West. The pertinence of this long period of antecedent development is ignored in the advocacy of global redistribution. It is ignored also in the insistence that Third World countries should promptly reach Western levels of income by a process of virtually instant development."[7]

Where Do History's Lessons Leave the Development Assistance Industry?

History seems to say that for fundamental structural reasons, we in the development industry cannot do very much directly to improve the material well-being of others in a sufficiently significant or sufficiently lasting way. Certainly, the large numbers of *direct* interventions on the ground that the industry has promoted over the last fifty years have been largely ineffective. We are only now beginning to see the possible value of indirect interventions (policy-level work, for example). But the development industry has all along been led by a production/engineering model. In this it has been grossly sidetracked into projects and programs and tinkering with inputs and technical assistance. Direct interventions within a planning/engineering model cannot work because they will always be thwarted by some of the lessons of history discussed above.

Why have we been unable to take in these rather evident lessons? Simply, it has not been in our interest to do so.

---

7. P. T. Bauer, *Equality, the Third World, and Economic Delusion* (Cambridge: Harvard University Press, 1981), 22–23.

The Helper and the Helped

1968–1989

ONE DAY in the late 1960s, Nate Stoppard, scion of an old Yankee family, summarily stepped off a career path that would have guaranteed him a position as the chief executive officer (CEO) of a major company, left the big city and started an NGO over a store in New Hampshire. He was thirty-three years old. The summer before he had accepted a challenge by the pastor of his family's church to volunteer in a hospital in Africa. He had never traveled to the third world and knew nothing about hospitals, but he had an MBA in addition to his Ivy League bachelor's degree and figured he could help.

When the summer was over he returned to his position at the company. But he was a changed man. He thought about what he had learned. He knew little about development but concluded that what Africa needed was not food or airports or factories but business management skills. A man of integrity and deeply held Christian values about charity and good works, Nate decided he could not live with himself if he did not offer to those in need something he had that could make a difference.

Using his own savings, he opened his office and hired one other person. Immediately he received a small grant from his church and soon other small grants as word of his own dedication and character got around the surrounding towns. In the same African country where he'd spent his summer, he hired a fellow Christian whom he'd met there, gave him a small budget, and directed him to set up an office, register it locally, and hire two individuals who knew something about management.

Gradually, staff members made contact with some small farmers. These were producers of palm oil, cocoa, or coffee. They barely made enough money to support their families, let alone invest in improvements. The staff began visiting the farmers, showing them how they could band together to form groups, share their labor, invest in some processing equipment, and do better. Stoppard's vision of transferring business management skills to local people began to be fulfilled.

Back in the United States, Stoppard went on the road to raise money, and after several years of tireless effort, his organization, called Management Tools for Africa (MTFA), had steady funding from a number of sources, including USAID.

January 1989

Nate Stoppard, now in his late fifties, enters the conference room of MTFA's U.S. headquarters and greets each of his staff by name. Almost everyone, from the receptionist to his three vice presidents (VPs), is there. It's Monday morning and the weekly prayer meeting is about to begin. Staff are invited to attend. It is not an obligation, but most, even the non-Christians, do, not because they feel it would look bad if they did not but because they are drawn by the sincerity and commitment of the founder. They do it out of reverence for him and for what he believes.

MTFA is now well established and well thought of by other development professionals and by the development assistance donor community, which supplies it with about $6 million in funding annually. The NGO has programs in nine countries, all staffed by local people, many of whom have business or management degrees. Altogether, there are 145 staff worldwide.

Stoppard visits each country program annually. He does so because he believes he must meet officials and especially because he feels he must personally reinforce the morale of local staff and keep them feeling part of the MTFA family. He does not really like these field visits, finding them physically and emotionally trying. He is not by nature a gregarious person, not a glad-hander, but a soft-spoken and private man. Moreover, as much as he had tried to in the past, he has finally given up his efforts to shed his Yankee roots and patrician upbringing. He is, and has always been, uncomfortable with poor people and abhors the physical encounter with raw third world poverty — the flies, dirt, and disease, but especially its smell. Yet his dedication to helping the poor has given him the strength to put the habits and prejudices of his upbringing in brackets and learn, however awkwardly, to seem like the easy and outgoing leader that he is not.

The prayer meeting over, Nate and two of his staff remain at the conference table, for this is the time of year his annual visits are planned, and decisions need to be made. Ben, his VP for Africa, is present, as is the new VP for fund-raising. This woman comes from the business world. She is the highest paid person in the organization, making twenty thousand dollars per year more than Nate himself. Stoppard and Ben discuss the schedule of countries to be visited, looking at a large calendar laid out on the table. As always, Ben will meet Nate at one or two of the stops, between other visits Ben has to make in the region.

The fund-raising VP interrupts as the other two pore over the calendar. She feels strongly that MTFA has for years missed an opportunity to capitalize on these visits. If Stoppard would agree to have part of his visit videotaped, they could use the edited tape as a marketing tool in a TV campaign scheduled for the following year, an attempt to reach individual private citizens who could become major donors to MTFA's work in Africa. Ben is against this idea. He feels videotaping will alter the character of the visits. Stoppard feels this too but is willing to listen, he says, if this will help bring more money to devote to the poor, the same reason he gave when the decision was made to pay the new fund-raiser such a high salary. But he is concerned about the cost of taping. This and other concerns are discussed in detail over the next hour, and finally Stoppard agrees.

The fund-raising VP also suggests that Nate should stop in Europe on the way to see a number of multilateral agencies, particularly IFAD in Rome. The effort to procure new contracts from this organization has been under way for some time now, and a clincher visit by Stoppard might be in order. At the same time, perhaps a visit to USAID's West

African regional office in Abidjan, as well as the USAID East African office in Nairobi, might be wise. They are major funders of MTFA's work, and courtesy visits by MTFA's president and founder, the VP for fundraising feels, will reinforce the goodwill required to ensure MTFA's financial health over the next five years.

The hardest part of these trips is the jet lag. Nate is an insomniac and suffers from stomach problems, which are always compounded by jet lag. A few of his key lieutenants in the organization, people who have been with him almost since the beginning and know him, have recently suggested to him that he should fly business class on these long trips, especially because he schedules each country for only two or three days and is again on the plane. That way he might get a little sleep. Ben brings this up. But Stoppard continues to refuse, feeling that MTFA's obligation to be good stewards of others' money, not to mention the egregious condition of Africa's poor, requires him morally to use the cheapest means of travel. He adds, as always, that "it helps build my character." (His staff wonder why someone needs to continue to build character at age fifty-seven, but they know he is serious when he says it.)

Stoppard's one recent concession to a modicum of comfort is his purchase of a Swiss-made water filtration system that comes in a plastic pouch and fits easily in his suitcase. This system will filter anything. The brochure explains that one can put the pump down in the gutter of a street in Bombay and within several minutes (pumping very hard to move the dirty water through the tube) out the other end of the tube will come a glass of water clean enough to drink without fear. But this little concession to Stoppard's delicate health comes with a dilemma. The standard ritual of his regular third world site visits always involves a stop in a village, where he will, sure as rain, be proffered a drink. African culture simply does not permit the visitor to refuse the offer of a drink, especially if it is water. His staff wonder how Nate will handle this. Will he take the drink, stoop down to his bag, take out the plastic pouch, unwind the tube, and for several minutes vigorously pump the water through the machine, the village elders watching?

The meeting ends, the itinerary is set. Nate's secretary begins talking to the local travel agent about the flight schedule. Faxes are sent informing each of the MTFA country directors of the founder's visit and asking their views on possible schedules of visits to project sites within each country.

February 1989

In Conakry, Guinea, one of Stoppard's stops, the local staff is in a tizzy. They have mixed feelings about these visits. They know this is the usual time of year, but they never know in what order Stoppard will visit each country until the fax from HQ comes in. On the one hand, they like the attention and feel stimulated by the sense that they are connected to other staff of the same organization far away, all doing the same work. On the other hand, the visit is a pain, a disruption of their rhythm, which is normally slower and easier paced when no one is there to observe them. But they are used to the Yankee culture of MTFA, and because their dedication to the work of helping the poor is equally sincere — several of the staff have been with the organization for seventeen or eighteen years — they take Stoppard's visits as part of the territory. They are good at putting their own selfish concerns aside. There has been a little rumbling of late because the Conakry office's longtime country director, an African, has just been replaced by an outsider, an MTFA employee from a neighboring country. Some suspect this decision amounted to a vote of no confidence. But no one complains openly. They are all good Christians, keeping their goal of helping the poor firmly in view, and get to work on the preparations for Stoppard's visit.

Several local staff are assigned to the task. Everyone wants the president's visit to be successful. To them this means that he must visit what is now their showcase project, a palm oil mill in the central part of the country, set up as a community-run business, and now, after three years of intense effort, beginning to make some money. Two staff members set out from Conakry by pickup truck to go to this mill, a full day's drive. These advance men arrive and let the local chief and the executive committee of the mill know that the founder of MTFA will be visiting from America. Though the chief and the committee have never met Nate Stoppard, they know what to do; they have been visited often by foreign delegations, including once by the American ambassador.

March 1989

Stoppard arrives, about forty-five minutes late, in a small convoy of three pickup trucks, each bearing the MTFA logo, an outstretched open hand holding a stylized toolbox. The community is waiting, not just the member-owners of the palm oil mill, but the entire community. Everyone is gathered under a tree, in a large semicircle. Tables have been set up, on which are plastic cups of water and some refreshments under a colorful cloth to protect them from the flies.

The villagers, about eighty adults and many children, have been waiting for several hours. It is not easy to say what this wait means to them or even whether they consider it a wait at all. For they seem happy enough; there is no sign whatsoever of annoyance. In fact, they seem delighted that there is festivity in the air.

Everyone is seated after much handshaking. The community leader, a retired schoolteacher and thus one of the few literate men in the village, also an English speaker, begins his speech.

He starts by addressing the crowd in the local language and stops every few minutes to translate, addressing his translation to Stoppard. The speech is unctuous to Ben's ears but does not appear so for Nate. The schoolteacher tells of the hopes that have been raised by the palm oil mill project and talks of the past, when others from the outside world had come offering help but had not stayed the course, as has MTFA. He continues, talking now about how the spirit of Christianity crosses all boundaries of race and distance and nationality and that it is an honor, indeed a great compliment, that the president and founder himself has come from so far away to be here. As he speaks, there is much head nodding. It is clear that the crowd is sincerely grateful for the help this organization has provided. The schoolteacher, wiping his brow with a cotton handkerchief, continues in this vein for some minutes, talking about self-help and its rewards, and finally finishes with his voice rising as he says to Stoppard, "Your organization, MTFA, is the savior of our village!"

As Ben looks with some distaste at the video cameraman taping this speech, he feels increasingly uncomfortable. Here and there in the schoolteacher's speech crop up such phrases as "the spirit of self-help," "giving us help with dignity," and "you are helping others help themselves." Ben has been to this area before and has known some of these people for several years. These are not the phrases of the schoolteacher, much less the villagers, but ones that have been learned in the course of the relationship with MTFA. Is Ben hearing them now for the first time because the teacher is aware of the camera and playing to it?

When the speech is over, there is loud applause and much smiling, then a hush. Everyone now awaits the response from the president and founder of MTFA.

Stoppard hates making speeches. But he has forced himself to learn and on occasion has even approached a certain fluidity. He stands. The speech he gives is unusually short — Nate is suffering from the heat and not feeling well. In about seventy-five seconds, Stoppard delivers a homily about self-help, invoking the number of years MTFA has been working in Guinea, the lessons that have been learned, without specifying what they were, and the progress that has been made. Knowing how much the local folk like to hear it, Nate tells them that their mill is known about in faraway places, in the great cities of Washington and New York. In this one line, he sounds for the first time more comfortable. But then he goes on, hurrying to finish. He tells them, somewhat sternly, that they must never give up hope, that if people join together as a community, there is nothing they cannot accomplish.

He sits down, exhausted. There is a hesitancy, for his entire speech is the equivalent of the warm-up that any self-respecting Guinean would give before a speech really got under way. But soon the audience catches on. Collectively, they seem to recall that white men are different and that the president's sitting down signals that he has finished. All at once, they applaud.

The meeting is now open. Anyone may say what they please. A man leaps up and says, in a wonderfully clear and loud voice: "MTFA has saved my life. Without MTFA, I am finished." The way he draws out the last syllable of "finished" is so dramatic that it sticks in Nate's aural memory for the rest of his trip. (Indeed, a month later, the VP for fund-raising has chosen this clip from over eight hours of tape to use in one of the commercials that will air in next year's TV campaign.)

As the group of visitors wends its way in a loose procession through the village to visit the mill and observe a palm oil extraction demonstration, the schoolteacher, who is walking alongside Ben, draws him aside. Without preface, he asks Ben if he could possibly see his way to convince MTFA's esteemed president to provide bicycles for himself and his wife. If MTFA could manage this great favor, he adds, it would make such a difference in their lives. It would enable them to extend their reach to several markets now too distant for them. This, of course, would be an investment in self-help, the teacher adds unselfconsciously. Ben, somewhat troubled by this, knows he must answer. They continue to walk in silence for a minute or two. Then Ben replies slowly and gravely that one of the cardinal principles of MTFA is that nothing should be given away; people do not, MTFA has learned, appreciate it if they receive a free gift. "We once gave away such things as bicycles and found that within a few short months, they were rusted and broken," he tells the schoolteacher. "People do not care for things they have not earned through their own labor," he adds.

The schoolteacher listens politely. When Ben finishes, the schoolteacher takes Ben's hand in his and shakes it. He does not seem disappointed or angry. He smiles as the procession continues through the village. Then he tilts his head toward Ben, leans forward, and, in a whisper, says, "But, of course, I know that MTFA has its many ways of doing things. I'm sure you will find a way."

Confusing Stakes

South Asia, 1991

"DAMN THESE FLIES. Time after time I've told these guys the fruit has to be clean before it's put on the drying trays. They still don't get it!"

"But that's the way they've always dried them. They like the way they taste, flies and all; why should they change?"

"Because if they want to make some goddam money for a change, they've got to get with the program. They have to compete. They think these crappy apricots are wonderful! Try selling 'em down country. Try exporting them. Ha! No way."

Malcolm is a horticulturist. He has been seconded to the government agriculture ministry to work on this project. IFAD is paying for him to be here, a high salary even by his own standards, tax free in Malcolm's home country, Canada. Plus he gets home leave every eight months, the full cost of housing, and a hardship differential of 20 percent. This last is because of the project's remote location in the foothills of the Hi-malayas. He's been up here almost two years, and his contract calls for one more.

Ben can see how frustrated he is. Ben knows Malcolm is right about the apricots, but he wonders if it matters.

"Well, they sure look pretty, though. All those round flat baskets filled with yellow apricots, lying out on the rooftops to dry in the sun. I wish I could take a picture of them from the air. . . . But look at the time, Malcolm. Let's go back to the office; we'll be late for the planning meeting."

Ben and Malcolm get into the Landcruiser. They are alone, so Malcolm drives. He's taken some flack about this from the "local" employees of the project, especially Hamidshah, the chief agricultural engineer. "You really must take a driver, Malcolm," Hamidshah had implored. "That's what they are here for (the project employs six of them). It does not look right, not right at all, to see a senior person driving himself. The drivers don't like it, the staff don't like it. Please, Malcolm, I beg you."

But Malcolm is an impatient professional. He loves his work and loves to work. His general impatience always gets the better of him, and when he decides to go somewhere, he wants to go right away, no forms to fill out, no going to the dispatcher to get a driver assigned. He knows that the dispatcher would make him wait while one of the drivers is sprung loose from his tea and cards in the drivers' hut. It's not worth the trouble. He just grabs a set of keys from the board, signs a slip, puts it on the dispatcher's desk, hops in a vehicle, and goes.

Malcolm is on the road a great deal, constantly visiting the farmers in the project, cajoling, inspecting, ordering them to change this or make that adjustment, and generally hectoring them. He's passable at the local language — no one doubts that he gets his point across.

His project — to institute an appropriate technology for the uniform sun-drying of the local fruit (virtually 100 percent of which is apricots) — is one of several undertaken by the Earth Way Rural Support Institute (EWRSI). Earth Way is a private development organization founded as an international NGO. It undertakes agriculturally related projects in seven countries in Asia. Through diligent salesmanship and networking among the multilateral agencies based in Europe (IFAD and the FAO in Rome, the ILO in Geneva) and a few bilateral development agencies, particularly those of the Scandinavians and the Dutch, EWRSI has developed a reputation for no-nonsense professional project work. So much so that since the early 1990s, funding agencies have been practically clamoring to grant funds to EWRSI.

Earth Way is cleverly and strategically managed. It rarely takes on projects that will not have a tangible, measurable benefit in good time. When these benefits appear, as they usually do, EWRSI takes the credit.

When it started, EWRSI had to do some hard initial convincing to ensure donors that poverty is as serious in places like the sparsely populated, high-altitude Himalayas as it is in Bangladesh, one of the undisputedly deepest poverty pockets in the world. Even professional development types tend to associate poverty with dense populations, chronic food shortages, and hot and humid conditions.

But here in this part of the Himalayas, not only do people have enough to eat but they also live in an area of great physical beauty and such unusually pristine air quality that the government has thought of putting in a laboratory for scientific experiments that require uncontaminated conditions. At the same time, people are uneducated. Disease rates and infant mortality are very high. But the real concern here is isolation. It takes a full day's travel by jeep to come from the nearest city down country, and that is when the road is passable, so there is no trade and people therefore here have no cash. They live on what they grow. But there is one local crop, apricots, that has cash crop potential.

Marketing tests in a city south of the area, conducted by EWRSI, showed high potential demand, even export possibilities, for good sundried unsulfured apricots, especially to the newly health-conscious high-end British and U.S. markets. But local farmers are not terribly keen on keeping up product quality, and no matter how much the project's extension workers, who answer to Malcolm, try to get across that high quality will produce high profits for them, farmers don't seem to get the message.

It is now the third year of the apricot project, and the original contract calls for a major evaluation to be done. Ben was hired to do this with a team of three others, who will be arriving in a few days.

Malcolm drives in silence and with great concentration. The road is narrow. There are large rocks everywhere, the result of landslides. These can and do happen anytime, and the road is never clear. Ben stares at the landscape. There is nothing green in sight. White, brown, and gray are the only colors — the white of the permanent snow on the mountaintops, and the brown and gray of the rocks.

"Rocks, nothing but rocks. . . ."

"Ha, you said it, Ben! Did I tell you about that stupid IFAD lady who came to visit last March? This was an official visit, mind you. The donor wants to see how the money is being spent. Well, this gal was a regular development tourist, wanted to go everywhere. And, get this, she wanted us to videotape her tour. Of course we did. So we're out here, right about where we are now, and she says just what you did: "Rocks, nothing but rocks." So I said to her, with all the seriousness I could muster, that we were studying the possibility of transporting these rocks south and setting up a rock export business, by air! "Really!" she said. "What an interesting idea."

Earth Way's project office, with its large staff and drivers and vehicles, has become widely known in the area. The local people know that it is there to help improve their lives. Their tangible daily benefit is the health clinic that the project has set up next door to the office. Anyone can come in anytime and get help. On most days, there's a line in the dusty lane leading to the clinic's main door.

The office is in Bulduur, the only town in the area. Earth Way has so quickly become the hub of activity in Bulduur that even when businesspeople from other parts of the country manage to get up here to see whether there are any ventures worth investing in, they stop first at the EWRSI office, because they know they can learn what is happening in the area, including the status of various local products. They know they will get more accurate information than from the government.

Once, a Frenchman arrived with a proposal to bottle mountain spring water and ship it to France. He wanted EWRSI to become a venture partner and convince the villagers to turn over their water rights to him. The head of EWRSI's operations in the region, Sadruddin Akram, told him that the organization was not in the business of doing business and while it could not stop him from his explorations, it would not help him either. He went away.

The Landcruiser pulls into the vehicle pool yard next to the project office. Ben and Malcolm are right on time for the project evaluation planning meeting. This will be Ben's first chance to hear what Malcolm's associates, all locals from the region, have to say about how things are going.

Malcolm introduced everyone and then gave the floor to Ben. Ben was uncomfortable. Before he boarded the plane to come out here, the IFAD rep in Rome had alerted Ben to a possible conflict-of-interest matter. Ben was surprised IFAD would know about such things, since their level of detailed project knowledge was always notoriously limited. If a conflict-of-interest problem had reached IFAD's ears in Rome, it must be serious. Ben knew some of the details from having read through the daily logs and other project files over the last few days.

He decided not to waste time and to get it over with. He turned to Ghazi Din and asked him point-blank what the story was.

Ghazi Din is Malcolm's right-hand man. He is from the region, a member of the area's dominant tribe (in terms of both political power and population). He is university educated and speaks three languages, including English. Personable, kind, and committed to the development of his region, this is his first postdegree job. In fact he was one of the first staff hired by EWRSI when it came into the area.

He explains that as the project is now about to enter its fourth year, the sunk costs of the experiments in fruit drying and the level of frustration about most local farmers' lack of interest in improving their product have been such that it was decided earlier in the year to set up a local marketing association aimed only at those growers who were committed to maintaining quality control. This decision, Ghazi Din added, involved an ideological compromise for some of the staff, committed as they were to the idea that no one was to get rich at the expense of others or to become richer more quickly than others. So no one was really happy about it.

Ghazi Din was assigned the task of getting this marketing organization started. He explained that not only Malcolm, his direct boss, but also the executive director himself, Sadruddin Akram, had made it known that this marketing association must be a success — that the venture must show a profit because the donors are watching. Ghazi Din therefore made this assignment his sole priority and worked tirelessly on it for months.

Using a small line item in the project's budget for "research," he rented warehouse space in a building in the local town and hired a watchman. Then he got the three most active and largest of the fruit growers in the area together and asked them to constitute the executive committee of the association. Because the three growers do not live in town, they suggested to Ghazi Din that he open the bank account for the association in his own name so that he would be able to sign checks and not waste their time going in and out of the town, which can take hours over the rocky roads, which are often cut off by landslides. The account was opened at a local bank. (Ben knew that the bank was managed by prominent members of Ghazi Din's tribe.)

Ghazi Din then traveled to the capital city four hundred miles away where the main exporters of agricultural products are. He had heard of a company that might be interested in sun-dried fruit and made contact with them. He offered an initial shipment at a price he arrived at by adding the cost of the fruit paid to the farmers and the projected cost of transport to the capital city and then adding 10 percent for profit. This turned out to be an unusually attractive price, and a tentative deal was made, pending a visit to the area by the company's chief executive.

On his return, Ghazi Din set about visiting the growers to tell them that they had a contract. The growers quickly realized that their own supply would not come close to meeting the order and it was decided to approach neighboring growers and buy from them. Transport was going to be a problem, so Ghazi Din offered to use the EWRSI vehicle assigned to him to gather up the product in burlap bags and bring it to the warehouse. For a period of three weeks, Ghazi Din and his driver were on the roads almost constantly bringing tons of apricots to the central warehouse.

The condition of the fruit was less than the quality the buyer had wanted since the contract Ghazi Din had signed on the association's behalf was so large that the member growers could not supply it. Moreover because the contract had a time limit on it and because the season was now over, everything had been done in such a rush that Ghazi Din neglected to set up the books for the association in a proper manner. The shares sold to members had been marked in pencil in a black notebook that Ghazi Din carried around with him, as had been other of the association's transactions.

Ben was surprised that Ghazi Din was being so forthright. It was almost as if Ghazi Din did not realize what he was saying. Now would come the touchy part. Just the day before, Ben had looked carefully at the account books for the association. Certain numbers just did not add up. Ben asked about these.

Ghazi Din explained that some share purchases had been pledged but not yet paid for. Yet the assets in the books reflected these as real. Without prompting, he went on to say that he and his cousin had bought shares in the association themselves and that Ghazi Din had lent money from the association's bank account to two of the richest of the growers, at no interest, with no term limit. These loans were not recorded in the black book he carried with him or in the official account books, which contained very little information. But Ghazi Din had not been concerned about this, nor was he now, he said. Indeed, Ben should realize this from the fact that he was not hiding these facts. He wasn't concerned because these men are relatives of his, and he trusted them.

Ben *was* concerned, however, and decided to pursue further the nature of the association and Ghazi Din's involvement. Malcolm's role in all this would come later.

After the meeting, Ben and Ghazi Din went into Ghazi Din's office, where Ben asked to see all the paperwork Ghazi Din had, on everything about the association. Ghazi Din opened the files quite willingly.

Ben saw that Ghazi Din had been in contact with a number of exporters, and in two cases, negotiations were under way for shipments at prices that struck Ben as well below market price. Ben asked Ghazi Din how he had calculated these prices. He replied that he had simply taken the cash outlays that he needed to make from supply point to delivery and added 10 percent for the profit. Ben asked him to run through these costs. It immediately became clear that Ghazi Din had not counted his own time, the time of his driver, or the use of the project vehicle. Nor had he counted the cost of renting the warehouse or hiring the guard, as these costs had also been paid for out of the project's "research" budget. The only cost that Ghazi Din had charged to the association had been the price paid to the other growers for the extra fruit needed to fill the order. It was clear to Ben that Ghazi Din was doing business but not thinking like a businessman.

Ben needed to talk to the executive committee of the association. He asked Ghazi Din to arrange it, and the next morning the two of them, plus a driver, went out to the village of the head of the committee, a distant cousin of Ghazi Din. The committee head is also a businessman who owns a local hotel. After they sat down, Ben asked the man to describe the work of the marketing association. He was effusive about the help that the project, in the person of Ghazi Din, had been giving the association and praised Ghazi Din's devotion to getting the association up and running and seeing to it that the first orders were filled. He added that Ghazi Din's hard work had permitted him and his colleagues to pay full attention to their other businesses. "I have to run my little hotel, you know. This is the season that the trekkers come through."

The next day, back at the project office in Bulduur, Ben was sitting in Ghazi Din's office, looking glum. As always, Ghazi Din was fresh as a daisy and ready to go to work, showing no sign of any shame or guilt. At about ten o'clock, a man from Western Fresh and Dry Fruit came in to see Ghazi Din. He said that he worked for the government in Oenergu, the neighboring district, and was acting on behalf of his brother, an entrepreneur with plans eventually to dominate the dried fruit market in the west. This man claimed that his brother's company had already been successful in marketing grapes and cherries west to Country X and in importing computers back into this country. He also claimed to have market connections in North America and South Africa and therefore "requested," as he put it, the project to supply him with ten thousand to twenty thousand kilograms of sun-dried fruits for these markets, at cost.

Ben sat there amazed at the scale of the man's scheme, but he was more amazed by Ghazi Din. Not missing a beat and in Ben's presence, Ghazi Din began negotiating with him.

After the man left, Ben couldn't hold it in any longer. He looked at Ghazi Din's earnest face and said right to him that his job was not to make deals; that the Apricot Project was not and could not be a direct supplier of commodities; that Ghazi Din's pricing was in effect a subsidy for people like his distant cousin, who did not need the favor; and that the whole way in which things had been done was, if not illegal — that wasn't for Ben to judge — certainly of questionable integrity.

Did Ghazi Din not get what the proper role of the project was? At most, Ghazi Din could set up a meeting between Western Fresh and Dry Fruit and the principals of the marketing association. It was the head of the marketing association who should be talking to this man, not Ghazi Din. "Tell your cousin the hotel owner to get off his rear end and work for his own association, instead of getting a free ride off the project!"

Ghazi Din listened carefully. Then he said that he understood all that Ben had said but reminded him that the leaders of the association were too busy with other things, and that's why they leave the handling of these things to him.

Ben got up and excused himself. He went outside and looked at the mountains while he calmed himself down and thought. Ghazi Din, while he certainly cheated, especially in lending money to friends from the marketing association's account, was not a thief. Nor was he entirely naïve. When the notion of "conflict of interest" was raised with him, he got the concept, offering to sell his shares in the association to his brother, who is not an employee of EWRSI. Ghazi Din was acting, by his own account, appropriately opportunistically and in the interests of his community, as he saw it. He was also responding to his boss's urging to get this enterprise moving toward a fast success. One could argue that he was being entrepreneurial in starting a side business using the resources of his employer — a not-for-profit NGO. After all, wasn't EWRSI a local resource institution? Isn't Ghazi Din yet another "service," available to the community, like the clinic? Or perhaps for Ghazi Din this is all about "self-help." It's just that he is one of the selves to whom "self-help" applies.

Ben had to ask Ghazi Din one more thing. He went back inside.

"Tell me this, Ghazi Din. Why, given your contacts, didn't you just quit your job at EWRSI and go into a straight business partnership with the other growers, without the trouble of a marketing association and all that? You know, there is a world of difference between starting a business while being an employee of an international NGO, using the knowledge you've gained and even some of the contacts, and starting a business on your own. And if you had done that, you would always know whether you were making a profit or a loss and you would know how to price your product to cover your costs. You would also have the incentive to make sure the customers kept coming back, and so forth. Why didn't you do that?"

Ghazi Din, for the first time, looked uncomfortable and perhaps a bit ashamed, though Ben couldn't really tell. He had been afraid, Ghazi Din said. "What if things didn't work out? Then I would have lost my money, and more important, my job with one of the few large employers in the region would be gone. It was too risky."

CHAPTER FIVE

The Consequences of Avoiding Certain Universals of Human Nature

In 1899, when he was twenty-five, Winston Churchill ruminated about colonialism in his account of the reconquest of the Sudan by the British in the 1896–98 "River War," during which he served as a cavalry officer under Lord Kitchener:

> What enterprise that an enlightened community may attempt is more noble and more profitable than the reclamation from barbarism of fertile regions and large populations? To give peace to warring tribes, to administer justice where all was violence, to strike the chains off the slave, to draw the richness from the soil, to plant the earliest seeds of commerce and learning, to increase in whole peoples, their capacities for pleasure and diminish their chances of pain — what more beautiful ideal or more valuable reward can inspire human effort? The act is virtuous, the exercise invigorating, and the result often extremely profitable.
>
> Yet as the mind turns from the wonderful cloudland of aspiration to the ugly scaffolding of attempt and achievement, a succession of opposite ideas arises. Industrious races are displayed stinted and starved for the sake of an expensive imperialism which they can only enjoy if they are well fed. Wild peoples, ignorant of their barbarism, callous of suffering, careless of life but tenacious of liberty, are seen to resist with fury the philanthropic invaders, and to perish in thousands before they are convinced of their mistake. The inevitable gap between conquest and dominion becomes filled with the figures of the greedy trader, the inopportune missionary, the ambitious soldier, and the lying speculator, who disquiet the minds of the conquered and excite the sordid appetites of the conquerors. And as the eye of thought rests on these sinister features, it hardly seems possible for us to believe that any fair prospect is approached by so foul a path."[1]

I am reluctant to label the development assistance industry "neocolonialist," but if we try to help others when they have not asked for it, are we in our own way "philanthropic invaders"? And what if these others want our help and do ask for it? Are we then off the hook? Helping others, whether they ask for it or not, seems always to be morally and psychologically problematic. At best, helping is a delicate matter; at worst, it puts us on Churchill's "foul path." Most human beings, both those who offer help and

---

1. Winston S. Churchill, *The River War* (New York: NEL Books, 1973), 13.

those who receive it, seem intuitively to know this and thus feel some ambivalence about helping or being helped.

The Hidden Fear of Creating Dependency

Most of us have an instinct to help others. Mundane opportunities to do so are before us often, as when we pass a homeless man holding out a cup. But we squirm and twist momentarily, consciously or not, caged as we are in our jaded time: "Is this the right thing to do?" "Will it really help?" "Am I being 'soft'?" "What about the next homeless person over there?" Even, "Does he deserve it?"

And if we let them, these kinds of questions escalate: "Will my help last?" "Can the homeless man change?" "Whose fault is it that he is there, anyway?" "Am I being foolish for giving?" "Am I being foolish for not giving?"

Questions like the above often mask a fear that one is doing more harm than good. One way of reconciling that fear is to employ the convenient mask of "self-help," and that has often been done in dealings with the poor, and not just in our own era. Here is Henry Mayhew, writing on the poor of London in 1861: "Philanthropists always seek to do too much, and in this is to be found the main cause of their repeated failures. The poor are expected to become angels in an instant, and the consequence is, they are merely made hypocrites. . . . It would seem, too, that this overweening disposition to play the part of pedagogues (I use the word in its literal sense) to the poor, proceeds rather from a love of power than from a sincere regard for the people. Let the rich become the advisers and assistants of the poor, giving them the benefit of their superior education and means — but leaving the people to act for themselves — and they will do a great good."[2]

The idea of self-help was invoked by Henry Ford in 1915: "I have little use for charities or philanthropies as such. My idea is to aid men to help themselves."[3] Andrew Carnegie used the term explicitly: "The rich man should give . . . in such a way as to encourage self help."[4] And John D. Rockefeller worried about it: "It is a great problem to learn how to give without weakening the moral backbone of the beneficiary."[5]

The development industry still hides behind the concept of "self-help" today, though perhaps there is a bit more awareness of the inherent contra-

2. E. P. Thompson and Eileen Yeo, *The Unknown Mayhew* (New York: Random House, 1971), 34.

3. B. Howe, "The Emergence of Scientific Philanthropy, 1900–1920: Origins, Issues, and Outcomes," in *Philanthropy and Cultural Imperialism: The Foundations at Home and Abroad*, ed. R. Arnove (Boston: G. K. Hall, 1980), 44.

4. Eugene Linden, *The Alms Race* (New York: Random House, 1976), 16.

5. *The World*, October 13, 1898.

diction in the concept (if the poor in the third world could help themselves, they would not need our help). But what exactly are we hiding from?

I believe we hide from the realization that helping others is very tricky business, to say the least. How do you give "in such a way as to encourage self-help"? How do you prevent help from being a veiled expression of power? How do you avoid help becoming an imposition? Then there is the matter of motives. Charitable motives are not always purely charitable, as social critic Thorstein Veblen noted long ago: "It is a matter of sufficient notoriety to have become a commonplace jest that extraneous motives are commonly present among the incentives to this class of work [works of 'charity or social amelioration']—motives of a self-regarding kind, and especially the motive of an invidious distinction."[6] Perhaps Ralph Waldo Emerson expressed the problematic nature of helping most eloquently: "The law of benefits is a difficult channel, which requires careful sailing, or rude boats. . . . We can receive anything from love, for that is a way of receiving it from ourselves; but not from any one who assumes to bestow."[7]

And yet our empathic instinct, perhaps even genetically predetermined, tells us we must do something. We must act. And our upbringing, all of ours, in all cultures and religions, reinforces that urge, as does the Judeo-Christian concept of charity for many people in the West.

Thus there is much force behind our instinct to help, our sense that we must take action. To resist takes more than self-discipline; it is simply counterintuitive, not to mention threatening to our self-image.

And let's be clear about development assistance. The instinct to help exists in all the institutions and agencies of the development industry, no matter how hard-nosed their organizational culture or raison d'être may be. Even if the World Bank casts itself as a tough-minded financial institution, the majority of those who work in it derive meaning in their jobs from their sense that they are helping those in need—they may work in an institution that likes to think of itself as a bank, but *they* are not bankers. Certainly, the steady rise in philanthropic giving in America (over $100 billion annually since the mid-1990s) is based on more than the loopholes in the tax code.

And so as an industry we too feel we must act. But we do so without much, if any, reflection on the dangers involved. For the seemingly sound instinct to help the poor of the developing world gets inevitably distorted and eventually corrupted when put into the service of long-term and sustainable development, as opposed, say, to emergency relief. And even when our motives are relatively pure, the result of that instinct is often dependency.

6. Thorstein Veblen, *The Theory of the Leisure Class*, Mentor ed. (New York: New American Library, 1953), 221.

7. Ralph Waldo Emerson, *Essays and Addresses* (Chicago: Scott, Foresman, 1906), 54.

Some Subtle Dimensions of Dependency

One of the reasons development assistance often crosses into creating dependence — to the extent it is based on the instinct to help — is that it stretches several of the natural human dimensions of the helping dilemma to extreme limits.

The Psychological Dimension

Sociologist Helmut Schoeck talks about the concept of "ressentiment," meaning the rancor expressed against benefactors. The helping relationship has two sides, often mirroring each other. The persons being helped may harbor the same kinds of doubts that the persons doing the helping have.[8] That rancor appears in one of the few modern novels to take place in a development project in the third world, *Mating*, by Norman Rush:

> Anyway, he said, so say we have some average collection of poor Africans, farmers, and here come some white experts to induce development, say by setting up an integrated rural development project in the most sensitive way anybody has figured out to date. Time passes. Things begin to work. But a funny thing: the best of the poor, the most competent, the ones doing best and the ones who're even the most like you spiritually, are the ones who are going to present you with . . . bouquets of ressentiment. Why? What can be done? I am talking about your mainstream development project here, by the way.
>
> No adult wants to be helped, I said.[9]

Not only stiff-necked Yankees in old New England are ambivalent about being helped. There appears to be something psychologically universal about being helped that makes one uncomfortable. That something is independent of whether or not one needs the help. If I fall down on the street and someone helps me up, I am grateful for the help. But even in that tiny instance — one where long-term sustainable development is not the objective — I may feel some sort of loss, even if it is only a bit of my dignity. Oddly, at the same time help gives, it also takes something away. The meaning of what gets lost will vary with culture. For some cultures it may be part of the soul or a sense of wholeness; for others it may be "self," "independence," or "dignity"; for yet others, "strength" or "role." And this is not to say that the thing to be given up or lost is always given up unwillingly. Having lost my dignity for a few minutes while someone helps me up is not so bad. I can afford it. I'll get my dignity back in other ways, another time.

But in development assistance the sense of loss is put under much greater stress. A two- or three-year-long project in a village, involving a score of

8. Helmut Schoeck, *Envy* (New York: Harcourt, Brace & World, 1966).
9. Norman Rush, *Mating* (New York: Vintage Books, 1991), 105.

"development workers," magnifies this inherently problematic psychological dimension. The potential for ressentiment grows.

The "Economic" Dimension

Anthropologists have long noted that there is no such thing as a pure "gift." A gift in all cultures is part of an implicit system of exchange. Built into it is an economic calculus based on reciprocity: something is returned (or exchanged) for the gift. In some cultures the obligation incurred on receiving a gift is calculatedly material. In others the tacit obligation is "made good" in the currency of ego, status, noblesse oblige, or plain power. A thank-you note is not just something that Miss Manners teaches the well-brought-up in our own culture — it is also an "instrument" in an intricate social clearinghouse of obligations.

In development assistance this complex dimension will also inevitably become stretched and magnified. I have often sensed that many people in developing countries have become so willing to take what we offer, and over and over again, because they have become used to repaying us in deference and obsequiousness. If they seem to bow and scrape, it is not because it is in their nature but because that may be the only currency they have to repay us in, and we, in turn, have become quite happy to receive it. If we sometimes worry about dependency, most of the time we do not notice how we reinforce it.

Sometimes the stretching of the economic dimension occurs in strange ways. Anyone with a few years of field experience in development assistance will have come across cases where they suspect that behind the proffered gratitude of project beneficiaries is a thinly veiled hope for more, and behind that an odd kind of anger. When this occurs it is not simply because someone is trying to take advantage of us. Instead, it is possible that they may feel the calculus has tilted, oddly enough, in their favor. The quantum of "feel-good" we get from giving them help is so large that they are getting the short end of the stick in the exchange. To make it right, they *need* to ask for more, and at some level they do not want to.

An example of the way the inherent obligation to reciprocate can be magnified is the current movement to forgive third world debt, on the grounds that to keep the burden on these countries is to make them worse off. While that is true in material terms and in the short term, forgiving the debt ignores the possibility that in some inchoate way these countries may come to feel they owe something else (other than money) in exchange for being forgiven what they owe.

The Irony of Duration and Proximity

It is dependency that underlies both the psychological loss and the unequal sense of reciprocal obligation discussed above. Part of what exacerbates that dependency is the duration and the proximity of the help the development assistance industry means to provide. We hang around just long enough to believe we are getting at root causes instead of just giving things to people. And because we believe we're doing more than giving things away, we justify getting organized to do that. But by being so close by and hanging around for awhile, we cannot help but contribute further to dependency.

If I drop a coin in an outstretched hand and then leave, I may or may not have significantly magnified the dilemma of dependency or the psychological loss of dignity in the person who accepted it. If the person's life is saved or the coin enables him to buy what he needs to present himself for a job, I may well have helped him genuinely. In any case, it is not likely that I will know, because I won't see him again.

In development assistance efforts, in the way we have seen them undertaken until now, we do not generally drop the coin and leave. We have become quite used to believing that dropping the coin and leaving is akin to giving a man a fish and feeding him for a day. John D. Rockefeller saw this as his second career as a philanthropist began to mature: "Instead of giving alms to beggars, if anything can be done to remove the causes which lead to the existence of beggars then something deeper and broader and more worthwhile will have been accomplished."[10]

Instead, we have convinced ourselves that we are in the business of teaching the poor man to fish or giving him the means to fish and thus feeding him for a lifetime. It sounds right, but it is more complicated than it sounds. Still, we have used this kind of thinking to justify and bolster our sticking around, in proximity to the problem, over just enough time (two to five years) to make our presence an expected one.

But in being proximate over such durations, we have not been careful to avoid the dilemmas built into helping. Rather, we generally skirt these dilemmas or dismiss their importance. First, as I noted earlier, one way around the dilemma is to call what we do "self-help." Second, because we perceive the need to stick around long enough to avoid just dropping a coin and leaving (we pejoratively call this "Band-Aid kind of help"), we need to organize our help. To be sure, dumping medical supplies off the back of a truck involves a degree of organization — indeed, intricate logistics — but development assistance, as it has evolved over the years, is a different order of organization altogether. Organizing development assistance has meant becoming permanent institutions, staffed by professionals.

And it is with this need to organize development assistance that we come to the reasons why the helping instinct inevitably becomes distorted. For the reasonable enough instinct to institutionalize and professionalize the act of

---

10. Bruce Bringhurst, *Antitrust and the Oil Monopoly: The Standard Oil Cases, 1890–1911* (Westport, Conn.: Greenwood Press, 1979), 26.

helping ironically results in magnifying the problematic nature of helping. One set of actions based on reasonably sound instincts begins to cancel out another set of actions, based on equally sound instincts. The mismatches are profound.

The Consequences of the Clash of Two Equally "Good" Instincts

About 150 years ago in London, Henry Mayhew had the idea of setting up a "loan office for the poor" through which

> deserving subjects might obtain either small outright grants or loans on easy terms of repayment in order to obtain the necessary stock or equipment to carry on their trades. The sums advanced were petty and the number receiving them amounted to only a few score.
>
> The largest sum advanced on loan was to C. Alloway, the crippled seller of nutmeg-graters, whose portrait and harrowing story [in the *Morning Chronicle*, for whom Mayhew was then writing a series on London's poor tradespeople] brought sympathy and recognition in the streets: "I am gazed at in the street," he wrote, "and observations made within my hearing with respect to the Exact likeness of the portrait." More than 9 pounds was advanced to him, to be repaid at 1 shilling a week, but he was beset at once with new disasters; he invested in a donkey, ordered a cart, and bought some hardware stock, but the donkey became ill, and the carpenter absconded with his money. The most ambitious effort of the "Loan Office" appears to have ended in failure."[11]

Mayhew's mistakes long ago are just what the development industry has worked hard to avoid. First, he was unprofessional. Second, his instinct was to help the poor help themselves, but in beginning with "easy terms of repayment," he made the error of being softhearted. Likewise, he did not choose his Mr. Alloway rationally but on the basis of sympathy. Moreover, poor Mr. Alloway was not an entrepreneur but someone whose harrowing story encouraged the loan office to lend him money so that he could try out a bunch of ideas without having had any experience. Not surprisingly, these ended in disaster. Finally, the amount loaned was too large. At the time, poor tradespeople, such as needleworkers, were netting two shillings per week, which came to about five pounds per year. Nine pounds was simply more than Mr. Alloway could handle.

Worse, we surmise from the account, Mayhew's idea, having been basically a charitable lark, was rather quickly abandoned. More important than the failure of Mr. Mayhew's loan office for the poor, poor Mr. Alloway went down the tubes along with it. End result: More harm than good was caused.

The development assistance industry *has* been on a learning curve, though the lessons learned have often been counterproductive to what we

---

11. Thompson and Yeo, *Unknown Mayhew*, 43.

would like to accomplish. By trying to think things through in a way the amateurish Mayhew did not, the field of development became much more professional, and virtually everything it did has become institutionalized. Even so, other agendas inevitably creep in, and the instinct to help becomes muddled; institutional and bureaucratic imperatives begin to weigh as much as the original intentions of the helpers.

Story 8 in this book illustrates how easily things become compromised. It is a demonstration, under almost laboratory conditions, of how innocently professional and institutional imperatives can take over the instinct to help. The purity of the couple's original vision, a desire to help linked to an unusual aversion to being an "organization," and their view of grant making as a simple and lean process are all rather quickly blurred, as different stakes (and stakeholders) begin to take a seat at their table. They then begin to move away from acting on their instinct to help and toward transacting business between and among their staff and possible new constituents (the web of contacts both the manager and Ben the consultant begin to make). Now the couple have put their foundation in a position where these transactions must take place before direct action (defined here as grant making) can take place. The process also greatly influences how they make their decisions to give grants. But the overarching change is that the possibility of not acting is greatly reduced. The institutional momentum has made that practically impossible. Ideally in development that wild card — the do-nothing card — should always be there; it is the ultimate ace in the hole. But it is almost never used. In this story the instinct to help was the reason for the couple to set up the foundation. That instinct is still there and has its own imperative to do something. Now institutional imperatives add pragmatic force to original moral basis for acting.

But the parties here (the two foundation founders, the newly hired young manager, and the professional consultant, Ben) are innocent of the far more complex mix of motives and constituencies faced in talking about a large multilateral institutions such as the World Bank or even a large private foundation like the Ford Foundation. And yet once the mix becomes the slightest bit complex, which is almost unavoidable if one wants to achieve more by expanding, then, paradoxically, one achieves less in the sense that the original intention is compromised — a case of more is less.

So what? the reader may ask. Does this basis for action differ from that in the corporate world?

The Commodification of Help

Just as in the development organization, the corporate organization has built up layers of structure and a series of transactions that must take place before the action does (the production and selling of a product), and in the corporation too decisions are often compromised. But unlike in the field of development, *not acting* — doing nothing — cannot be a stratagem. Because the corporation must survive, it must (indeed, it exists to) fulfill its goal.

The structure of a for-profit company can be thought of as a wedge. The whole corporate endeavor, as complex and bulging as it may become at the wide end of the wedge, must end in a fine point. The thin end of the corporate wedge is the utterly clear, measurable goal of profit: making more money by selling a product than it took to produce or deliver it. And if that happens consistently it does not much matter how thick and complex the wide end of the wedge has become.

Furthermore, if the product is produced, if the equipment has been designed and purchased to make it or move it, if the demand is there or can be made to be there (through advertising), not to take action is not to supply that product to the marketplace. This is tantamount to corporate suicide. One will never see a company deciding not to sell its products because its managers have come to realize that it might be more "meaningful" and have more value for customers' self-esteem, or be more "sustainable" in the long run, if customers learned to make the product themselves.

Again, development is not business. In development, there is no naturally built-in compunction to sell a product. But inevitably, as an industry, it begins to behave as if such a compunction exists. And, in story 8, when the couple's foundation began to expand in Eastern Europe because the founders sensed that there was a need they could fill, they switched in a very subtle way from the act of offering their help to the act of seeking market share. And that "commodification" of help is what has happened increasingly in the development industry.

Communal Benefits and Enforced Equality Are Not What Most People Want

The world has always been an unequal one. There have always been what the French historian Braudel calls "disparities of strength or situation." Even with the extreme enforcement of egalitarianism under Soviet communism, inequalities reasserted themselves. People re-created invidious distinctions in a society that was based on eliminating them.

The development field since the 1970s, in its heartfelt caring for the plight of the poor, has deplored inequality and tried directly to alter that condition, often with considerable urgency. During the days of "basic human needs" in the 1970s, the development industry went into poor villages and dug wells and irrigation ditches, built clinics and schools, gave out seeds and tools. Many development agencies got involved in political advocacy in defense of those who were downtrodden and consciousness-raising among poor people to make them aware of their condition. Many NGOs promoted redistribution of wealth as an answer to poverty. And a great many grassroots development projects were based on the idea that poor people should work together to eliminate their own poverty.

But development field workers will recall that when material benefits began to flow as the result of the project's external funding, people's solidarity with one another often began to dissipate. It seems that once people begin to have a little wealth and some sense of possibility, they tend to act in a more self-interested manner. This human tendency also explains the failure of so many development efforts aimed at keeping people from migrating to the third world's growing cities. Why has the development assistance industry designed so many projects that are based on a denial of the truth that it is hard to keep people "down on the farm after they've seen Paree"?

Many a poor young peasant, to the extent he has been even the slightest bit exposed to modern Western popular culture, begins to covet it. While he is out in the field, poking the earth with his stick, he is listening to a tape of the Rolling Stones on his Chinese-made tape player. He may dream of coming to America, and when he meets an American traveler or a Peace Corps volunteer, he wants to marry her. And if he senses that his dream is just a dream, he is nonetheless making real plans to move to the big city.

What more and more poor people want is the culture of "bright lights, big city"—to be where the action is. And this appeals to more and more people as they have more contact with each other in a shrinking world. Certainly, people move in the first instance to seek work. When they can, people look to improve their lot. We have seen in the last thirty years a massive movement of people from farm to city, from slow-paced, traditional rural life where subsistence was all there was, to seek wages, piecework, any kind of work, even street begging, in urban areas.

Quite simply, when people see that they are lower on life's totem pole than others and stop believing that it is meant to be, then they want to move up. Braudel has put it nicely: "Nothing has ever been effective against the passion to move up in the world."[12]

Yet a huge amount of the development effort has been predicated on a different kind of human nature: not only the belief that people will stay on the farm if only their livelihood can be improved but also the belief that people in the third world are naturally less self-interested, more community-minded, or more naturally solidary than we are. Thus we have invested in "community building" and in projects that depend on group forms of behavior ("village banking" efforts in microcredit are a good recent example).

Our utopian projections about community, collectivity, and solidarity have almost always turned out to be just that—utopian projections. After a

12. Fernand Braudel, *The Structures of Everyday Life*, vol. 1 of *Civilization and Capitalism, Fifteenth–Eighteenth Centuries*, trans. Siân Reynolds (New York: Harper and Row, 1982–84), 311.

while the groups we development professionals help form do not hold together cohesively. Often they are solidary in part because we held solidarity
out as a condition of their receiving something from us. We have consistently believed that we can remake a world for the third world's poor, helping them hold on to a past we (perhaps nostalgically) wish we still had.

As Ortega y Gasset said: "You want the ordinary man to be master. . . .
Well, do not be surprised if he acts for himself, if he demands all form of en-
joyment, if he firmly asserts his will . . . if he considers his own person and
his own leisure, if he is careful as to dress. . . . Was it not this that it was
hoped to do, namely that the average man should feel himself master, lord
and ruler of himself and of his life? Well, that is now accomplished. Why
then these complaints of the liberals, the democrats, the progressives of
thirty years ago? Or is it that like children they want something, but not the
consequences of that something?"[13]

Incentives: Can People Be Induced to Change?

Why hasn't the development assistance industry learned that people will not
change just because we tell them change is for their own good or because
we show them new ways of doing things that we think are better for them,
even if they agree when they first see them? Again we have avoided facing
something basic in human nature: the way incentives work.

For almost all the years that humans have lived on Earth, they ate by hunting and gathering. Virtually all humans lived on wild food. Then, about ten
thousand years ago, the cultivation and growing of food (agriculture) on
land cleared and prepared for that purpose began. The practice spread for
the next eight thousand years, and by two thousand years ago almost all
people ate by farming. Historians who take the long view consider this
event — the long and slow spread of agriculture (often called the agricultural
revolution) — one of the two most important developments in history to date,
the second being the industrial revolution. Thus development as change
toward greater control of one's environment — a modern definition — seems
to have been around at least for ten thousand years, though not, again, as an
"idea," intention, or conscious endeavor.

The debate about why humans made this dramatic change ten thousand
years ago began when a few scholars made some plain observations. First,
hunters and gatherers still exist today and, by their own lights at least, manage quite well. Second, analysts of diet have concluded that agriculture does
not provide a better-tasting or a higher-quality diet than hunting and gathering. Third, agriculture before the machine age was not any easier than
hunting or gathering (ask any berry picker if she'd rather be bending over a

13. José Ortega y Gasset, *The Revolt of the Masses* (New York: Norton, 1932), 155.

hoe). Since today's hunter-gatherers know about agriculture but choose not to use it, we have to conclude that all things being equal, it is not inherently superior to hunting and gathering. So what made most people change? Scholars found one main comparative advantage to agriculture: it provides more food calories per unit of land and time and so can support larger populations. The current theory holds that agriculture was taken up because population pressures required it.

The lesson is not only that incentives matter. In prehistory, population pressures provided the incentives, but those incentives were both attractive and compelling reasons for change. Development assistance thus far has basically assumed that incentives are carrots: simply dangle them in front of people, and people will covet them and thus do what is necessary to get them. But incentives that work have two sides, carrot *and* stick. People do not generally make a lasting change in the way they do things until the carrot and the stick are in the "right" relationship to each other. Of course, what that "right" proportion will be is very difficult to know, and thus all the more reason we are unlikely to be able to engineer the desired change.

Innovation is also related to the two-sided (carrot-and-stick) structure of incentives. Innovations occur as the result of trying to wrestle with a problem; the incentive to solve it is provided by the nuisance quotient of the problem. The degree of innovation and the motivation for it will be in direct proportion to the perceived need to solve the problem. Often, innovations (the solutions to problems) come from outside. But the insiders, those who have the problem, need to seek them out. Imposing solutions from the outside before there is a perception of a problem is much harder.

The distinction made earlier between development professionals as secondary actors and primary actors who have a direct stake in outcomes is nicely illustrated historically. Braudel and others show us that modern economic life starts to take off (albeit slowly) once the exchange economy begins. There is an acceleration of sorts or at least a layering of one phenomenon on another. As exchange economies increasingly interact, more transactions occur, and so do more problems. Seeking to solve the problems leads to identifying some gaps in the system. Innovations come into play. But these innovations are not created by secondary actors, disinterested parties whose major purpose is seeing to it that development occurs for others. On the contrary, when solutions to complex problems are found, they are found by institutions or persons who have something to gain in solving those problems. They are interested parties, primary agents.

To sum up this chapter, just as the development assistance industry has had a strong unhistorical bent, so has it avoided certain aspects of human nature which appear to be universal. It has been in our interest to avoid both history and human nature. Were we to take them fully into account, we would not do much of what we do.

Spare No Expense— the Very Best

Pakistan, 1994

BEN'S HEAVY-DUTY ear protectors muffled the sound of the helicopter blades. He was uncomfortable enough sitting in the big machine with the six prominent members of the Program Development Committee with whom he'd have to behave so diplomatically over the next week. Not being able to talk for the next hour was a relief. Anyway, they were busy looking out the chopper's windows as they flew up the Indus valley. Ben had done the trip a few times before, and as he was in a middle seat, he just closed his eyes and reflected on what he had learned about this hugely expensive development effort.

In the very early 1980s a wealthy royal patron became deeply concerned about the poor quality of much of what passed for development in the "third world," particularly in Africa and parts of southern Asia, areas he knew well. In the royal patron's view, almost everything having to do with development in the "third world"—education, transport, financial markets, government, laws, health care, even tourism—suffered from a pervasive mediocrity. To some extent he saw this as an inevitable lag between what the industrial "north" had accomplished in its head start on modernization and the well-known disadvantages and handicaps of the "south." But lags can be overcome, he believed, especially with investments in training and "institution building."

In the royal patron's view, institution building as a development strategy had been generally neglected in the 1960s and 1970s. If development donors had thought about this at all, they had concentrated on the institutions at the top, those of the state, and then more with the bricks and mortar of those institutions than their structure or content. To redress this would mean a much broader approach. But he also saw mediocrity in development as a subtle plot, the outcome of the development industry itself not being willing to put in quality work to get quality results. For the royal patron, it was as if the mainstream actors in development really did not care enough to give their best.

So the royal patron set up a foundation, with headquarters in Europe, to redress the problem of mediocrity. No expense was to be spared, since the royal patron recognized a first principle of quality: You get what you pay for. He therefore hired to run his foundation a core group of ten people who had decades of experience and in every other respect were top-drawer professionals. In the early 1980s, when the foundation's work began in earnest, these ten people had an average age of about forty-five, all had worked in development for most of their careers, all had spent time with some of the most prestigious institutions in the industry (such as the World Bank), and all had high graduate degrees (M.D.s or Ph.D.s). To attract (and keep) them, he set up a salary scale that bore no relationship to salaries in the rest of the industry. Instead, it was pegged to what senior professional managers would make in the private sector. This meant salaries from one and a half to three times the norm in the development assistance industry. The royal patron had to answer to no one in making these policies and decisions, because he provided the overhead for the foundation's operations and most of its initial grant funding, at least during the first years of operation.

But since his ambitions were grand and his awareness of the seriousness of the problems he wished to address very realistic, he knew large efforts would be required. To that end he also knew he would have to leverage funds from other sources. He set up branches of the foundation in major industrial nations, putting in place chief executives and staffs whose main function was to raise funds from bilateral agencies for the foundation's projects. These offices were also funded from the royal patron's own pocket.

Branch offices of the foundation were also set up in the developing countries themselves, where loyal captains, handpicked by the royal patron, would receive and bank the funds and see that they supported the projects the foundation favored. The initial projects were schools and hospitals. These were relatively straightforward efforts, but again no care was too great and the program officers in the foundation's European headquarters understood that their fundamental role was that of quality control. If a school was to be built in a remote area of East Africa or a hospital constructed in a large south Asian city, it was going to be the best, and not just by local standards but by Western ones. And this meant in every respect, from the design of the building to the construction, to the ultimate guarantor of quality, the human resources involved in running it. These institutions would be showcases, yes, but not simply for the glory of the royal patron. Rather, they would serve as examples, as inspiration, as a local standard against which, henceforth, other efforts in these arenas (health, education) would have to be measured.

The royal patron understood too that efficiency and cost effectiveness were not really appropriate tests when efforts like these were being mounted — efforts at changing a whole mentality. He believed fervently that one could not calculate what the cost of institutional leadership should be. It's a bit like asking, How long is a string? he liked to say.

And so the officers in Europe worked long hours, evenings, and weekends. Telephone calls between the project people on-site and the officers were extensive and daily, and in the late 1980s, when fax machines were installed, faxes came into the European headquarters by the minute. Each officer had a secretary, and no limits were set on communication costs. Sixty-minute phone calls between Europe and Africa were common. Daily, packages were expressed to seven or eight countries in Africa and Asia, with revised drafts of project plans. And, of course, the officers traveled. Each year they would have a budget of between fifty thousand and sixty thousand dollars each for airfares. And if they traveled over a certain number of days each year, they would get a bonus. Most of the staff used their entire budget and traveled between 130 and 160 days per year. Even a one-day trip to New Delhi or Nairobi was not discouraged. And because of the royal patron's belief in the relationship of quality to cost, whereas others in the development industry traveled economy class, the foundation's officers traveled business class and stayed in the best hotels.

The royal patron's work in education and health became well known very quickly. Within a few short years the foundation had established a reputation for high quality. Soon, the foundation was ready to expand its activities to more challenging areas—in particular, rural economic development in remote parts of Asia and Africa.

"More challenging" is actually an understatement, Ben thought. From education and health to rural economic development is a quantum leap. Education is a building block. Health is a fuel; without it people cannot function and thrive. But rural economic development is the whole ball game of development all at once.

The foundation's most senior officer was put in charge. A brilliant man who had studied development history and saw what had not worked over the decades, he set about creating a model program, something that would accomplish what other efforts had not. Picking a remote area in Pakistan, where development had not yet reached in any way, the foundation's early efforts would be undertaken in a test tube, without fear of contamination from other effects. But this was a risky strategy, because if it failed, no one else would be to blame.

Resources again were essential, and they were forthcoming from the royal patron. The foundation's senior officer went to Pakistan to recruit someone to lead the program on-site. He had in mind a well-known and charismatic man of the elite, someone loyal to the royal patron, a friend of top government officials, with an impeccable education. Together they hammered out a set of tactics that eventually became the model. In the remote north of the country, they would hire a staff of persons who could go out and mobilize whole villages to participate in the program. The idea was that villagers would be taught to see that they had hidden resources, their land and their environment, but, most important, their own energy and the capacity to organize themselves. Villages would be encouraged to form village organizations (which soon came to be called "VOs"), and each member would be encouraged, by the rules of these VOs, to save money in a common fund, a village organization bank. With this capital, eventually they would be able to start new endeavors that would create wealth.

Recognizing that the program had to become "owned" by the villagers themselves, members of the foundation would concentrate their efforts on facilitating, to providing support, not just financial but moral and educational as well. But the foundation's senior officer knew that in reality such a program had to be jump-started. He knew that while the principle of "ownership" was all very well and good, people did not just sign on and devote their energies to something new, however grand, without seeing some sort of immediate gain. The incentive, the carrot, would be the foundation's contribution of a "productive physical infra-structure" project in each village, once the village had formally organized itself into a VO. The area's irrigation systems, for example, had fallen into chronic disrepair and needed to be revitalized. Roads to link one village to another could be built, and improved varieties of crops introduced.

The foundation would pay for both the productive physical infra-structure projects (or PPIs) as well as the engineering that was required to ensure that the PPI was well constructed. Thus if a check dam was required on the bank of a stream to prevent repeated flooding of an otherwise productive adjacent field, the foundation would ensure that it was built in such a way that it would last. An engineer would design it, and someone would supervise the construction. The villagers would contribute their own labor. Moreover, the senior officer and the local project leader both knew that the villagers had to participate in the decisions about what was to be built. The VOs would say which PPIs were the most important for their villages. After all, they knew their own environment far better than any outsider.

The idea caught on rapidly, and by 1987 hundreds of VOs had been formed and the program's staff had grown to meet the demand. The senior officer traveled almost monthly to the area and was proud of the physical sacrifices he had made to get up the often treacherous 375-mile road to the area from the capital city.

In the program's office, located in the main market town in the mountainous region, a chart had been put up showing the projected growth in the number of VOs and their membership. The goal was ambitious — within ten years virtually the entire population of the region would be connected to the program. More ambitious still was the objective of doubling the per capita income of the area in ten years. For the first time, one of the major criticisms of many grassroots development programs would be overcome: lack of scale.

Meanwhile, back in Europe the foundation had sent word to its executives based in London, Washington, and other major capitals that funds for the future of the program were to be raised. The foundation's executive director, an elegant man, who had the complete trust of the royal patron, knew that initial grants would be relatively easy to get because the foundation's reputation for quality in the health and education field would carry weight; he called these first grants "the low plums." But as time went on it would be harder to get bigger money and less restricted funding. Still, the money began to build, and by 1988, the rural development program in Pakistan had over $50 million committed for the next five years.

The royal patron himself was more and more excited about this new effort. Word was getting back to him that indicated that the donors too were excited. A few had sent representatives to see the work in the field and claimed they had never seen anything like it before. Here was a mobilization effort, at the grass roots, on a massive scale, that had real promise to create development that would last.

The observers appreciated the logic of the program's design. The local villagers were agriculturists, but their livelihood could not be improved until they could produce more and produce better quality. The program aimed to decrease losses, increase crop yields, build local savings, and open opportunities for marketing. A key to all this was the training of local specialists in livestock management and plant protection. Unlike traditional agricultural extension agents who came from government and were notoriously unmotivated and often ill-prepared, these local specialists would be members of the communities they served.

But the backbone of the program was really the emphasis on institution building—each VO would become a permanent local development institution. The royal patron's program and the VOs engaged in a contract specifying the sovereignty of the VO, the support obligations of the program, as well as the responsibilities of the VO. A great deal of effort went into preparing the VOs for these partnerships, and this was reflected in the fact that the most important program staff were the "social organizers," a cadre of young, energetic, and articulate people who went regularly to the VOs to explain and discuss the plan. The difficulty of their role was not to be underestimated, since the terrain alone made travel difficult.

As visiting observers spread the word, the number of requests to visit the program increased. Within a couple of years, visitors were coming from other donors and, most important, from other development agencies in the south who wanted to see this new model. The director of the program, needless to say a busy man, would take time out to greet visitors and explain the program's principles. Visits to the VOs would be arranged. Other staff would be assigned to show the visitors around. By 1990 it had become clear that a visitors center would be needed, and so one was built. This had facilities so that guests could see a video of the program before going to a field site. Visitors also benefited from traveling, in many cases, to the area by private helicopter, making the trip from the capital in about one hour instead of the ten to fourteen hours required by road.

The royal patron had understood from the outset that the creation of VOs on a large scale was essential to the program's success. Those first VOs would constitute a critical mass. But the terrain was a serious obstacle. Therefore, early on he had supplied a helicopter that would be used to contact the VOs. This made it possible to reinforce the partnership idea by allowing the program's director, a very charismatic man who spoke eloquently, to visit each VO repeatedly.

Inevitably, the helicopter trips became a regular part of the program director's schedule, requiring a more systematic preparation of each village organization for its comings and goings. The social organizers were assigned the task of requesting that each village or cluster of villages (if they happened to be near each other) designate a landing area and clear it of stones. These areas were then circled with stones painted white, and a large letter *H*, following international aviation practice, was painted in the middle of the circle, to make landing the helicopter easier.

When the program director's schedule of visits was set, the social organizers would go to the VOs on the list and announce the visit, asking the VO leaders to prepare for a meeting. The entire village would turn out for the arrival of the helicopter. Dust would fly up in a great cloud, and hundreds of men, women, and children would shield their eyes. But the crowds kept coming each time the helicopter arrived. Most had never seen anything like it before and were awed. Within months of the introduction of the helicopter, children were drawing helicopter graffiti on the mud walls of village buildings. The helicopter became part of their allegiance to the program, a symbol of their lives to come.

By the late 1980s, however, the helicopter was breaking down often, and the royal patron decided that a more serious operation needed to be mounted. In keeping with his view that no expense was too great to ensure quality, a helicopter "wing" was now created, with its own administration, two new aircraft, a maintenance crew headed by a European on contract, and a cadre of six full-time pilots. The foundation's logo would be painted on the helicopters' tail and repeated on the pocket of pilot uniforms, these having been especially designed for the "wing."

By 1991, about four-fifths of all the villages in the entire region had formed VOs, and PPIs had been completed in almost all of them. Savings accumulation had been spectacular, and large amounts of money were in the bank, invested in government bonds that earned a good rate of interest. Some new crops had been introduced, and some new methods had been taken on. Village agricultural specialists had been trained by the hundreds. Production improved, as did household income.

Pleased by these successes, the royal patron's foundation hired an outside agency to evaluate the program. After an extensive review that involved ten experts, one of whom was Ben, the evaluation report pointed out, quite diplomatically, that while much had been accomplished, much more needed to be done. The institution-building component, the backbone of the program, especially needed shoring up. There were signs that VOs did not hold together well unless the program continued to bolster them with visits and concrete support.

But there were other, internal problems. The staff of the program had grown large, to several hundred people. Because needed skills were not always available in the region, many senior staff came from elsewhere in the country; the local staff resented them as interlopers, and not just because they were not from the region. The program had become an important employer in the region, and its potential to absorb larger numbers of young people into its ranks — often the relatives of existing staff — was threatened when it brought in people from outside. And after a while, owing to the size of the organization and the amounts of money now involved, there were small but frequent instances of petty corruption, diversions of funds, borrowings from VO savings, and misuses of the credit facilities. Most important, a general malaise was beginning to permeate the program staff. This was in marked contrast to the early days, when everyone was enthusiastic and worked from dawn to dusk seven days a week, devoted to their tasks. So much had been accomplished so fast. Now, with the VOs having been formed, the PPIs completed, savings mobilized, new skills created, and surpluses in production, many staff began wondering what the program's next moves would be and whether their skills would be relevant.

It was now clearly necessary to embark on a new phase. The program would have to move into more difficult and taxing territory, switching from fostering quantitative changes — such as more goats, more fruit trees, and more VOs — to qualitative changes. It would have to find a way to move the villagers away from the age-old household economy that was still at the heart of their livelihoods, to a truly modern, more diversified economy that could be integrated with the rest of the country. That would be economic development.

But the broad base of the program staff seemed to pale in the face of the challenge. Some said it could not be done. Though the whole pro-gram was only a decade old, many were by now wedded to the old ways of doing things. Not a few had internal doubts they were afraid to express openly.

In an effort to ease the program's transition to its new phase, the foun-dation's European headquarters felt that consultants should be hired to advise the program. Because Ben had been part of the larger review a year earlier, he was hired along with other consultants to be part of one of these advisory teams. As Ben began visiting the program in Pakistan regularly, he noticed a pattern that bothered him. Consultants require contracts specifying their terms of reference, but experienced senior people require only a good, solid briefing before going into the field phase of their work. But in the case of the royal patron's foundation, much more than this was routinely done, and Ben had begun to realize that the stakes must have been felt to be very high, the sensitivities so tender, the risks to the royal patron's reputation so great, that every step of every visit was second-guessed and chewed over to the point of ab-surdity. Ben's team — and he guessed this was the case with others too — would be called to the foundation's headquarters for a previsit briefing, then find that foundation officers would accompany them to the field, and be asked after their work was done to stop in Europe on their way home for a thorough debriefing before they wrote their reports. Need-less to say, the helicopters were so full that scheduling their use had be-come a problem.

But after a year of such advisory team visits, the foundation's senior of-ficer and its executive director met with the royal patron and decided that a committee needed to be set up, to be called the Program Devel-opment Committee. It would be comprised of six very senior people, loyal to the royal patron, who would volunteer their time to manage and coordinate a series of studies. The royal patron directed this committee to report back to him in due course. Ben, to his surprise, had been asked to go back to the program area with one of the foundation's senior offi-cers. This time they were to assist in briefing the Program Development Committee on their fourth visit to the area as a full committee.

It had become clear to Ben that the royal patron was worried. Matters now had to be even more delicately handled because so much donor money had been committed and much was now at stake. The program was not only no longer unknown but also widely publicized within the international development community. Many persons of high office in the development industry had visited it and read about it. The committee had been directed to undertake its work very carefully and take the time necessary to ensure it had covered every conceivable aspect of the program's future. The investment was going to be considerable, but the royal patron had not hesitated to assure the committee that it would have both the financial and human resources and the time required for the task.

As he sat in the big chopper, Ben realized that it was now almost two years since the committee discreetly and cautiously had begun its deliberations. He guessed, no he was almost sure, that in all this time of advisory team visits and committee ruminations, pretty much all aspects of the program's transition had been put on hold. And he wondered if in the meantime the morale problem his advisory team had detected a while back had deteriorated further. He wondered if the cohesiveness of the VOs would begin to show some fraying at the edges.

Of course, during the last few years, Pakistan had not been standing still. Events outside the area had taken a toll on the amount of attention the world and the government of the country had been paying to the program. Civil strife, religious animosities, corruption in high places, and international tensions were growing, shaking the country politically and economically. Things were not going well. Even if the program had moved into its new institution-building and economic development phase with firmness and dispatch, the results, which would increasingly have to depend on smooth links with the economy of the rest of the country, would have been compromised. Ben surmised that these changes had made the royal patron, his committee, and his foundation even more worried and cautious.

After a week in the program area, Ben's suppositions had been confirmed. But what he had not anticipated was that for the program staff up here in the mountains, there was a silver lining to these cautious delays. By now so many of the VOs had become inactive that the regular maintenance of village-level roads, dams, and irrigation channels had been neglected. The general deterioration was of such an extent that many of the productive physical infrastructure projects in the villages needed repairs and not a few needed complete rebuilding. Now, with clear-cut tasks again before them, the staff of the program had forgotten their squabbles and their doubts and had begun attacking these familiar problems with new energy. They felt that they were back in the old days of the mid-1980s, when such tangible, achievable projects as roads and check dams had held their attention. And so they set out to do what they did best: they went out, reorganized the VOs, held new meetings, and made plans to repair and redo many of the same infrastructure projects they had done years before. Ben could see morale improving immensely, right before his eyes.

For the People, By the People

Bangladesh, 1994

BEN WAS DOZING; by noon the heat was getting to him. He was in the front seat of the lead jeep. There were three jeeps altogether, carrying ten visitors, not including the drivers. This was yet another of the over-organized development tours Ben had come to dislike. Along with his colleague on this evaluation assignment, Ramesh from Nepal, there was a USAID project officer (USAID was the lead donor in this multidonor community development program), two officials from the Bangladesh government, a local government official, and three senior staff of the Bangladeshi NGO Village Mobilization whose job it was to ensure that the genuine voices of all the villages in the project would be heard and their true needs and wishes reflected in the final design of the next phase. Village Mobilization (VM) was just one of several organizations involved in this complex project. It had been selected because of its long experience in the technique called Participatory Rural Appraisal (PRA).

They pulled into a village. At the end of a lane Ben spied a bit of shade provided by a few trees. Though the heat of the day was getting close to its high and normally everyone would be indoors, about ten people were waiting under the largest tree. The vehicles stopped. Ben thought, "Not bad, ten visitors for ten villagers. Could be worse." But it was worse. Three of the people under the tree were full-time VM staff: a Participatory Rural Appraisal trainer and two village-level workers (VLWs); two others were not even Bangladeshis but trainees from Bhutan, assigned to VM to learn the PRA technique. A PRA session had been under way that morning, and the two visitors were observing it. The other five people were genuine villagers. Apparently everyone was taking a break while waiting for the visitors to arrive.

The three jeeps began emptying, and the group approached the consultants and the VM staff. Ben and Ramesh were introduced, and everyone went around shaking hands. "Don't let us disturb you," Ben said to the PRA leader. "Please, please, go about your work," he added, feeling awkward. Ben knew that protocol and plain politeness required everyone to stop and greet the group. But how he longed for something he had never once experienced — the chance to be a fly on the wall, to arrive quietly and unnoticed and observe what people were doing. Because this was never allowed to happen, Ben always felt uneasy drawing conclusions about what he observed. He had, as good evaluators in this business do, learned to discount some of what he saw, to pick up tiny clues and extrapolate from them, using triangulation to approximate what was real. But what he most disliked was the point in each visit that he thought of as showtime. The villagers themselves are supposed to be the center of attention, especially in this new participatory technique. But showtime inevitably made the visitors the focus, especially when they represented a development assistance agency. At any rate, now he felt it coming. Sure enough, the leader cleared his throat and began briefing Ben and Ramesh on what PRA is. Both listened politely, though both knew quite a bit about it. Ben had taught a PRA course the summer before, and Ramesh had practiced it regularly in Nepal and Sri Lanka.

Ben cocked his head toward the PRA trainer to make it seem he was listening attentively. It would have been impolite to interrupt and tell him not to bother with the lengthy briefing he had so obviously rehearsed. Meanwhile, Ben's eyes roamed as he looked around for the familiar PRA props. There they were, on one side of the tree.

The ground had been carefully swept to create a rectangle about ten feet wide by twenty feet long. Here and there within the space were different shapes made of twigs, as well as conical piles of sand. Some of the piles had tiny flags stuck in them, made with bits of cloth. One of the five villagers had gone back to the space and was squatting in the middle of the rectangle, carefully forming a mound of sand into a volcano-like cone about five inches high.

Since the late 1980s, PRA had spread around the development industry. Today, there is hardly a village-level project being undertaken anywhere that does not involve it and few remaining field-level development workers who haven't been trained in or exposed to it. The technique had caught on, Ben thought, because it promised to make the abstract notion of "bottom-up" development tangible, while also being an efficient technique.

For decades, development projects had been planned and designed by experts and outsiders. When the industry began to realize that these projects had been failures, one of the accepted reasons was that no one had consulted the "people," hence the new concern for people-oriented and bottom-up development. But the question of exactly how to involve "the people" remained. Do you simply ask them what they want and need? Do you conduct a survey or have them fill out questionnaires? A few thoughtful development types felt that such approaches were themselves too culturally biased. They believed what was needed was something that came closer to the way poor people in third world villages thought and acted. An approach that involved physical action would be a good start. Ideally a village would get together under a tree and "reconstruct" not just their village but their society and economy as well. With twigs and stones, pebbles, sand and bits of cloth, people would map out their village on the ground. Then with a trained "facilitator" posing leading questions, their problems would be expressed in three-dimensional physical form on the "map." A simple lead question such as "Who is the richest person in the village? Where is his house?" could lead to a long and animated discussion of caste and privilege, landownership, and politics. The facilitator might point to a spot between two twigs (representing mud huts) and ask, "What happens here during the monsoon?"

If things went the way they were supposed to, the interaction of the villagers around such questions, often involving corrections and disagreements, would have two results. First, the villagers would have their reality "mirrored" to them by the exercise itself. In theory, they would see more clearly the dimensions of their problems. Some of them were chronic and thus familiar problems such as annual flooding, but a few would be more gnawing, under-the-surface dilemmas that they had only vaguely sensed before. If the villagers had had an inchoate grasp of these before and now saw things more clearly, it was hoped that the second result might ensue: a sense that something could be done. An earthen check dam could be put "here," a path redirected "there." Or if a rich man in the village was exploiting people but they only now learned the full dimensions of exactly what he was doing, those gathered under the tree could (again, in theory) agree to get together and act collectively to resist him.

Finally, because the development industry is a formal endeavor with experts and funding, the results of the PRA would give the experts a far more realistic understanding of what the village was about and hence enable them to plan the project more sensibly. With local reality and needs understood, there would be, as the theory went, few surprises down the line. And since a set of these exercises might take no more than from three to five days and involve only one trained facilitator, the return on the investment was seen as cost effective.

When Ben was first exposed to PRA, he had thought it was one of the few really interesting, creative, and promising things in a plethora of otherwise anodyne interventions the development business had devised over the years. Still, he had worried that, like so much else, it might become a fad, adopted mindlessly by donors and development organizations alike, simply because it sounded both promising and politically correct. Indeed, as he began observing PRA exercises in practice, he rarely saw it work very well. And he was never sure if that was because it was driven by fad, because it was applied as a form without content, or worse, because, as with other ideas, it was good in the abstract but became diminished when it ran up against reality, just one aspect of which was that poor people had better things to do with their time than play games.

The PRA facilitator was now through with his introduction to the theory and was telling the consultants that this afternoon's exercise was going to be a "wealth ranking exercise" during which most of the households in the village would be represented on the map relative to each other's wealth. And the villagers' own criteria would determine what constituted wealth.

Ben and Ramesh thanked the facilitator and then stood waiting for the exercise to begin. They had both noticed that there were now about fifteen people unconnected to the village standing about and only five villagers anywhere in sight. "Not much participation in this participatory exercise," Ramesh whispered to Ben.

The PRA facilitator seemed not to have noticed. He pushed on doggedly with his work. He and the five participants began, with the two VLW trainees and the two Bhutanese attentively listening on the edge of the rectangle. Ben saw now that the villagers were not all adults. Three were boys about ten or eleven years old. Quite a bit of gesturing was going on, with the two adult villagers, both older men, directing the boys on the ground where to put various bits and pieces of twig and stone and how to arrange them. The facilitator was interrupting the two village men, making corrections to their instructions ("That pile should be higher!") and all the while talking to the two Bhutanese and the VLWs, who nodded respectfully as he explained to them what they were seeing. As he talked he was rapidly pacing clockwise around the perimeter of the rectangle, waving his arms as if impatient to have all the parts of the exercise fall into place in the order he was taught them. It was soon apparent to Ben and to Ramesh that this fellow was a dullard for whom form was everything. His training had not succeeded in teaching him the art of PRA but rather a technique and a form. The example he had been taught in his training became for him the art itself. It was a set piece, and in pushing it forward, he inadvertently subverted what PRA was supposed to be accomplishing.

The USAID officer was the only other person in the little train of visitors who seemed to feel even slightly uncomfortable about what was happening. "Perhaps we should move on," he said to Ben and Ramesh. "I think we've seen all there is to see of this."

CHAPTER SIX

The Mismatch of Organizational Imperatives and Money

Any large-scale effort that is in the slightest way complicated needs to be undertaken in an organized form. Indeed, organizations have become the quintessential framework for much of modern life (factory, corporation, government body, military, voluntary association, and so forth). In the development assistance field, organizations are so self-evidently necessary that no one has questioned the form, and rightly so. Yet the more development assistance takes place through the medium of organizations, the more the natural imperatives of organizations run counter to the real mission of development. What are these imperatives, and how do they arise?

The Inevitability of Organizational Imperatives

The core characteristics of an organized form of activity in the modern world are obvious. Complex actions need to be planned, carried out, and paid for. Specialized functions come into being, such as production, supervision, management, administration, bookkeeping, public relations, research, and human resources. In a modern society, some of these functions will be dictated by laws (e.g., those spelling out the fiscal and other responsibilities of corporations or of nonprofits). To carry out these functions, people need to be hired, a place to house the activity needs to be found, and things need to be bought.

To ensure that the work of the organization is uninterrupted, its work must not depend entirely on particular persons but rather on defined functions that any qualified person can fulfill. Thus rules, procedures, and systems arise and begin to take on a life of their own. The organization can even develop a "personality," culture, or style, just as if it were a person. Often this is inadvertent; sometimes it is designed.

After a while an organization becomes something greater than the sum of its parts: a living entity with its own needs and demands. Though an abstraction, the organization is capable of imposing demands and obligations on the people who work in it. Whether the organization is governmental, a multilateral agency, a foundation, or an NGO, its functions carry expectations, and these exist in a framework into which people are asked (even obliged) to fit. The everyday language we use to talk about our jobs attests to the organization's independent life force: "A position is to be filled," "Your function is . . . ," "I've changed positions," and the like.

To the extent the missions, functions, systems, and procedures of the organization have the capacity to dictate action, they are imperatives. Daily the organization says "do this, do that," "behave this way or that." Moreover, it says to those who inhabit it that the organization's survival and perpetuation are part of what the individuals who work in it must be responsible for.

There is no nefarious design behind these imperatives. They evolve naturally. A primary — if not primal — organizational imperative is sheer survival. Even though an organization is not in itself tangible, it is harder to tear down an organization, reducing it to nothing, than it is to tear down a large building. Organizations, like persons, resist death.

Today, in addition to survival, other common organizational imperatives are to grow, to become more important, to become more "legitimate" (achieve higher status), and to have greater "market share." Indeed, the metaphor of resisting death is translated into common phrases in today's organization culture, such as "grow or die" or "change or die."

All this seems obvious in talking about Boeing, Microsoft, or General Motors.

These corporate organizations must compete with others that make similar products. For them, market share — the number of customers from the available pool of potential customers who might buy the product — is an essential imperative. One must drive everything toward achieving more of it. But what is "market share" to IFAD, the World Bank, USAID, or CARE? What does "grow or die" mean to CARE or Save the Children?

When I joined the Peace Corps in 1964, one of our most coveted beliefs was that we were going to the third world "to work ourselves out of a job." This was not just a slogan but official policy as well. It reflected a clear (if touchingly innocent) understanding that if development is successful, development organizations (and Peace Corps volunteers) will no longer be needed.

We do not hear development agencies (including the Peace Corps) talking like this today, and it is not just because they realize the "job" is not done. We do see much evidence that the organizations in the development industry are acting more and more like Wal-Mart or Microsoft or the Great Widget Manufacturing Company. They are seeking market share, though they do not yet call it that. But they do talk about "customers" and "products," and they certainly feel that if they do not grow or change, they will die.

During the last twenty years, development assistance agencies, large and small, publicly and privately supported, have become increasingly focused on their own survival. To be sure, they recognize that one of the things they need to do is be more effective. And to that end many development assistance agencies have undertaken serious internal reviews, asking themselves hard questions about their effectiveness.

Among NGOs and multilateral agencies, self-examination retreats and strategic planning workshops have become regular additions to the calendar. Wanting to ensure objectivity, development organizations engage hundreds of outside consultants in reviewing organizational performance, assessing "capability gaps" or "mission gaps." "Working groups" are set up. "Review panels" are brought in. And questions like these are asked: "Are we responding to needs?" "Do we have appropriate decision-making mechanisms at different levels?" One large NGO brought together top staff from twenty of its country programs and asked itself, "Are we value-driven, open/empowering, risk-taking, learning, innovative, flexible, result-oriented, happy?" Another asked, "Are we adequately/excessively accountable to all/some stakeholders (in particular our donors)?"

Such self-examination is laudable up to a point. But these organizations miss the compelling logic of their mission—to be more effective is to shorten the organization's lifespan, not lengthen it. The imperative to survive, however, does not permit this kind of logic. What commonly happens, therefore, is that the imperative to survive takes on greater weight than the goal of effectiveness. In practice, more of the discourse within these self-examination retreats is about the prospects of survival and gaining market share than it is about the initial concern for effectiveness.

The language of such self-examinations more and more reflects that of the freshly minted MBA. The World Bank has been talking since 1996 about "customers and clients." And other large development organizations are concerned, as one NGO was, about "optimizing the benefits of our international identity," as if they were a brand name like Dunkin Donuts. Today, practically all development assistance organizations talk (and worry) about competition. Almost all seek ways to gain competitive advantage over others in the same industry.

Three Conceptual Traps

First, there are no "customers" in development. When I give my "custom" to Macy's, it implies I go there to shop repeatedly. But the World Bank does not want Sierra Leone to come knocking on its doors regularly and repeatedly. CARE does not want to provide relief supplies to Somali refugees forever. If Wal-Mart were to say that it is actively seeking customers and actually trying to create them, we would not bat an eye, but if CARE or USAID said the same thing, it would strike us as quite an odd goal. The concept of "customer" in development is counterdevelopmental.

And yet, strangely, the last two decades have revealed more and more development assistance agencies actively looking for more "customers" (more often called "clients") and new markets. It is interesting, for example, that the nonprofit organizations of the development industry (from the World Bank to international NGOs) seem to have paralleled the for-profit corporations in moving into Eastern Europe, Russia, the "Newly Independent States" of the former Soviet Union, and China. McDonald's went into Hungary to find new markets. The Peace Corps also went into Hungary to find a new market. McDonald's is in business to seek new markets. The Peace Corps is in business to respond to needs and foster development. Did Hungary need the Peace Corps, or did the Peace Corps need Hungary?

Second, unlike corporations, development agencies do not exist to make a product to sell. They may loosely call some of what they do a "product," such as a method of promoting development (like microcredit, health clinics, or the training of agricultural extension agents), but it is not for sale. Ford Motor Company exists to sell its products. Selling its products and its mission are one and the same. But development agencies *do* have a loftier mission, and that is to alleviate poverty and help nations grow economically. And even if that mission were to be construed as a product, the jury is still out as to its success.

As I have noted earlier in this book, the gloomy facts of development are not hard to find. The failures far outweigh the successes. Those who work in the field, who are at the front, so to speak, generally know that while little things might improve, long-term sustainable poverty alleviation, much less reduction, is not happening much. We know that the likelihood of a project's failure is generally greater than its chances of success. Moreover, we all know that those broad successes of economic growth in the last fifty years and the few signs of poverty reduction (such as the decline in population growth rates) are very difficult to attribute to our own work. Yet organizational imperatives being what they are, an unsuccessful product (the work of those in the industry) continues to be "sold."

Finally, corporations are constantly assessing the "demand" for what they sell. But what is the nature of the demand for what the development industry offers? And how is it measured? No clear market feedback exists for our mission, other than the rhetoric of our clients. If you ask the government of Mali if it wants the development assistance of the World Bank, the Food and Agriculture Organization (FAO) of the UN, or UNICEF, it will, of course, say "Yes, we want to develop." And "Yes, we accept your premises about development," and "Yes, we will support the methods you are promoting." But do we in development know if this constitutes what economists call "effective demand"? "Effective demand" means a demand backed up by a willingness to pay a price for the thing sold that covers its costs and offers the seller a profit. If what we do is provided free or partially subsidized (which much of development assistance is), then there is no effective demand for it, only rhetorical demand. This dilemma is exacerbated because the product (development or a method of promoting it) is usually not what is actually changing hands. Most of the time what is actually changing hands is money, which governments, communities, and people all want. Thus, while our money may be in demand, we still do not know if our "product" is really appreciated.

It is easy to see why the development industry has subconsciously begun to envy (and imitate) the for-profit corporation. The Great Widget Manufacturing Company (GWMC) has things easy. It makes widgets. So do other companies. If people do not buy its widgets, GWMC can do many things. It can improve the product, advertise it more to change or enhance its image, raise or lower its price, or invent a new, improved widget. If all that does not work, GWMC can reduce the number of widgets it makes and begin making something else. Or the company can merge with another widget maker to gain greater market share or economies of scale. It can hire new people and fire old ones; downsize and decrease costs and become more efficient; renegotiate with its raw materials suppliers; tinker with its inventory timing; change its distribution system; and so on. The number of things the company can do is limited only by the imagination and cleverness of the MBAs who work for it. But no matter what it does, the value of the outcome will be known quickly because the bottom line will be a good proxy for effectiveness. The GWMC may never know exactly which factor improved profits, but it will know whether profits improved.

In contrast, the development organization is in a constant state of anxiety and ambiguity. For here we are, with no proven product, facing, to say the least, a rather flawed sort of "demand," committed by the very nature of our mission to seeing fewer rather than more "customers." Meanwhile, we are seeking greater "market share." Rather odd.

The question to pose is not "Why does an industry that has not produced much continue to survive?" but "Why does it not only want to survive and perpetuate itself but also grow and become more important than ever?" The short answer is that the development industry simply "cannot help it," such is the power of organizational imperatives. The moment the idea of deliberately induced development took root in formal fashion and required organization and money to begin its work, it was on the path to becoming as concerned with its own survival as with its mission.

Getting Caught Up in "Doing"

The above conceptual traps aside, the very structure of the relationship between the development organization and its constituents dooms it to doing things, a function deeply mismatched with the mission of development. Clinics, schools, and roads are tangible. A road cannot be cajoled into exis-

tence; someone, actually a bunch of someones, has to "do" something—
survey it, grade it, mix and pour the concrete, and so on. Community development projects or microcredit projects, though less tangible than a road
or a school, in the hands of development organizations, are also about "doing" something, and inevitably the doing also involves tangible things. Thus
the microcredit project hires and trains people, operates vehicles and computers, owns blackboards for meetings, contracts the printing of passbooks,
and the like. The daily bread and butter of development assistance organizations large and small is doing things.

Development professionals continue to hedge the question of whether
development assistance is about doing things. Increasingly we know that the
real keys to development are neither tangible nor involve much "doing."
They are about institutions, attitudes, laws, and human resources. And yet
we continue to "do" development as if it were largely about doing things and
doing those things, moreover, for others.

If development were successful in fostering institutions, attitudes, and
laws and in enhancing human resources, we—as professional developers—
would not have to do things like build schools or roads. The institutions of
a functioning society would see to it that they got built. Additionally, if development can be undertaken at all on behalf of others (which I doubt),
then it must be about these intangibles, and whatever action might be taken
would not be direct action but more in the nature of fostering and support.

Surely, if development can be fostered, it is, like good teaching, an art
form and not a science. A good teacher does not "make" the student learn.
Teaching is not doing, and neither is development. Nor can we say when
the process is done. The teacher may test a student and then grade the test,
but that grade is a proxy for learning. It conveys neither precisely how much
the student has learned nor how well she has learned it, nor can it predict
how soon or whether she will forget what she has learned.

By its nature, then, the mission of development means that we as "actors"
must be once removed from the desired action. We should not be "doing"
things. But being once removed from direct action is a stance less well
suited to an organization than is direct action. So we continue to "do" development directly.

A second mismatch arises because the essential artfulness of development almost guarantees that the time element will be unpredictable. We
can say that development takes time, but it is not possible to say how much.
Some aspects of development might require six or forty or seventy years. But
open-ended time is a parameter ill suited to an organization. And so we
compound the first error—that of assuming we must be doing things for/on
behalf of others—by then acting as if development is time bound, which
also fits well with an organizational form.

An organization requires that endeavors be broken down into small enough bites to be put on a finite time frame, bites that can thus be planned, staffed, budgeted, executed, completed, and accounted for. In development we call these bites "projects," and the project form, after fifty years, remains today the basic unit of development organizations despite its being deplored by many development professionals.

The development industry has evolved methods to ensure that the project is a finite bite that can be properly accounted for. One of these is the "log frame," the logical framework, a method invented by USAID originally (and much adapted in other organizations) of laying out the objectives and goals of a project, against a time line and a set of indicators that will tell when those goals have been met. The logical framework is a way to ensure that the project does what it is meant to do and that the outcomes are measurable.

If the "project" is to train agricultural extension workers in the Philippines or Mali, the log frame requires the agency bidding for the money to say how it will train, when it will train, and how many people it will train. This seems very responsible, and of course it is. Who would give $3 million to an agency to train agricultural extension workers if it merely said, "Give us the money, and we will do the job"? After all, we need to be held accountable. The problem is that the time-bound, direct-action project, a made-to-order convenience for an organizational imperative like the accountability promised by the "log frame," is a bad match with the mission of development.

The Power of "Other People's Money" Reinforces the Doing Trap

This question leads us to the most compelling of the reasons why doing things in development persists, and that is the kind of money we use. Development does not usually proceed with money made by the development agency but with other people's money, or OPM.

Other people's money and my own money (MOM) are different. If I want to use my own money my own way, I'm free to do so. I can give it to the poor and walk away, never seeking to find out what it was used for. But the vast majority of development organizations depend on OPM. Because it is not theirs, OPM carries powerful constraints. Virtually all sources of OPM demand accountability, and this demand is increasing and becoming more stringent as new philanthropists enter the marketplace.[1]

OPM reinforces the project form. The "project" becomes its own imperative. Projects are the logical bite-size quantum in which to gauge the effort to be made. The process is circular. Public funding cannot really go to "de-

1. Bill Gates and other new philanthropists in America increasingly want to apply business principles to giving — they want results, and they want them guaranteed.

velopment" in the abstract, so development is put into an organizational form; the organization, as a legal persona, can receive and spend the money. And because the donors want to know both how it is going to be spent and how it was spent, the time-bound project becomes the appropriate fundable bite.

If development is an indirect art form, something we foster, encourage, and convey, and if it is, then, neither clearly time-bound nor easily measurable, why do we try to break it into projects and measure it so that we can say to donors "we did it" when we know we have not? In a sense we act as if we are in a bottom-line business (like widget making) when we are not. (It is significant that the idea of the log frame comes from the corporate world and modern management theory.)

So the "beltway bandit," or the NGO that has won the USAID contract to train agricultural extension workers in Mali, fills in the blanks in the log frame and at the end of twelve months sends its report to the AID project officer in charge of this effort. The report tells the officer that "we have trained 7,486 ag extension workers, as specified in the log frame." The officer checks a box, stamps "approved," and sends a copy to the file, and another copy to USAID's disbursement department, which then releases the next "tranche" of funding to the contracting organization. Everyone is happy: "Objectives achieved, no problems, project successful."

This is a shell game. But why? What is so wrong with training 7,486 agricultural extension workers?

Again, it is not *our* job to do so but that of the appropriate institution in Mali. If they do not have such an institution themselves, then perhaps the training offered is premature and perhaps the appropriate development effort should be directed at fostering such an institution. Second and more important, training these workers is not the same as saying that they have internalized the training. But it is harder to measure output (effectively using what one has learned) than input (training). Third, the ways in which these ag extension workers are made use of by the Ministry of Agriculture of Mali is as important to the long-term improvement of Malian agricultural production as the degree to which the trainees internalized what they were taught. But we know from experience that the Ministry of Agriculture in such a country as Mali likely does not function well in this regard. In many places such an entity is not really an institution yet but often just a building that the World Bank paid for. So these new human resources, if indeed they did absorb what was taught, are likely to be wasted. The objective of ag extension worker training may fit the project framework like a glove, but if there is no articulated system to deploy the workers, then they hang on the shoulders of the Malian government like an ill-fitting suit. On the other hand, to foster an articulated system in which these ag extension workers could be deployed would not fit well with the project frame. It would, however, be more developmental, even though infinitely more difficult. And so it goes.

The project imperative is also reinforced by the multiple constituents in development. The first are the donors who provide funds. If you are an NGO like Save the Children, you will have multiple donors: some will be individuals, some will be public institutions such as USAID, and some will be foundations. If you are the World Bank, part of your finding comes from member countries. You are beholden in part to them, and especially to the biggest ones. If you are USAID itself, your money comes from the citizens of the United States via the allocation process that is the negotiation between the executive branch and the Congress. You are beholden to the Congress and to U.S. citizens. In the particular case of USAID, congressional influence further distorts the development mission. As one observer pointed out: "Over the years . . . Congress has foisted onto the Agency for International Development more than 40 different missions, from disposing of American farm surpluses to strengthening the American land grant college system. No wonder . . . that AID has trouble accomplishing its real mission — promoting international development."[2]

The organization will also have its internal staff and board of advisers or directors; they are constituents too. And, finally, the poor in the developing world are a constituency whether the direct relationship of the organization is with the government of a country or with the poor themselves. Each of these constituencies derives comfort from the project form.

Imagine a "task manager" at the World Bank (the term used for the people who manage/supervise projects). She wants to be recognized for good performance in that function. She has a stake in having her task designed in project form because if it were open-ended, no one would or could know whether what she instigated produced results that could be linked to her. But the more truly developmental the effort, the longer it will take for the results to be evident. If it took twenty-five years to know if the results of an effort were lasting, getting "performance feedback" would be difficult; no one would remember what the original effort was or who "task-managed" it. The finite, bite-sized project is therefore in the best interests of most constituents.

One more thing about OPM: development organizations have to ask for it. And since there is never enough OPM, particularly public money, given all the possible uses for it, competition for OPM arises in the development industry. In the world of the for-profit organization, competition improves the product, and a good ad campaign enhances (and differentiates) the image. More people buy the product. Profits rise. But in development

2. Paul Glastris quoted in the *New Republic*, October 11, 1993.

assistance it is very hard to link advertising to what the product should be — that is, real development — in part because we are not achieving much of it and in part because development does not lend itself to easy description. What we can advertise are the short-term results of projects (schools built, latrines dug, wells installed, smiling faces). And so, unlike in the world of widgets, where competition should lead to a better product or at least a better price for the same product, in development, competition leads to image creation that is unrelated to development. When the organization becomes hooked on the cycle of needing to have the projects that produce the sellable images, its distance from true development increases.

In the commercial world, competition tends over time to reduce the number of firms in the same field (by eliminating them or combining them). In development the opposite is true. For OPM, even though it is by definition a rare commodity, attracts new entrants to development. The rate of founding of new NGOs, for example, went up in the 1990s.

Here is how one cynical insider critic of the industry views the matter:

> Many assume they [the private agencies] are making good these claims (to alleviate poverty, etc.). Funds have been kept flowing on that promise. No agency seems to quit the field, and more agencies professing such purposes enter it every year. Yet this may reflect not the strength of performance, but one of gravest weaknesses; funding is only poorly linked with actual outcomes — if it is linked at all. Agencies are regarded chiefly for spending and being active; they are almost never punished when that spending and those activities come to nothing, or entail unwelcome side-effects. . . .
>
> One reason is that agencies can just keep moving. Staff can often "escape into the future" through a succession of short-gestation, photogenic projects and partners. Sustainability becomes somebody else's problem. It is easy to disclaim responsibilities of paternity of their projects, left in the care of local people. . . .
>
> Moreover, aid fashions change, new staff arrive, a new crisis spot grips world attention, and it is time to assemble a new portfolio — appropriate technology is out, small scale credit is in; public administration is out, natural resource management is in; Somalia is out, Rwanda is in, and so on.[3]

Many organizations in development, in competing for OPM, have taken to imitating certain tactics of the commercial world, with lucrative results. Ian Smillie, one of the few insider critics of development, talks about growing similarities between transnational NGOs (CARE, SCF, PLAN, Oxfam, World Vision, and so forth) and transnational corporations. He notices an adaptation into the development world of the phenomenon of "transfer

---

3. David Sogge, "Settings and Choices," in *Compassion and Calculation: The Business of Private Foreign Aid*, ed. David Sogge, Kees Biekart, and John Saxby (London: Pluto Press, 1996).

pricing," that is, taking advantage of being global, and talks about "transfer fund-raising," where transnational development agencies take advantage of donors' grant requirements by opening offices where the overhead costs are lower. If they are applying for matching grants, they can thus invest in fund-raising at a lower cost and request a match to the funds raised from a donor. An example is PLAN International, which in 1991 raised $28 million in the United States but $58 million in the Netherlands. World Vision raised less than $1.00 per head in the United States in 1991 but $1.50 in Australia and $1.78 in Canada.[4] Thus new markets are aggressively sought.

Sometimes the impetus for "transfer fund-raising" is donor saturation in the home countries of the international charitable organization. One "marketing" executive for a large development organization explained to me that by going to "more naïve well-off countries" that had not yet been "tapped" (e.g., Italy, Greece), the costs of recruiting new donors would be lowered and the prospects of continuing to mine these for the foreseeable future that much greater.

In the end, poverty alleviation is not a product. And this fact remains the fundamental flaw in these seemingly benign adaptations from the commercial world.

The Vicious Cycle of Development Funding

If money is something development agencies have to ask for, that does not mean money is always and necessarily a wallflower shyly awaiting a suitor. It does not sit in a cache at USAID, the Ford Foundation, or the World Bank waiting for needs to come along that require different sums. Money in development has become (and I argue again inevitably) an active, pulsating organism with a desire. It seeks ways to be spent. It wants to be spent. And it wants to be spent in "this fiscal year." In many instances, it would rather be spent wastefully than not at all.

To some extent money's need to be spent is a legal matter. By law the Ford Foundation must give away a fixed percentage of the income from its endowment in order to qualify for its status as a charitable foundation. But with most other donors we cross quickly from legal requirements to other concerns. By legislative mandate USAID must spend (or at least "obligate") the budget amount Congress has allocated to it in each of the line items or lose it next time around. Norway, if it wants to maintain its top position in the ranks of industrial nations in terms of percentage of its GNP devoted to development, must, as a matter of policy, gear its annual spending accordingly. The World Bank could not hold up its head as the premier develop-

4. Ian Smillie, "Interlude: The Rise of the Transnational Agency," in Sogge, Biekart, and Saxby, *Compassion and Calculation*.

ment organization or justify its members' contributions if it did not lend its annual billions. Whatever the reasons, you get zero points for holding on to money. Everything in the development industry conspires to have money spent annually, from the moral imperative to "help" to laws and public policy, to the accountability that makes the short-term project necessary, and to performance appraisals of key staff and the right steps on the career ladder.

But development, again, does not respond well to this kind of spending. As I have tried to show, development is staggeringly complex; by historical definition it is not a "task" or an "endeavor" but a much larger phenomenon that "happens" as a result of an intricate buildup of and interaction between different kinds of resources: cultural and social "capital" (mentalities, beliefs, values, social institutions); physical capital and infrastructure; and public capital (the political, legal, and economic institutions of society). We cannot "engineer" development, if only because the number of variables is beyond control. We could instead undertake more subtle and indirect interventions, stimulating, encouraging, and cajoling.

Ironically, though there was enormous shortsightedness in the past when we thought building things such as hospitals, schools, and airports *was* development, at least our "projects" were linked to finite constructions of bricks and mortar or to such physical tasks as vaccinating children. But the more we have become aware of the intricate complexity of development, the more we have tried to incorporate and adapt those intricacies to our old way of doing projects. Whereas we used to make a building into a project, now we tend to make an entire historical process into a project.

Development, as long as we continue to "tackle" it as a set of problems to be solved urgently, poverty being the most egregious of them, cannot in any case make much of a "dent" in these problems with the kind of money we have, as an industry, traditionally thrown at it (roughly $60 billion a year), or, certainly, given the short timing of that money. But I am not implying that we could do much more with more money, because real development is not about money.

Who knows what amount of money would be significant enough to really "do " something about poverty? I'm convinced that at any level of public expenditure we would be going down the wrong road (see chapter 5 on the pathology of helping as a starter set of reasons why). But let's say fifty times the amount we currently allocate, or $3 trillion annually, might do it. And let's say that the only way to build up that powerful sum would be to stop budgeting for annual spending and allow moneys to accumulate for a single big bang. Would the Ford Foundation, for instance, be allowed to spend nothing at all for ten years but merely reinvest its investment income each year and then at year 10 have tripled its endowment, thus freeing it to give ten- or twentyfold what it gives now? Would Congress allow USAID to spend nothing for years, saving its budget year to year? No. Clearly, once administrative and organizational structures are set up, they have to be used. The beast has to be fed.

But forget that $3 trillion is unrealistic. Forget that if such sums were available from the public coffers the best we could do would be literally to "buy" the physical accoutrements of development in one shot for all of Africa, in the unsustainable way Saudi Arabia has bought green grass in the desert, watered by pipelines and sprinkler systems at enormous costs. Focus instead simply on the "how" — the requirements of development grant making and lending — and on the institutional monstrosities that would need to be created. For, just as in the commercial world where it takes money to make money, in the development world it takes money to spend money. The money it takes to spend money attracts other users of the money along the way like a magnet attracts iron filings. In the same way the magnet does, a development organization creates a host of other users who line up to attach themselves to the money (travel agencies and consultants are two such ubiquitous users).

This need to spend money in order to spend money is neither unjustified nor frivolous. It is done in the name of accountability and responsibility. It is not simply the law that requires probity in the management of public moneys but also the unwritten rules and structure of organizations — the organizational imperatives noted earlier. But managing the money, especially large amounts of it, requires more staff, more accountants, and more functions. And even though, with large grants, projects might achieve economies of scale on the money management side, there would still be the need for more spending on the implementation side. There would thus be more field-workers, more evaluators, and more contracting specialists.

And because management of public moneys generally has to be geared to annual budgetary cycles, the industry would have to work harder to find more absorptive capacity, that is, more "projects" that matched the kind of money available and the time spans for that money. The result would be not more development but more projects — more frameworks that can be wrapped around a concerted effort in a three- to five-year time span and use larger sums. Finally, because it is impossible to know in three to five years whether anything lasting has occurred, it would be fairly easy to declare short-term success based on short-term achievements. The cycle would keep going.

Some Casualties of the Mismatch between Development and Its Organizational Imperatives

As the organizational imperatives in development have grown in strength (with more organizations extant), so have the mismatches with its mission.

And as these have become entrenched, the damage to the mission increases. Among the most important casualties are rigorous thought and integrity.

The Loss of Usable Memory

One of the casualties of this vicious cycle is usable memory. More than a few thoughtful development professionals may remember that the reason a given project had problems or did not work was that it was too much a project and not enough an open-ended process. But having remembered that, they are not free to create an open-ended process the next time around because someone will ask "when will it end" or "how do we budget for it." From the standpoint of the conventional wisdom of responsible funding, these questions have to be asked. The result is that the objectives of an open-ended project will be stuffed into a temporal vessel too small for it — a short-term project. Increasingly, we do this kind of thing knowing the contradictions involved.

The Inability to Analyze Need and Impact

Development assistance organizations ought to ask themselves regularly, and soberly, whether they are having any real impact and whether they are truly needed. Given the nature of the organizational ego, that is a lot to expect. But once moneys begin to be granted to development organizations on an annual basis and if these organizations are large enough and politically supported, it becomes even harder to question their existence.

The Peace Corps again makes a good example, especially so because it is a fine institution. It is probably one of the most leanly run U.S. government agencies. Through it have passed about two hundred thousand Americans, the vast majority of whom are genuinely dedicated to development. After its glory days during the Kennedy administration, the Peace Corps has had a low profile on the public and congressional radar screen. It's director is rarely a known name, and its budget (which over the decades has hovered between $100 and $140 million annually) has been too small to be attacked with heavy artillery. While it has a few detractors, it has no real enemies. Moreover, no one would get any credit for killing it.

In March 2001 the Peace Corps was forty years old. As it aged it willy-nilly created a series of supporting structures that all act to preserve it. There is a National Peace Corps Association, in its own right a registered NGO. There are many separate state and local-level Returned Peace Corps Associations. There is a national magazine and several newsletters. There are annual conventions. Virtually no one asks anymore why the Peace Corps is still needed or what impact it is having; they assume it is a useful organization.

For at least thirty years of the Peace Corps's existence we have known that twenty-four months (the length of the volunteer assignment) is a poor match for the reality of the learning curve that most PCVs go through. But knowing that has changed nothing. Moreover, the Peace Corps, once installed in a country, often stays despite changing conditions. Take Morocco, a country that opened its doors to the Peace Corps in 1961 and to which PCVs still are assigned. The country has changed enormously in those years: It is far less isolated from Europe and much more physically developed. And in some ways conditions have worsened. But it is certainly now a more mature developing country and in some rankings considered "second world" as opposed to "third world." One thing it does have is native skills in abundance. Why continue to have the Peace Corps?

The inertia of the Peace Corps (and the agency is one of the best in development today) is such that we no longer ask such questions or make judgments about it. The Peace Corps exists, and will continue to. It will evolve, but many of its adaptations will be responses to the need to compete in the marketplace of development, rather than to the need to be more relevant to development.

Getting and Spending Money Equals Performance

Many if not most development organizations now exist in a global "marketplace" where altruism has become commodified, just as other cultural and social phenomena have (perhaps an inevitable effect of "late capitalism"). In the development industry competition for attention, voice, prominence, roles, and even grassroots venues for project work (without stepping on each other's toes in the field), as well as government contracts, has become intense. More and more, private development assistance agencies assess their organizational health by checking with their fund-raisers first. The key question for many now is not "Are we doing a good job?" but "Are we continuing to grow our donor base?" Large questions of performance that might address long-term goals like poverty alleviation have been bracketed, put on a shelf. Instead, we measure performance by spending.

The nature of OPM obliges development agencies of all types to be continuously in the process of seeking new or renewed funding. They must therefore sell their accomplishments: number of individuals trained in x, y, or z; number of institutions supported; number of farmers whose incomes rose; number of bags of wheat produced from newly introduced seeds. Intangible "products" are also sold, and these often are geared to appeal to current trends. Women's empowerment is one example, thus the photos of smiling women meeting in groups.

As with all advertising, the image is what counts, and the tendency to embellish the image is strong. In the past an organization in development was not afraid to admit failure. Nor was an organization uncomfortable using the words "experiment" or "pilot effort." Today those two concepts are "out." They do not sell. It used to be OK to experiment; to see if a new approach might work. That rarely happens in development anymore. No one questions the inherent value in experimentation, but no one wants to pay for it. Donors do not want to hear that an organization is experimenting or developing a "pilot." They want their money to "count" for something that can be measured: an outcome, an output. To sell a small experiment as a "pilot" would be like selling a relatively small egg in a grocery by calling it "tiny" instead of "extra large."

The way in which organizations sell varies, but one thing is clear — more energy and money is increasingly spent on selling. Many American NGOs used to have offices in only one place. Many NGOs were headquartered in smaller towns and cities. But in the last decade many have recognized that you have to be close to the money and have therefore opened Washington offices, which enables them to drop in regularly on those donors with large sources of money. Much time is spent on relationship maintenance, just as is the case in the private sector when sales representatives call on customers, "just to say hi."

The annual reports of development assistance organizations have become increasingly slick, expensive, and, interestingly, similar. No one can risk not saying the right things and not using the appropriate buzzwords.

Finally, there are more and more publications in general, and these too are part of selling, a way of saying "we are legitimate, we are serious." Many agencies now have departments that devote themselves to publications, brochures, reports, field papers, occasional papers, and the like. The flood of publications has led to considerable personnel growth and bureaucratic expansion in agencies.

Our Organizations, Ourselves

The more we in both the north and the south have been competing for position and money, the more we have become victims of the imperatives that come with being an industry. In such an industry we must, to survive, vie for donor attention, donor grants, and donor contracts. And the more we do that, the more we are forced to follow some if not all the bureaucratic imperatives of these different donors. Inevitably, we take on staff to do more work on paper. We get involved in a world where writing the proposal and bidding for work can take up almost as much time and energy as the eventual work itself. Then, once finally launched, our projects are subject to constant review and evaluation. No sooner has one evaluation been completed than another team is preparing to arrive. The cycle continues, all in the good name of accountability. The stakes and the focus in all this can imperceptibly shift to our own selves, our own jobs, and our own organizational survival. We end up looking at our own navel. We have little time to contemplate or to ask ourselves whether what we are doing makes any sense.

In the nearly fifty-year history of government development assistance programs, their public constituencies have intended aid to be of real help to poor countries. While these publics implicitly understand that we want something in return for our help (friendship, thanks, influence, even allies), there is no widely held cynical view that aid is necessarily a quid pro quo arrangement, much less a kind of bribe. Thus from the beginning development aid has meant fundamentally just that—helping others develop.

A remarkable number of the people who staff these agencies are sincere about development. They do not, any more than the rest of us, want their agencies to be involved in things that do no good, harm people, or waste money. They do implicitly agree on a set of goals vaguely defined as development, meaning something that brings a country forward, toward progress—something that creates a foundation on which one can grow and build. Whatever metaphor or mental image these staff members have of development, it implies solid movement forward. Band-Aid solutions, addressing symptoms rather than deep problems, helping to go one step forward and two steps back, are not what they want. But there is a consciousness that development is not easy, and as the first steps taken in the early days were often missteps and gradually recognized as such, development agency staff have become aware that things have to change, that methods need improvement.

But one thing was clear in the beginning. The work of development was not to become a permanent endeavor embodied in bureaucratic institutions that would last forever. This was to be help that would end, sooner or later. If development assistance needs to be given continually, it is by definition not doing what it is supposed to. Many development assistance agencies give lip service to the notion that their goal is to work themselves out of a job. This goal is not met though, and it is not just because development takes longer than expected. The imperatives of our organizations and our dependence on other people's money account for a large part of our failure.

Position, Not Condition

India, 1996

KENDRA WAS INSISTENT. "We've got to have an AC car, Ben. We must make sure they order one, otherwise we can't go. Ben, I know Uttar Pradesh at this time of year. It simply has to be AC."

Ben and Kendra were scheduled to fly the next day to Uttar Pradesh. Ravi, the executive director of Humankind's India office in New Delhi, would have a car waiting at the Varanasi airport to drive the consultants to the project area, three hours further away, on the border between Uttar Pradesh and Madhya Pradesh. Record high temperatures were killing people all over India, and Kendra did not want to take the chance that the car might not be air-conditioned. As soon as they walked into Ravi's office to go over the arrangements, Kendra glared at Ben and lifted her eyebrows once. "Ravi, would you mind terribly arranging for an AC car?" Ben asked, on cue.

When Humankind first contacted Ben to evaluate its funding partnerships with local NGOs in India, he was pleased, even a little excited. Humankind was one of the largest international NGOs in the world, with a presence in thirty countries. Though their slogan — "A world without poverty? It's up to you" — was too glib even for the true believers, he had heard good things about Humankind and was looking forward to getting to know the organization. And, so far, he liked the idea of working alongside Kendra. Like Ben, she had years of experience and was known as an advocate for poor women. As she put it whenever she introduced herself as part of the evaluation team, Kendra was "responsible for gender."

At the domestic terminal at New Delhi airport the next morning, Prakash, a Humankind program officer who would be accompanying Ben and Kendra, introduced himself and handed them a briefing paper. Prakash was a husky, self-confident, tall man in his midtwenties, with a square jaw and a strong handshake. Immediately he addressed Ben and Kendra by their first names, asking them more questions than they asked him. He also admitted forthrightly that this was a jaunt for him. When he traveled to the GS project area, as he was required to do twice a month, he always took the overnight train, third class. To go by jet plane was a treat.

They would be visiting one of Humankind's "most successful" partners, a local Indian-registered NGO called Grameen Sarvodaya, which everyone referred to as GS. Ben and Kendra's official assignment was to evaluate GS's readiness to "graduate from the Humankind family" and replace the funding it received from Humankind with money raised locally. The first step would be a visit to GS's home base, followed by a further visit with GS staff to its main project, in a remote area a further hour and a half by jeep.

GS had been a Humankind partner since 1991. As the thorough briefing paper Ben read on the plane showed, the "target" families in the twenty-five villages covered by GS live in extreme poverty. They are landless; even those who "own" land, lack secure title to their land. They farm the poorest-quality land and lack whatever could make it more productive. Fertilizer, knowledge, and good management of the local water resources are in short supply. Moreover, the tenacity of the local feudal system (in cahoots with corrupt officials), the caste system, and the inferior place of women, rather than diminishing after independence, has been reinforced. As if to give a textbook-perfect example of poverty, the briefing paper went on to note that "these problems are exacerbated by physical remoteness and the government's standard neglect of its responsibilities." One could almost write out a recipe: take uneducated people living on barely fertile land, add a coterie of feudal landlords to take away their property rights, render all legal protection useless and all government services inactive, and then isolate the whole package by making sure there are no passable roads leading to it.

As he read on, a couple of large doubts arose in Ben. For one thing he had begun to see more and more clearly that if nothing really changed in the position poor people were often forced to occupy in society — and what could keep people in their place more forcefully than a caste and feudal system — direct interventions in their day-to-day condition often made little lasting difference. The lack of secure property rights and protection of those rights were central elements of poor people's *position* in UP and needed to be seen as a priority by any organization wishing to make a difference. If GS were focusing instead on such things as fertilizer and water — elements of the condition of the local poor — that would mean they had bet their (or rather Humankind's) money to place or show, not to win.

The other doubt Ben had was about the Humankind-GS relationship. While the evaluation was supposed to judge whether GS was ready to be on its own, Ben wondered whether Humankind was ready to *let* it go. In a way, Humankind needed GS more than the other way round. Humankind's funding base was child sponsorship. Middle-class people in the United States and Canada bought a basic Humankind sponsorship "package" for twenty dollars per month. One of the things they got for that contribution, besides inner gratification, was some sort of communication from the child — what Humankind calls a "message," because the child might not be literate and might therefore send a drawing. Since many sponsored children in the developing countries were by definition very poor, their families often moved (or, more proper, "migrated") seasonally. Also, each year some children died. Besides dealing with migrating and dying children, the other dilemma Humankind had in keeping the sponsors connected to "their" children was that in the developing world, children do not remain children for very long. Inconveniently from an administrative standpoint, they grow up fast and thus could be expected to remain viable sponsorees for only five to eight years. Thus Humankind was in the strange bind of constantly needing to find replacement children for seemingly eager middle-class sponsors to relate to. Besides those dedicated to harvesting the biannual "messages," Humankind also had staff dedicated to opening new areas with high densities of potentially sponsorable children. For decades Humankind had done all this work itself, with its own resources and staff. In a sense, by picking children community by community, family by family, and child by child, Humankind was stuck in a retail rut. But once local NGOs such as GS became more prominent and professional, all kinds of new efficiencies became possible. By making these local organizations partners and funding much of their work, Humankind ridded itself of the tedious work of renewing the pool of sponsorable children and maintaining the regular communication with sponsors. Such arrangements allowed the organization to move to the wholesale level, so to speak. Wouldn't Humankind, Ben wondered, have an interest in keeping its partnership with GS going in perpetuity?

GS was founded in 1968 by a Dr. Mukherjee Das, a Gandhian and former member of the Communist Party of India. Dr. Das had studied sociology and modern Indian history and had come to believe that the key to a just India was land rights. Like Gandhi (whom Dr. Das physically resembled), he lived simply and strongly believed that the peasantry was, and would remain for some time, the heart and soul of India. In the early 1960s he had returned to one of the most remote parts of UP, not far from his own birthplace, and founded GS, devoting his spare time and savings to helping the poor farmers in his area. His little organization, registered under the Indian Charities Act, was run on a shoestring for many years by Dr. Das and a few friends who volunteered their time. As he approached retirement age, Dr. Das began spending longer and longer periods in the area. He built a simple mud house and passed his days with the peasants, doing what today might be called "action research" but which amounted to engaging them in conversations about their lot in life, during which Dr. Das never lectured but asked many questions. He regularly published quite original papers on the central role of land alienation in the history of UP's poverty.

Dr. Das was so unassuming that Ben didn't realize who he was when he met him. When he and Kendra arrived at the large tented open pavilion that serves as GS's headquarters, they were hurriedly introduced to the staff. They were an hour late, and GS had scheduled a long day for them, beginning with a briefing. The wiry old man reclining near one of the main tent poles had raised a weak handshake during the introductions, and Ben had taken him for a visiting farmer. During the two-hour-long formal flip chart–filled introduction to the work of GS, Dr. Das never moved from his spot near the tent pole, said nothing during the whole time, and seemed not to notice whenever his name was mentioned.

Ben knew many NGO founders. Whether South Asian, African, or American, most had big egos and little inclination to let go of the reins.

The test was usually how they behaved when visitors came to call. Even when they allowed their associates to begin the talking, their impatience to hear their own voice eventually won out, and they took over the discourse. But over the two days of the consultants' visit, Dr. Das said nothing. Could it be that he really had let go of the reins and had no personal investment in his creation? Ben remained skeptical well into the second morning. At the tea break, he caught up with Dr. Das near the well pump and asked him about various NGOs and donors that Ben assumed he would know of. It was soon clear that Dr. Das knew little (and cared less) about the rest of the NGO scene in India. Had GS remained under Dr. Das's leadership, it would never have found out about Humankind.

In the late 1980s Dr. Das brought in Govinder Singh, who had been one of his students, to help him run GS. In 1990 he turned over all operational responsibility to Mr. Singh and since that time had acted only in the capacity of an informal sounding board.

It was Govinder Singh who brought GS into the wider world of NGOs. He began approaching international NGOs for funding. He had read about Humankind in a fund-raising guide to international NGOs and in 1994 wrote a proposal. Funding followed, linked to GS being able to "supply" a significant number of children to Humankind's sponsorship department. With the funding, GS began to hire new staff, eventually reaching one hundred people, many of whom are involved in the business of keeping up the numbers of sponsorable children. These all continue to receive some kind of training through the Humankind network.

When running GS by himself, Dr. Das had concentrated on getting the farmers to understand how their alienation from the land they worked was at the heart of their poverty. At the same time, he learned more and more about the critical connection between property rights and poverty, eventually gaining some of his published papers the attention of sympathetic government officials. This twenty-year-long process had not really yielded noticeable results, but at least the rhetoric of the local government officials and even the federal Ministry of Rural Development was changing. Ben had come to believe that changes in rhetoric do eventually translate into changes in beliefs and thus can have consequences for policy and action. In this case such changes had not yet yielded results in this part of UP. But that did not mean GS had not been on the right track. Indeed, the more he learned about Dr. Das's research, the more he saw how Dr. Das had penetrated to one of the root causes of the region's poverty. Land alienation, the absence of secure title to one's own land, was the issue to pursue first. He wondered whether GS, in taking on Humankind's more urgent and direct approach to poverty alleviation in exchange for funding, was in the process of throwing out the baby with the bathwater.

For it was evident that GS had changed. It now presented itself as an integrated rural development organization "empowering local people to take on development themselves."

Being "integrated" meant that GS undertakes and initiates a large number of direct projects. The empowerment agenda is fulfilled by beginning everything with the formation of a village community organization, called a "sangatan." Its brochure explains that GS staff "work to transfer in a transparent way to the people themselves first an understanding of their condition . . . followed by a series of plans to undertake solutions to their problems." Those solutions, therefore, can be anything, and as the astoundingly long list in the brochure noted, GS is involved in everything from the formation of savings and credit groups to leadership development, local governance, training in bookkeeping, rights awareness, legal support, watershed planning, soil and water conservation, tree plantations and nurseries, cattle care, crop loans, loans for reviving traditional occupations, health awareness camps, immunization camps, cataract camps (where eye surgery is performed), diarrhea prevention, the digging of wells and springs, traditional birth attendant training, adult education centers, preschool classes, motivation programs for education, setting up libraries, anti–child marriage rallies — the list continues.

All GS staff except the director and a few others live and work near the villages. The majority are "rural animators" (RAs) who work under "cluster coordinators." The RAs are recruited from the villages themselves and usually have had some elementary education, enough for basic reading and writing.

After the briefing a new, larger group was constituted to get ready for the first field visit of the afternoon. Now Kendra, Ben, and Prakash were joined by two of GS's cluster coordinators: Lal, GS's director of communication (who had given the flip chart briefing), GS's director of training, and Mr. Singh himself. This group required two jeeps, so there were two drivers as well.

They set out at about 12:30, hoping to make the first village by 1:45 or 2:00. The two vehicles bumped violently over the dirt track. Because Kendra and Ben were in the lead jeep, they ate less of the fine red dust than those in the second, but even Kendra, who wrapped part of her sari around her face and hair, had changed skin color within twenty-five minutes.

The land would have appeared flat from the air, but in fact it rolled slightly, with hillocks up to thirty or forty feet high. It was mid-May, and the temperature was somewhere between 100 and 105 degrees Fahrenheit. There were no trees left, only thorny bushes in a sere, endlessly brown landscape. For the first hour they saw no people, no animals, no crops. Talking was close to impossible with the racket of the jeep and the muscular exertion necessary to keep from getting banged on one part of the vehicle or another during the bumpy trip, so though Ben and Kendra valiantly began asking a few questions, everyone soon grew quiet.

Ben gratefully retreated into his head. Without the obligation to talk, he could look around. Participant observation, the classic method of cultural anthropology, was a bit like trying to pat your head and rub your stomach at the same time. Either Ben participated or he observed; it was hard to do both together. The bumpy track gave him the opportunity to "observe" and again try to sort out what he knew about the third world from the vast amount he did not know. In the privacy of his head he was free to admit that poverty fascinated him, not morbidly but as an impregnable subject. After thirty years in the "poverty business," he still couldn't figure it out satisfactorily. Despite having studied the economists and the historians and knowing most, if not all, of the theories and their variants, he wasn't satisfied. They all missed somehow. He recalled his first awareness of poverty and its mystery. It was on the New York Central train ride into New York City from the then new suburbs of Westchester County—this would have been in the late 1940s, when Ben was eight or nine. Ben was sitting next to his father. They had moved up from the city a few years before, so his father commuted every day. Ben stared out the window as the train slowed coming into the 125th Street station. They were passing scores of people looking out of the windows of Harlem tenements. Ben was sure, though he didn't know why he was, that these people were not happy. He felt that they were looking at him, in the train, and that they envied him. He understood that they were poor and that he, who lived in a large house surrounded by trees, was rich. "Why are they living here?" Ben asked his father. "Why don't they move?"

Decades later, Ben caught a late-night TV comedy hour and watched a frenetically obnoxious comedian making jokes about the famine in parts of Africa at that time. As the comic riffed on, his voice rose to a scream. "No wonder you people are starving, you live in the goddamn desert!! Why the hell don't you live where the food is?!"

As they rode on through this weirdly empty part of the second most populous country on the planet, Ben had again to ask himself why some people feel they have choices and others, though they share the same conditions initially, do not. One answer was how hard or easy it was for people to change their position in society.

They arrived at the first village, two dusty lanes with some trees at the end of the principal one. A cluster of people awaited the group. Before they got out of the jeep, Ben suggested quietly that he, Kendra, and Prakash might go to meet some people in their houses and that they needed only one of the GS staff to come with them.

Singh designated the director of communication, Lal, who spoke the dialect of this area quite well, to go along. The four started walking away from the trees and down the single central path of the village. There were mud houses on either side of the deeply rutted path. One had a small metal sign on the wall advertising condoms.

Ben asked Lal about AIDs. Yes, it existed, he said, and yes, it's getting worse. "But people don't like to talk about it." "You mean men don't like to talk about it!" Kendra said sharply.

"Tell us about child sponsorship in this village," Ben said to Lal. "Do you happen to know how many 'case histories' (Humankind's term for sponsored children) you supplied from here?" As director of communications, Lal was also in charge of administering the child sponsorship connections with Humankind. "Last year was the second year we developed case histories from here. Altogether there are now forty-three children being sponsored." "Do you include a photo of each child in the initial communication with the sponsor?" Ben inquired. Lal replied that they did. Ben then asked if they could stop at a couple of houses, at random, and, if those households had a sponsored child, talk to the parents. Lal was game and right away stopped walking and approached a doorway.

An extremely thin small woman, perhaps in her thirties, came forward, and Lal spoke to her for a couple of minutes. She motioned to a boy in the shadows behind the doorway. He came out. Perhaps thirteen, he was taller than his mother. His left arm was badly twisted so that his hand was permanently curled in a fistlike position. He was a sponsored child. Lal asked the mother if his photo had been taken. It had. Ben asked Lal to ask her if she knew why. She said she had been told that doctors needed to see a picture of the child if he was to be helped. What was she expecting to happen? Ben wanted Lal to ask her. Without hesitating, she answered that she was hoping a series of operations could make her son able to use his arm and that eventually the project would give her the money for this.

They stopped at the next house. There were two sponsored children here, about eight and ten years old. This time the father of the house spoke to Lal. He said that photos had been taken and he had been told that the project needed the photos to track the progress of his two children through their primary schooling. What was he expecting from the GS project? Ben had Lal ask. The man replied that GS was helping the village in many ways, They had been told they had to work together to solve their own problems. But GS would supply them with materials, like cement and tools. Did he know where the money came from? He wasn't sure but thought that it came from far away — "from foreigners," he said.

Ben and Kendra were a bit surprised. They had been told at Humankind headquarters that "transparency" was one of Humankind's cardinal values. No one was to be fooled, least of all the poor people of the third world.

Ben turned to Lal. "Why are people apparently being told different things about the reasons for the photos? Why is it they don't know that their children's photos go directly to the sponsors, who then send money to Humankind?"

Lal shrugged. He was clearly aware of the compromise, but if he saw its moral implications, he essentially dismissed them. "We have to be realistic," Lal said. "If we tell them the exact truth, the parents will expect the sponsor's money to come to them directly. But we can't do that, since we are committed to a community approach. The only way we can ensure that the money is available to benefit the whole community is to change the story a bit."

Ben recalled leafing though the sponsorship manual when he had visited Humankind's headquarters. He had been given it as an example of how thoroughly professional Humankind's operation was. He had been impressed, first, by its detail and length (over two hundred pages) and, second, by how difficult sponsorship management seemed. The result of years of experience on Humankind's part, the manual showed the seemingly infinite number of pitfalls sponsorship can entail, such as missing or mismatched photos, children moving on, children dying, the transferal of case histories from one sponsor to another, inappropriate messages, wrong signals given to the community, inappropriate symbols, how to deal with a sponsor who decides to become a "development tourist" and drops in on the local Humankind office, hoping to visit his child (always with many gifts), and so on. Only now, in a dry and dusty village in India, did some of these matters come to life for Ben.

Ben especially remembered his skepticism when he read the chapter of the manual with the "sample letters" that sponsorship personnel could use to respond to sponsors' questions or to inform them of changes in the child's status. There was one, addressed to a fictional "Mr. Wilson," reporting that his sponsored child had migrated and offering him another child. As if to anticipate Mr. Wilson's wondering what his money had accomplished, the letter went on to assure him that "Abdullah benefited fully from your contribution while he was in the village." There was also the gruesome "death letter," telling the sponsor that though Humankind was doing its best to improve the lot of the people, including their life expectancy, the direst consequences of poverty could not always be avoided, and so little Hakim or little Mohini had died. To be sure, little Mohini *had* enjoyed a fuller life while she was alive, thanks to Mr. Wilson's kindness.

Humankind had tried to convert its sponsors from giving to an individual child to giving to a community. Sponsors seemed able to make the cognitive switch, but only up to a point. At the same time that they "got" the value of working with a whole community, they wanted to retain the emotional connection with a real and specific child. So Humankind straddled the fence, continuing to find real children and match them up with sponsors. But the children did not receive the sponsor's money; their communities do.

What Ben and Kendra now understood more vividly than before was that the children were ironically a cost to the sponsor and a burden to Humankind. They needed to exist to keep the sponsor interested, and though they were unnecessary from the standpoint of the development agency's work, specialized staff and the time of general staff had to be devoted to recruiting these "case histories," taking the photos, collecting and sending the twice yearly "message," and writing the various letters found in the manual. And while the sponsor was being told that her contribution was a kindness to a specific child in a community context, that child was being "retained" as a kindness to the sponsor's sensibilities.

Ben was amused. He turned to Kendra. "At least Humankind provides equal treatment—if we accuse them of patronizing the villagers, they can always say they patronize the sponsors too!"

It was now 3:30 in the afternoon. The visitors had come to this village to see a typical "sangatan" and observe GS's interactions with it. A gathering of the villagers had been planned, and it was time to go over to the village center, a low flat-roofed mud building with a single doorway and four window openings, but no windows. The building had been constructed using village labor and GS-contributed materials. Ben and the others now rejoined the larger group and Mr. Singh led them to the center.

Inside, Ben was surprised to see a large mass of people sitting on the hard dirt floor of the center. About fifty women sat on one side of the space and an equal number of men on the other side. Everyone stopped talking and chatting as the visitors entered. "Namasté," cried the women, bringing the palms of their hands together and bowing their heads. The men did the same, though it seemed to Ben less vigorously.

Kendra immediately went to sit among the women. Ben turned to Mr. Singh and Prakash and told them he wanted to talk to both groups. He would, he said, spend fifteen minutes with the women and then come over to the men.

Ben joined Kendra, squeezing himself in next to her. This was not easy; the women were sitting so close together that he could only see disembodied heads bobbing on a sea of sari cloth. Kendra was already in animated discussion with the women. She looked up, surprised, and Ben asked her to explain to them that the American man was interested in hearing about their savings group. Ben knew that such a specific topic would seem appropriate for him to be interested in. He'd only take up fifteen minutes, he said to Kendra, knowing she had other areas to explore with the women.

Ben asked if the rural animator who helped them form and run their savings group was present. A young girl of about eighteen raised her hand shyly. Who is the treasurer? Ben asked. Another, much older woman, raised her hand. Ben asked if someone would tell him the history of their savings group and how it works.

The women's savings group was begun in March 1994, twenty-six months earlier, with the help of GS and the RA assigned to them, the treasurer explained through the translator. Each member of the group contributed five rupees each time the group met, their monthly meeting being on the twentieth. The group had a bank passbook, and records were kept of the meetings and the accounts. The amounts contributed are put in their group bank account. Ben asked how many of the women sitting here are members of the savings group. Most hands were raised. Ben guessed the group had about forty members. "How far away is your bank?" he asked. Some discussion was required here, and the treasurer finally said it was about four kilometers away in a larger village, where there was a small branch of the Badra Rural Bank. (Since the 1950s India has had a government-mandated and -subsidized system of rural banks. Unlike many third world countries in which banks are few and far between, India has thousands of bank branches.) Who goes to the bank to make the monthly deposits? The treasurer replied that she did. "Do you regularly make deposits?" Ben asked. Again there was some discussion. The treasurer replied that she could not always get to the bank and that she had last made a deposit three or four months back.

Ben had studied small village savings groups like this before and had learned that asking to see the actual record books was rarely if ever taken as intrusive or insulting. And while he didn't like playing the role of auditor, examining the books was one way to get a real picture. "Do you have the account books and bank passbook here?" Ben asked. The treasurer did not but immediately got up to get them, rewrapping her sari as she extricated herself from the group. The houses being close by, she was back in several minutes, with a small bundle of school-size notebooks tied in a gauzy cloth. She unwrapped the books carefully and handed them to the translator, who handed them to Ben.

In the meantime Ben had made some calculations. If everyone contributed their five rupees regularly, the books should show over five thousand rupees saved. Some of this might have gone out again as loans, but if GS had been disciplined in its monitoring of this fledgling savings fund, these loans should have shown interest payments and in some cases have already been fully repaid. Ben knew, however, that no group saves 100 percent of the time. There are always other competing needs for five rupees, and someone will always be absent. So he guessed that half the amount of his estimate would be reasonable.

With the help of the translator, Ben found the main account book and began to decipher it. The meeting date column showed clearly that not one of the recorded meetings had taken place on the twentieth of any month. Ben looked up and asked again when the group met. The treasurer repeated that they met on the twentieth. Ben asked the group to verify, unembarrassed in the event they might think he did not trust the treasurer. "Is that right?" he asked. Several women responded that it was. The book also showed that three or four months would go by without a meeting and that when one was held, there were many blanks next to members' names, showing a sporadic record of contributions.

Ben flipped through the small pile to the group's bank passbook. He opened it. It was virtually blank, except for one entry — 220 rupees in March 1994, the date the savings group began. Ben looked up. He explained slowly to the translator what he had found and asked her to repeat this to the group. He then asked Kendra to speak directly to the RA, whose job it was to monitor the savings group. He wanted to know how much had actually been saved and why only one deposit was made to the bank, so long ago. The RA did not know. The treasurer then spoke and said that altogether 800 rupees had been saved, but it was not in the bank. It was in the treasurer's house. Additional discussion revealed that the group's savings of 800 rupees had been loaned out to various members. None of the books he was holding showed these transactions. Ben asked to see where these loans had been recorded. More discussion ensued. Ben turned to Kendra, who was looking a bit perplexed and annoyed. He whispered to her: "It doesn't appear the group understands this savings concept, nor has the RA played any role at all in seeing that they do."

Kendra's annoyance, it now became clear, was with Ben. "Look, Ben, these women are not only illiterate, they are not numerate either. Written records mean nothing to them. You and the whole development endeavor keep wanting to put some Western, and largely male, template on this savings and credit business. I've said for years that what we need is a gender-sensitive accounting system, one that accepts that written records with columns and dates and regular entries are inappropriate for these women. They may not be able to keep records on paper, but they know who's paid what and who's borrowed what, believe me!"

Ben nodded and without replying suggested to Kendra that they should discuss this later, at dinner. Right now, he wanted to get over to the group of men. He asked the translator to thank the ladies, clasped his palms together, said namasté to the women, and got up.

Ben was as attuned to cultural differences as most development workers, but over the years he had begun to see some universal truths that trumped these differences. Two plus two equaling four was one of them. The ostensible point of GS encouraging the formation of a savings group was to enable the women to have some equity of their own, some small fund of money they could use to smooth out the awful bumpiness of their material ups and downs. Everything was always hand-to-mouth; there was always a child getting sick or a goat dying, and no one was ever financially prepared for these small disasters. A women's savings group was meant in the first instance to help them gain a tiny bit of control over their fate. And research had shown that even the poorest women could save small sums. Five rupees a month — twelve cents — was possible. What was lacking was a system to keep the money safely and to pay — in the form of interest — for the loss of the chance to use the money immediately. Ben didn't buy that even without good records the women necessarily knew exactly what was what financially. He had seen countless cases of poor people being ripped off not only by exploitative outsiders but also by members of their own group.

A contractual obligation was also at stake here. Humankind brought in money and granted it to GS, its partner, to do things like form savings groups. Part of that money was to pay the RAs, who in turn were to monitor, coach, and supervise these new activities until such time as the villagers could handle matters themselves. In the case of the women's group he had just sat with, the road to that goal was looking like a dead end.

Ben sat down among the men. The space seemed larger because the men were not sitting on top of one another. On the wall was a colorful chart with several columns. Each column had a symbol on the top, easily recognizable pictures of, in turn, a shovel, a water well pump, a bag of cement, and so on. Ben asked the translator to ask the men what the chart was about. A young man stood up and nodded formally to the visitors. He explained that this was a plan for the activities various members of the village group would undertake during this month, May. The main activity was the construction of a check dam, to prevent erosion and retain moisture in the soil. This would involve twelve people, but three people were to build a well, several others would repair houses, and so forth. Over here in this column, the young man pointed, is the date the project starts, and here is the number of days it is expected to take. The sangatan spent several days last month devising this plan, on which everyone had had to agree. Then once agreed, GS was given a list of materials to supply. In this way, the young man said, concluding, we will become self-reliant. Ben nodded to the young man, whose sincerity he did not want to offend. "Who is this?" he asked Prakash, next to him, in a low voice. Prakash, who had visited this village often, said this young man was the first RA to be hired by GS and was now a "cluster coordinator." He had gone on several training and exposure visits to other NGOs and projects. "As it happens," Prakash added, "he is also the son of the village head."

Ben nodded to Prakash and turned to the young man. He had a number of questions. "Did the villagers have to pay GS for the materials?" No, the young man replied, they were a gift. "Did the villagers have to provide their labor free?" Part of it is voluntary, the man replied, but part of the labor is paid, by GS. "What rate are the men paid?" Ben asked. Forty-seven rupees per day, the man answered, adding that this was in conformity with the legal minimum wage. "We are proud to teach the villagers what their legal rights are." "You mean," Ben said, "that this rate is not what people around here are used to getting?" "That's right," said the young man.

Ben looked again at the chart. The plan was so well wrought, so beautifully presented, and in color, that it seemed too good. He had to know if it was really being followed. Today was May 12. He saw that the check dam was to have begun on May 4 and the well on May 7. It soon became evident that neither project had begun, despite the incentive of a paid wage. A third of the way into the month and the plan had lost ground.

General Eisenhower used to say that planning is essential but plans are useless. Ben knew that rigid adherence to a plan was unlikely, especially in this context. But was it also possible that some members did not really seem clear about what these plans meant or, to use the parlance of participatory development, that they did not have "ownership" of the plan? But for both the villagers and the rural animators, perhaps merely making the plan was a sufficient enough achievement, as setting up the account books and opening the bank account seemed to have been for the women's savings group.

On the opposite wall, also in bright colors, was a chart depicting the progress of the Crop Loan Scheme, yet another of GS's projects in the village, now in its second year. Twenty-five names were listed down one side of the chart. Next to each name was the name of the plot of land being farmed, then the amount of the crop loan, and then the term of the loan (one growing season). Finally, the last column for the year showed the total amount to be repaid, including interest. Ben understood from having seen such schemes before that the initial crop loan fund was provided by GS. The idea was that once repaid the fund would revolve and, with the buildup of interest, sustain itself as future loans were made in later years. The loans were small, averaging about twelve hundred rupees (twenty-eight dollars), but Ben noticed that most of the boxes in the repayment column at the end of the first year were empty. A bit wearily he turned to the young man and asked him to find out if the empty boxes indicated that those loans had not been repaid.

The young man turned to the group of men and entered into a discussion with one of them. He then told Ben that most of the farmers had difficulty repaying on time — weather had been a factor — but that eventually they would repay the loans. "I see," said Ben. It is easy to get the sense that form was substituting for content, and not just on the part of the villagers. GS personnel seemed to have the same tendency.

This was reinforced when the meetings broke up for a tea break around 5:00. Ben and Kendra were told with some pride by Mr. Singh that in addition to all the other activities GS had instigated in its commitment to integrated local development, a grain bank had also been established, again, as Singh explained, "the result of the villagers' own analysis of their problems and their conclusions about how to solve them." Singh insisted that the consultants see this, since it was in the back room of the newly built community center where they were. They opened a door and there in the corner was one standard size sack about two-thirds full of grain. Ben nodded. "Is that the grain bank?" he asked Singh. "Yes," Singh replied, adding, "It is, of course, early days, and our hope is that soon the grain bank will grow." GS had been working with this village for two years.

Singh knew that the consultants had come to Uttar Pradesh to evaluate the relationship between GS and Humankind. Why, then, had he wanted them to see a half-filled sack of grain? Was Singh more concerned about the checklist of promises GS had made in its contract with Humankind? Line item 26a: "We will, by the end of the second year, have helped the village establish a grain bank." Perhaps Singh was covering himself — GS has done what it said it would, even if in token form.

It was becoming clear that while GS tried to adhere to the spirit of consensus and participation — gathering villagers together for meeting after meeting — at the core of the relationship between GS and the people was a flow of material or cash. When a check dam is constructed, to be sure the villagers have established why and where it is to be constructed. But they also receive material and are in the end paid for part of their labor, at the legal minimum wage, which is double the prevailing real labor rate. Then a portion of that wage is deducted as a contribution to a village fund. The project offers an incentive, which is a distortion of local reality, and then, in the name of community, takes part of it away.

When a well is to be built, a spring rehabilitated, or a nursery to be started, material costs are involved, even when labor is contributed. There is material for blasting, and in the case of a drilled well, there is outside "skilled" labor to be paid for. In each case the budget and plan is worked out with the villagers, and the plan is posted on paper on the wall of the village center. Even these charts (which are prepared with the help of the GS staff) involve a small budget. It may be as little as one hundred rupees to cover tape and drawing materials, but it goes to the group.

Ben began to worry that after two years of help from GS, few signs existed to show that the villagers had absorbed the "development process" that GS was counting on them internalizing. People come to meetings, though without full enthusiasm, perhaps because they felt it was part of a deal — if they want the cement, tools, fertilizer, crop loans, they had better show up. And the plans, even after all the analyses and meetings, and despite some material incentives to carry them out, were not followed very well.

Ben asked himself why he got the impression that good intentions were substituting for sustained activity. Was GS simply trying to do too much at once and thus dissipating its and the community's energies? Or is poverty itself simply demonstrating its intractability? People's needs are simply too great and too immediate, the level of poverty too extreme, the vested interests too entrenched, and the temptations to smooth out the bumps in villagers' lives too great not to juggle a bit with cash, as Ben thought was probably happening in the women's savings group and the crop loan scheme.

Ben felt sad. He saw how dedicated Dr. Das had been and saw that dedication reflected in many of the GS core staff, who worked long hours for small wages. But had a bargain been made here that served Humankind and GS more than the villages? Humankind was able to make its management of the relationship between children and their sponsors more efficient. And GS, having agreed to be a cog in the great wheel of child sponsorship in return for more money than it had ever had before, was inevitably drawn to trying to deal more directly with the conditions of local poverty. But in so doing, GS was losing its focus on the local people's untenable *position* in society. Worse, having chosen to deal with the conditions of poverty by trying to tackle so many of them at once, in the service of an "integrated" approach, GS was accomplishing nothing of any real significance. Finally, not only were there no signs of any but the most mediocre material progress, but all the rhetoric of building self-reliant institutions and systems was just that — rhetoric. At the end of the day, all the development projects undertaken in this set of villages seemed to be at risk of reinforcing if not increasing dependency, whereas the real foundation stones for self-reliance — secure property rights, good basic infrastructure, and a governing regime that upholds the laws — were simply not there.

Headless Chickens

World Bank, late 1990s

BEN HAD GOT USED TO IT. Every time Charles Taber forgot to do something he said he would, didn't respond to a query or a memo, lost a report in one of the piles around his desk, or in any of his myriad ways screwed up, he'd slap his palm on his forehead and say, "Oh, what a flake I am!" Ben couldn't get mad, even when he saw how much his disarming style was intended to disarm. Nor could others who worked for Charles. That was the surprising part.

Ben was not building a career at the World Bank but simply doing some long-term consulting work that interested him. Charles's own full-time staff, a growing number of professionals as he moved up in the hierarchy, people with careers to build and a lot on the line — such as Raoul from Peru, who had just got his daughter into one of Washington's most prestigious private schools, whose wife was just learning how to shop, who clung with every breath to the status of being part of "the Bank," a rocketship ride from where he had started ten years before — just took his scrambled management in stride.

It took Ben a while to figure it out. It was not that these people were any thicker skinned than others, that his failings didn't mess them up, or that they had learned to work around his shortcomings as a manager. The answer was that they knew these managerial flaws didn't matter.

The Bank, at least in the 1990s, was an institution always in "transition." This fact came to Ben viscerally, when in the first year of his routine monthly visits to the Bank he would find that a third of the people he'd been working with the month before had moved to other departments and that the department to which he was assigned had changed its name, location, and office arrangement. When this kept happening in the second and third year of his consulting contract, he began to see that it was chronic.

One day, while lost trying to find someone who had moved, he wandered into a gigantic space on the ninth floor of the M building, the Bank's newest building, just completed and significantly over budget. The space was vast and open, yet it appeared oddly cluttered. Everywhere were aluminum flip chart stands and movable partitions, placed seemingly at random. And huge posters were taped on every available surface.

On a large table sat a cardboard box with three half-eaten muffins and a chocolate-covered doughnut. They looked about a day old. Ben took the chocolate doughnut and walked around the labyrinth of flip charts. There were magic marker red and green arrows and black circles and yellow squares and blue triangles; organigrams and matrices; lists of "attributes" and "desired qualities." Ben took in the various headings, trying to find a logic, a place to begin: "WHERE WE ARE—WHERE WE WANT TO BE," "A CHANGING WORLD," "OUR MARKET," "CLIENT RESPONSIVENESS," "CROSS-DISCIPLINARY LEARNING," "TEAMING AND CLUSTERING," "CONSULTATIVE AND PARTICIPATORY PROCESSES," and on and on. After twenty minutes Ben was confused. But he did see that here was one of the epicenters of the Bank's effort to "transit" to a new kind of institution.

It seemed a sincere effort, not just because of the earnest way in which each poster and chart was worded—or because senior staff nodded gravely when they spoke publicly about the Bank's new, more-sensitive-to-the-poor culture—but also because a huge amount of money was being spent on it. Ben had become used to missing some of his regular colleagues (the few who didn't end up being transferred to other departments) when he was in Washington because they were "on mission," but now he began to see a new pattern. Their secretaries—sorry, the new term is "team assistants"—were more often saying that Charles or Ishiko or Piet or Istvan was "on a retreat" or "in training."

By 1997 quite a few people at the Bank were coming into the office only sporadically. Besides their regular mission travel, they were now doing lots of two-week-long retreats and participating in the "VIP," touted as one of the most expensive parts of the transition to the "new Bank." Of course, Ben wondered how a more sensitive Bank could be pushing people into something called "VIP." That would smack of the "old" Bank, the very-important-person Bank, the Bank that routinely flew everywhere first class. But Ben soon found out that VIP stood for Village Immersion Program. Every professional at the Bank was to spend a week to two weeks living in a real third world village somewhere, so he or she could experience poverty firsthand. This would bring poverty home; this would make it front and center in the Bank's mission.

But, as Ben was beginning to discover, these sheaves of urgency and hand-wringing taken from the Bank's very own Little Red Book were not, for all their outward form, a cultural revolution. For, while up close the changes looked like violent waves frothing on the water, the underlying sea of the Bank's work and especially the deep entrenchment of its approximately six thousand "regular" staff remained calm and steady. (In addition to "regular" staff, that is, career appointments, the Bank employs several thousand "consultants" full-time.) The business of lending about $20 billion per year continued. Projects were proposed, negotiated, designed, and "task managed" until the "completion date" said they were over.

At lunchtime Ben would sit with different people connected with his project. He'd begun asking people, obliquely at first, then point-blank, what they actually did. Forsythe Shuttlefield, a senior industrial economist from Jamaica who'd been at the Bank for twenty-two years, in his dry smoker's voice had no trouble reeling off his day-to-day work without embarrassment or self-consciousness: "Well, I review documents pertaining to projects, organize consultants, do the Terms of Reference for them, coordinate incoming missions to the division (meaning visitors), and, these days, go to training courses. Except for the last, it's pretty much what I've always done."

Piet van Drumpt, a Dutch environmental economist in his ninth year at the Bank, was less resigned: "Boy, I don't like to think about it. I came here to do development work, but I see more and more that most people don't see themselves as development workers but as professionals—economists, engineers, social scientists. We're intellectuals. We write and read, like academics. We're all in our boxes, doing intense work in short spurts, not sharing with each other because we're afraid someone else might see that what they do isn't important. Then our work goes into the great pipeline. But it's a mystery — somehow it always gets stuck before it goes anywhere, or it gets radically altered. We rarely see our work come out the end of the pipeline in any way that's recognizable. We make high-quality products that get stuck in limbo."

Claudette Orzul, an anthropologist in her late thirties who was raised in Paris by a Turkish father and a French mother, just rolled her eyes and laughed: "I spend my time going up and down stairs that lead nowhere."

So nothing much was changing. The great core of the Bank, its mid-level career people, accepted the calls for yet another "transition" with resignation tempered by cynicism. They know that "this too shall pass." In fact, they count on certain things not changing. Certainly the perks. Bank staff still get five weeks annual paid vacation. And though first-class travel was officially dropped in the mid-1990s (the Bank's manual cryptically states that travel shall be "by less than first class"), the Bank's clout with the airlines is such that in 1997 at least seven major airlines had made deals that when Bank travel was booked with them, the traveler would get an upgrade on most long-distance routes. Ben himself, a mere consultant, had been expecting a routine business-class trip to attend a conference in London the first spring he was working for Charles on the project. He remembers the day he came up from the M building sub-basement, level C, where the Bank's own American Express travel office was, in a daze because he was holding a ticket to London on the Concorde, the result of a special deal British Airways was offering the Bank.

So new layers replaced old, and new titles were given out. But deep down in the Bank, its "DNA" seemed to guarantee that the thousands of cells within it, the professionals, would be free to read and write in the way they always had, impervious to rigorous judgment about performance or development outcome.

This is why having a "flaky" manager didn't matter to Charles's staff. Much of the work in the Bank consists of tasks that exist in part to justify one's position, in the form of reports and papers written in isolated cubicles, next to "stairs that lead nowhere," so that whether or not the work is carefully managed is irrelevant.

When Ben was first put in touch with Charles Taber, he had already heard quite a bit about him. He knew he was one of the rising stars at the World Bank. Charles had a winning style. When he was disarming, he was also warm, funny, and irreverent. And he was smart. Though he wasn't an economist, he had picked up the key concepts of the Bank's majority profession — he could talk to the economists in their terms. It went without saying that the reverse was not true; the economists could not quite get the "grassroots" perspective that Charles had earned in his years of working directly with the poor. Changing that imbalance was one of Charles's crusades. Little by little, through his presence on an endless series of committees and poverty "teams," Charles would convey the poverty-centered point of view in such a way that the economists would not only for the first time hear it but also eventually begin using his terminology (whether they embraced the terms is another question).

And though Charles was a tireless crusader and devoted to his work, deep in his heart he battled some doubts about the institution he worked for. He had doubts about the integrity of the Bank as a development institution, about its clumsiness and size, its mix of incompetents and brilliant misfits, and especially the Bank's strong tendency to pull its professionals in fifteen directions at once. He justified having stayed these twenty years by acknowledging that if you want to make a difference in the lives of the poor, you can't do it from the margins. And all, or practically all, organizations in development, compared with the World Bank, *were* marginal. Only the Bank had real power to command people's attention. The Bank not only can dangle big sums of money in front of big people but, with its prestige and world-class economists, can also engender respect among governments, which, when combined with its money, could make governments do things they would otherwise not be inclined to. The Bank was where the action was in development, plain and simple.

Besides, Charles was a natural-born optimist. He had faith that he could make a difference. The challenges were immense, and he loved them. Not just the sheer developmental ones but also the political economy of the institution he worked in. The Bank as the subject of a crusade was by itself all-consuming. Charles thrived on the continuous battle to create light at the Bank — to get economists and others to understand the reality of development problems, to shift their perspective more to the poor. Though he was capable of seeing through some of the sham in the Bank's latest incarnation, he routinely chose to ignore most of it and excuse the rest. For him the Bank was coming around, slowly to be sure, in fits and starts perhaps, but "moving in the right direction."

Charles had the energy of a twenty-one-year-old. He put in twelve- and thirteen-hour days at the Bank and seven days a week when on the road, which was often. Travel is as close to sacred in Bank culture as anything can get; it is so much a part of Bank life that no one questions it. "She/he is on mission" is the first phrase new secretaries at the Bank must learn to say when the phone rings. Charles traveled perhaps even more than others — 130,000 to 160,000 miles per year. And like others he complained about it, though Ben always suspected that most Bank staff secretly loved traveling. It broke the boredom and routine of the office. More important, travel reified the mission. Sitting in the front section of the plane, being picked up by someone who has your name on a wooden sign ("Dr. Taber, World Bank," with brass bells and other doodads hanging under it), five-star hotels, dinners with high officials, taxis everywhere — these seductive symbols were self-referential, messages sent to you about your place in the world. To be unaffected by all this, you would have to be morosely and unrelentingly cynical, which Charles decidedly was not.

By the time Ben came to know him, Charles had become well known in the Bank hierarchy without having pushed himself into a special corner. He was known as an advocate of the poor, but not of the warm and fuzzy sort. He could be a member of a team without being a solid team player. He could play the gadfly role at the Bank without being marked by it.

But until the project for which he had recruited Ben, he had never been in a position of real authority and control. "The Project," as it was portentously called by those associated with it (as in "the Bank," another word regularly overloaded with great meaning), was a trust fund project, Bankspeak for something that is undertaken by the Bank but paid for by outsiders. Oddly, the Bank was cheap when it came to those things which a commercial company would put under the rubric of "research and development." For certain kinds of research, it liked to get outsiders to kick in a small fund. In this case the Swedes and the Dutch had agreed to put up the money (a round $1 million).

Charles and an economist in another division had been talking for some time about the growing number of programs offering small loans to poor people in the developing countries. By the early 1990s, the trick of lending money to poor people who had no collateral and getting repaid looked like it was beginning to be mastered. Many programs that lent money to the poor had surprisingly few loan defaults. Charles and a few others at the Bank felt that "microfinance" held real promise for improvements in the lives of the poor, especially women, even though they recognized that most of these programs were still in their early stages. What they did know was that the Bank had no real solid understanding of this new area, and as a result a "microfinance component" was often being tacked on to Bank projects as a faddish afterthought.

Charles's contention was that because it rarely listened to what outsiders had to say, the way to help the Bank get its act together in this new field was for a major research and documentation project to be undertaken by the Bank itself—the Bank would tell itself what to do. The Project would entail a comprehensive series of case studies from which a set of "best practices" would be derived, resulting in a procedure manual for microfinance. In this way the Bank would not only create for itself a basis for rigorous decision making about backing microfinance projects but would also be doing a service to the whole field by setting right many myths and misunderstandings about what microfinance was and was not.

The Project was to run for three years, with Charles managing it. Budget in hand, with his division manager behind him, Charles began recruiting staff. Ben was one of his first calls. He agreed to work half-time as a consultant and adviser. To run the Project on a day-to-day basis, Charles recruited Luis, an economist at another agency in Washington who he knew was looking for a way to come to the Bank.

Within three months of beginning work on the Project, the original team of Ben, Luis, one other principal consultant, and three people on Charles's staff began to break up. Cindy left to work on a big environmental project in China. Philibert switched (or was switched, it was never clear) to the Africa division to work on rural infrastructure. And both Charles and Luis quickly began getting involved in many different things at once. Ben would come into Washington for several days for planning meetings related to the case studies and would notice Luis and Charles running off between and during their meetings to meetings in other departments and divisions. Ben would show up at the Bank early at 7:15 A.M. and find Charles at his computer wading through scores of e-mails asking for his participation in this or that initiative or project or to serve on a committee. "How can I possibly do all this?" he'd ask in exasperation. "You can't," Ben would say. "Why don't you just say no?" But it didn't make any difference. Charles would choose the offers that interested him and run off. Luis began accepting offers to come along on missions for other departments, a process of internal consulting that was supposed to provide a degree of cross-fertilization of ideas at the Bank.

Increasingly, Ben found that the project he was hired to work on was becoming an orphan. Nobody was supervising it, no one controlled it.

Once the Project had been signed and funded, the key people moved their energies elsewhere. Ben and Alice, the other principal consultant, ended up moving the work forward, as it were, in a managerial vacuum. They worked on the design of the data collection, planned the field-work, and handled the negotiations with the organizations and agencies whose operations were to be the cases studied. Luis or Charles would have to sign off on the contracts for the cases and the travel moneys. Whatever was proposed, they signed. The work proceeded, and in the first year and a half considerable work got under way. Some twenty-five case studies were commissioned, and two very energetic new consult-ants were brought on to assist in processing them.

Ben would go home, continue his work, write some more plans, and make some phone calls for the Project. He did three of the case studies in the first eighteen months. Every month, Ben would tote up the time he'd spent, submit a bill to the project secretary, Louise, who would pro-cess it. Three weeks later he'd get a check in the mail. In the beginning he'd routinely send a weekly memo to Luis and Charles keeping them abreast of what he was doing and offering them opportunities to com-ment. He soon sensed that these were a bother to Charles and Luis. No one asked what he'd spent his time on.

When in Washington, D.C., Ben would occasionally bump into Charles's boss, Clyde, the division chief. A gregarious man, always smiling, he'd pass Ben in the hallway, quickly pump Ben's hand, and say "Project's going well I hear. Great, great, keep it up" and continue on his way.

As the case study work began, it was soon clear that there were not only no hard guidelines about cost but also no real deadlines — no sense that the cases had any sort of "sell-by date" if they were to be use-ful. Ben came back from a three-week trip to West Africa where he had done a case on one of the local NGO-run microfinance projects. In two weeks, Ben wrote a fifty-page case study. He knew the data would be old fairly soon. He also knew that the problems this NGO was facing at that stage in its work were remarkably similar to those many other practitioners faced. Ben sent off his draft to Luis and Charles, noting that getting this case study — one of the first — published in a timely fashion should be a priority. Weeks passed. Ben e-mailed a reminder. This time Charles wasn't on "mission" — he was at Harvard attending a three-week management course with a bunch of other Bank staff. Luis had been temporarily seconded to another project. "We'll get back to you," he e-mailed Ben. Ben's case, along with, eventually, all the others, would end up sitting in the Bank's "pipeline" for up to two years before coming out the other end, and a few never made it.

The Bank, from a managerial standpoint, is a fragmented, almost anarchic institution. It doesn't hire professional managers but rather skilled specialists in particular subject matter areas. Most Bank professionals have Ph.D.'s. There are far more "chiefs" than "Indians."

But this is only one reason why even Management 101–level concepts such as "follow-up" are unfamiliar at the Bank. The other reasons have to do with the development industry itself. A project is initiated and gets funded; the objectives, or the "outputs," that were initially proposed change, or they do not. It doesn't matter. At the end someone verifies that the money was spent. And since there is no true demand for the project in the way demand exists in a real marketplace, no quality standard by which to judge it, no feedback in terms of sales figures, there can be no abject failure. Therefore, what's to manage?

As no one really watched things like time, expense, or outputs, the Project began to resemble a set of amorphous amoebas — a nodule in process here, with a new pod taking shape there, while over here nuclei were splitting. A paper that was due from one consultant kept being delayed; no one called him. Another set of cases was completed, but no one could get it together to finish the editing process, so they were never published. As for the first case Ben did in West Africa in 1995, it did not come out of the pipeline until the end of 1998. Of the other two he did (in 1996), one came out in early 1999, and the other just fell through the cracks. Eventually, the organization whose operation Ben had studied for that "lost" case, which had regularly contacted him to ask when "their" case was coming out, just stopped asking. They too had forgotten.

Of course Ben and the other case study consultants got paid for the time they worked, whether it led to anything or not. And the Project money kept on being spent. Interestingly, as the third and final year of the Project came and went, neither the Swedes nor the Dutch seemed disturbed. In their institutions the people who had signed on to the original project had moved on. Those who succeeded them needed only some perfunctory note to plug into the proper place in the file so that their bureaucratic structures would be assured that various supervisory checklists were covered. But Charles and Luis *did* recognize that the Project wasn't finished. They asked the donors for an extension of the Project and more money, and they received both.

By the fourth year, it was clear to Ben that the field had changed.

Many of the original premises of the Project were stale. People who had backed it at the Bank had moved on to other positions. There were other priorities. The cases that were produced were finally disseminated. The microfinance manual was completed, to take its place on the shelf along with a dozen others that other institutions had by then produced.

The Project's true insignificance became clear to Ben some time later when a surprise contact from Charles caused him to recollect the fate of one set of the case studies. In 1994, Charles had commissioned five cases on microfinance organizations in South Asia, to be done by an Indian organization. Twelve months later these studies came in. Charles felt more could be done with them and began talking to one of the Project's consultants about rewriting them. The consultant rewrote all five. Nothing happened.

Then, in late 1996, Charles recognized that the data were stale and authorized a trip to the region for the consultant to update all five studies. After a two-week-long trip, the consultant updated and rewrote the cases.

Meanwhile, Charles had received a promotion (the Peter Principle could have been invented for the World Bank) and was now managing several hundred staff in three countries in Asia. He was busier than ever, in the throes of getting to know everyone, and heavily involved in bringing in new staff and putting together a planning retreat. Luis had moved to another division. The consultant sent in her final draft of the five South Asian cases. Ben knew the consultant and had confidence that she had done a professional job. He had written a memo telling Charles that he hoped this set of cases could now be completed, as the Project was officially nearing the end of its one-year extension.

As each month went by, the information in the cases was increasingly irrelevant. The consultant sent in her bill and was paid. Ben stopped pestering Charles. His work had been completed, and he went on to other consulting assignments.

A year went by, and one day in the fall of 1998, Ben received a call from Charles, who acted as if they had spoken the day before. Would Ben be interested in going to South Asia to update those five case studies? Surprised, Ben asked Charles what the point was. He replied that this work could be of use in his new role. Ben reminded him that the cases had already been done three times– (if one counted the first rewrite) and that if tallied up the Bank would be paying to do the same work four times over. And besides, Ben added, the Project was over. No matter, said Charles, just tell me how much time you'd need, and I'll try to get the money.

Four months went by without a word, and then Ben got an e-mail from Charles saying he had been busy with other things but thought he could find some money for the work. Ben had to decide whether he should, five years after the original case study work, go off to revise data that had been revised two years earlier, and one year before that. Was this good money being thrown after bad, squared? Or was this déjà vu all over again?

Ben declined, and Charles probably went looking for someone else — that is, if he remembered to follow-up. It didn't really matter. As the Project faded in everyone's memory, Ben realized that all that remained was a happy glow. The Bank, the Swedes and the Dutch, and, of course, Charles all felt quite good about the outcome: yet another successful project.

CHAPTER SEVEN

The Professionalization of Development

As with getting organized to do something complex, so with becoming professional — it seems folly even to question such trends, much less suggest they have negative consequences. Yet in the case of development assistance, they do. In this chapter I focus on the professionalization of development: the ways in which the people who "do" what has become the "work" of development have come to think of themselves as trained professionals; the ways in which the language of development reinforces specialized knowledge, and how these tendencies have created another set of imperatives that is counterdevelopmental.

From Calling to Career

I may be romanticizing the past, but many people used to go into development as a kind of calling or vocation. Today, development is a professional career. Originally the movement to professionalize had some positive consequences. But of late, these have given way to negative ones. It seems somewhat obvious that once development became a career to which young people would aspire and for which they prepare themselves professionally, that career would begin to have a life of its own, a set of stakes and interests as in any other profession. One of those, of course, is to ensure not only that the career continues to exist but also that it is widely perceived as effective and commands respect.

From the 1940s through the late 1950s, development itself was not a profession. People came from other professions to work in the early institutions of what became the development industry. In the more formal institutions such as the World Bank, those professionals were engineers, hydrologists, geographers, geologists, physicians, and the like. Generally speaking, they were experts in technical or scientific fields. For some, no doubt, going abroad to underdeveloped countries to help develop them was not much more than an interesting job. But for a large percentage there was an element of idealism, and for not a few, an old-fashioned sense of calling.

In the less formal and smaller institutions that later became part of the industry as NGOs — the early voluntary organizations such as CARE and Oxfam — their voluntary character attested even more clearly to the aspect of calling. Indeed, many who joined early NGOs were not salaried.

The term "calling" carries the connotation of a strong inner impulse toward a course of action in the world. You are "called" to work in development by something inside you — a need to help, a sense of duty, an ideal about how the world should be. A related term, "vocation," comes still closer to this sense of being called. One of its original meanings referred to a "summons from God" to undertake a particular function in life. A calling, then, was sort of a secular version of a vocation. But whichever term one uses, there is (or was) an implied noble quality to such work in the world.

In the 1960s many people went into development work because they were idealistic, in some sense felt called. They thought of such work as deeply meaningful.

In terms of skills, many young people who worked in NGOs in the late 1960s and 1970s were different from the professionals in the World Bank and USAID or other large bilateral agencies. Whereas the latter were technical or scientific professionals, many if not most of us on the voluntary side of the development field were generalists. Still, both kinds of people, the young idealistic generalist and the older technical professionals, were bringing what they had to offer *to* development as opposed to coming to development as a profession in its own right.

And the sense of calling persisted, especially among the NGOs. One executive director of a midsize NGO in the early 1980s was famous for his marathon job interviews. A candidate for any but the lowest clerical jobs in his organization would spend an entire eight-hour day with the director. He would ask endless details about the person's parents, sisters, and brothers, about the individual's childhood and children. He'd ask the person if he or she had ever lied. He would probe into the candidate's beliefs. Around lunchtime he would tell the candidate what he was doing: he was looking for character, for idealism, for commitment. He cared much less about what the person knew. Two days later, if he had decided to hire the candidate, he'd get the person's salary history. Then he would make an offer, which was usually 15 to 20 percent lower than the last salary of the person. This, he'd say, was to make you put your money where your mouth had been.

Such an approach to hiring people is hard to imagine today. Development has changed. For one thing, one is not asked to starve to work in the industry. Although salaries in the for-profit private sector are higher, they are not so bad in the development field in general. A senior World Bank professional with twenty-four years of experience may make $130,000 or more. A USAID field officer or the country director of a Peace Corps program with about twenty-four years behind her may earn between $80,000 and $100,000. A twenty-six-year-old fresh out of school with a graduate degree in development studies may make $60,000 or more working for a development consulting firm, or if he chooses to go with an established NGO, he might have to start at $35,000 to $45,000. The chief executive officer of a medium-size NGO with an annual budget of $10 million may make as much as $160,000, while the president of a large one such as CARE may make over $250,000. The top daily rate for consultants at USAID is pegged to an annualized salary of about $100,000. Some short-term consultants at the World Bank may earn as high as $800 per day or $100 per hour.

This change also reflects broader changes in the world at large. The whole of the twentieth century has been a movement (most visible in the advanced economies) away from the so-called primary and secondary occupations (agriculture, mining, manufacturing) to service occupations and finally to what we now recognize as the mark of the twenty-first century— "knowledge" occupations. The economies of scale necessitated by capitalism's march and aided by technology mean fewer jobs in the older occupations and the need for more and more jobs to be created in the newer ones. This trend by itself explains the creation of some new professions, including those in development.

In the distant past we used to farm to live. We did not have to create the occupation of farming. Today we are actively creating occupations and subspecialties (along with new professions). But some of them have no more value than the fact that they provide work and to some extent status. Think about the new professions of marriage consulting, event coordination, or executive compensation analysis. Not too long ago these were jobs that one either did oneself (families planned weddings instead of paying someone to do it) or were simply part of another broader function. These are only a few examples of new professions that are as much responses to the need to create professional status for people entering the knowledge job market as they are responses to new needs in the marketplace.

Finally, idealism itself seems to have changed. If you were an ambitious sort thirty or forty years ago, you did not go into development. The development field, especially the NGO side of it, was often self-consciously "anti-ambition." But today, while most young people who choose careers in development still have ideals about helping others, they are also ambitiously concerned about their career and levels of remuneration. Let's call them "ego-idealists."

Thus, one of the things that has largely gone out of the NGO world is the voluntary character of staff. U.S.-based NGOs (and some prominent ones in developing countries) now seek to hire MBAs and others with postgraduate professional degrees, especially in management. There is a further irony: Those few (usually older) organizations which are still staffed by retired professionals who contribute their time to the cause are the organizations that are increasingly "out of the loop"—organizations viewed by the new professionals as irrelevant, ineffective, and, indeed, nondevelopmental. It is telling that such voluntary staff are seen, in the end, as mere "do-gooders," a term that has become one of denigration among those whose business it is to do good.

The Two Sides of Professionalization

I am not simply being nostalgic for an earlier time—lamenting the loss of calling and the professionalization trend in development. Everything has two sides, and for a while professionalization in development was a breath of fresh air. It did have a positive side. To understand that, it might be useful to go back briefly to the origins of the modern notion of a profession, in the nineteenth century.

While leadership in the military and work in the church had long been incipient "professions" embodying a "calling" (the core meaning of "profess" is religious in nature), it was the linking of these callings with lengthy formal preparation—and in turn with the rise of higher education—that resulted in the professions as we have come to think of them. The classic "learned professions" in the nineteenth century were theology, law, and medicine. But by the last quarter of the century, others were joining the professions, such as engineering and soldiering. All the professions now required some sort of "learned" preparation. As such they had considerable status; they were honorable. Yes, one made a living by practicing a profession, but that was almost incidental. The professions were more than mere work and certainly were not labor. Labor, from the Latin for "exertion," carried the connotation of toil. And though labor, or certain kinds of it, would come to be seen as respectable, even ennobling, no one confused labor with calling or profession.

As the kind of work one did in the world began reflecting notions of status and class, and as these were linked with kinds of monetary gain, it also became common to think of labor as a class of workers who earned wages, as opposed to profits or fees. Profits were the fruit of the entrepreneurial class. Members of a profession were still different: they received fees or compensation, neither wages nor profits. In every way, then, professionals stood apart.

No Longer Amateurs

We often use the term "amateur" as the opposite of the professional. The term is particularly interesting when we apply it to development. For one of the impulses for the professionalization of development was growing criticism (often from within) about how amateurish many of its institutions and practitioners were. And as development practitioners came to understand in the 1970s how much more there was to development than we had thought, the demand to professionalize became greater. This was especially so among the NGOs. They were often rightly criticized for being amateurishly run. "We need more specialized expertise," the NGOs said to themselves. "We need to be better organized, be more deliberate, institute systems for project planning, do less shoot-from-the-hip kinds of interventions." The larger agencies too told themselves that they could be more accountable, better managed, and more comprehensive in their mix of expertise and skills. It was no longer enough to have crossover engineers, geologists, and economists. Agencies began to adopt new management theories (it was during this phase that the "logical framework" came into being) and hire such new types of professionals as sociologists and anthropologists. As we in development began to sense that we were accomplishing less than we had hoped, it was natural to blame ourselves rather than the nature of the endeavor. So, across the board the perception grew that development itself needed to become a speciality — yet another profession that required formal training and preparation.

Soon, the demand was being met by academia. Many organizations and universities set up institutes or centers with specialized courses on development. Some offer postgraduate degrees in development. The Institute of Development Studies at the University of Sussex in the United Kingdom and the School for International Training in Brattleboro, Vermont, are examples. And the courses evolved as distinct from the international relations courses that traditionally prepared diplomats or political scientists. For example, the Agricultural Extension and Rural Development Department of the University of Reading (United Kingdom) International Development Centre offers, among others, the following for development professionals: an M.A. in "rural social development"; an M.Sc. in "agricultural education and training"; and a diploma in "rural extension and women." There are also short courses in "management skills for rural development" and "communication and extension for rural people." Other institutions offer the courses Poverty Alleviation Techniques, Famine Relief, Participatory Development, Population Policy, and Impact Assessment, along with, by the score, courses on development project management.

And, as in the older professions, professional development associations began forming, and with them, attending conferences became a standard part of everyone's calendar. Seminars on new techniques began to attract staff from many organizations. And specialized journals and publications became part of the "to read" pile next to every development professional's desk. From the late 1960s on, these proliferated: *Journal of Development Planning* (1969); *IDS Bulletin* (1969); *World Development* (1973); *Development and Cooperation* (1974); *Development Policy Review* (1974); *Journal of Development Economics* (1974); *Africa Development* (1976); *Public Admin-*

istration and Development (1981); *Asian Development Review* (1983); and *Development in Practice* (1991), to name a few. Specialized journals arose in the south too, such as *Lokniti* (the journal of the Asian NGO Coalition).

And all this was a reasonable response to a strong feeling that we had to do better. Indeed, whenever a small voluntary organization used to "throw money" at problems in the third world by indiscriminately doling out cash, seeds, or tools, it was right to accuse them of amateurishness. A strong dose of professionalism seemed warranted.

But making amateurs into professionals had and has other consequences. For there is a second meaning to "amateur"—loving what you do. Being an amateur in this sense does not mean that you are not good at your work but, as in sports, that you are not a member of an exclusive club and are not paid.

Creating Indispensable Expertise

A certain clubbiness, complete with its own codes and jargon, began to characterize development, just as happened with most movements toward professionalization in other fields. Social historians such as Burton Bledstein noted some of the negative consequences of the late-nineteenth-century movement to professionalize some other, older vocations: "The more elaborate the rituals of a profession, the more esoteric its theoretical knowledge, the more imposing its symbols of authority, the more respectable its demeanor, the more vivid its service to society — the more prestige and status the public was willing to bestow upon its representatives. Common sense, ordinary understanding, and personal negotiations no longer were the effective means of human communication in society. . . . Now clients found themselves compelled to believe on simple faith that a higher rationality called scientific knowledge decided one's fate. The professional appeared in the role of a magician casting a spell over the client and requiring complete confidence."[1]

Professionals also began, quite naturally, to have a stake in making themselves indispensable to society. They found ways to do so, according to Bledstein:

> The pattern of dependence was the most striking . . . consequence of the culture of professionalism. Practitioners succeeded by playing on the weaknesses of the client, his vulnerability, helplessness, and general anxiety. . . . Professionals tended to confide the worst, often evoking images of disaster and even a horrible death. The physician might hint at the possibility of an undetected cancer, leaving the patient to his own thoughts. The lawyer might threaten the client with high bail, a long trial, and visions of being locked up. . . . The insurance man might warn the client of sudden destitution and moral irresponsibility toward

1. Burton Bledstein, *The Culture of Professionalism* (New York: W. W. Norton, 1976), 94.

one's family. The accountant might confront his client with the discovery of fraud and financial disgrace. . . . The culture of professionalism tended to cultivate an atmosphere of constant crisis — emergency — in which practitioners both created work for themselves and reinforced their authority by intimidating clients.[2]

I don't want to carry the analogy too far. Development professionals do not intimidate clients; one of the ethics of the development profession is kindness and gentleness toward clients. In the current culture of development work, to intimidate would be "unprofessional." But development professionals do play a role in creating dependence on their expertise, even when, in the name of participation, they try to downplay their expert status or even because as professionals they are increasingly well paid.

Foreign Experts Get Paid Well

When, for example, it becomes difficult to find local counterparts (who are themselves supposed to be professionals) because low pay scales provide them with little incentive to work for their country's development, it is the foreign development professionals who fill in the "incentive gap." Over time the buying power of the wages of public servants in a great many developing countries has fallen to the point where even a high official cannot feed a family of four for more than half the year on his or her basic salary. Poor incentives for public servants is an endemic problem in many countries, especially in Africa. Any development professional from the "north" has entered a government office at 11:00 in the morning only to find that the key people he or she needs to see to make progress on a policy agreement or a development contract have left for the day because they are selling things in the marketplace to supplement their salary. As a World Bank study points out: "Difficulties in getting highly qualified nationals to work in the public service (low salaries, unsatisfactory working conditions, etc.) . . . increase the demand for short term TA [technical assistance], while impeding the process of long term institution building. . . . Government's working environment for local professionals is not attractive and is deteriorating in most . . . West African countries, prolonging dependence on foreign aid."[3]

Robert Klitgaard relates a case of a five-year development plan prepared under the auspices of the United Nations Development Programme (UNDP) for the government of Equatorial Guinea (West Africa) in the mid-1980s which "noted a vacuum of skilled people in government, which in the plan's eyes, would continue to justify the presence of high priced technical assistants from abroad." These foreign experts earned from forty to eighty

2. Ibid., 99–100.
3. Quoted in Robert Klitgaard, *Adjusting to Reality — Beyond "State vs. Market" in Economic Development* (San Francisco: ICS Press, 1991).

times the salaries of their Equatorian counterparts. Klitgaard calculated that the relatively few foreigners involved in this project were earning, in total, 2.6 times the government's entire payroll.[4]

It has become one of the great ironies of foreign development aid that some of its professionals are kept in business at the expense of or on the backs of the public servants in the developing countries who are supposed to be their "counterparts." But it is hard to see where the motivation to solve this problem would come from, either on the part of those poor governments or on the part of the foreign development assistance establishment. This is one of the many Catch-22s of development: the incentives for one group (the high pay and fringe benefits for foreign experts) are likely to prevent them from noting that the lack of incentives for the group they are trying to help lie at the heart of the problem they are trying to solve — the development of that nation.

The hard thing to accept in this and other examples of what really happens in development is the lack of a blameworthy culprit. Foreign development professionals are not to blame for the inability/unwillingness of developing country governments to pay public servants properly. But they have, nonetheless, become part of the problem they are there to solve.

And this example of dependency resulting from the "incentive gap" just skims the surface of the development professionalization dilemma. The kind of dependency creation in law, medicine, or accounting that Bledstein refers to is not half so serious. When a lawyer makes much of what will happen without his services or a doctor dramatizes the consequences of not following her instructions, there is no fundamental conflict of interest, only an effort to enhance status and authority. But because development is a different kind of endeavor altogether, to professionalize it — to the extent the process increases status and authority — risks awakening a dormant conflict of interest. For example, if it is in the best interest of the "client" to achieve self-reliance, then creating dependency on outside experts conflicts with that interest. Development, it cannot be emphasized too often, is *not* about doing things for clients or rendering them a service. As Klitgaard says about the use of experts, "Long-term advisers should be considered primarily as teachers: the justification for their great cost should be the transfer of their skills to nationals, not carrying out a specific assignment."[5]

The Need of Professionals to Take Action

The tendency to carry out "specific assignments," certainly part of the organizational imperative discussed in chapter 6, seems even further reinforced

4. Ibid., 94.
5. Ibid., 112.

once a field such as development becomes professionalized. For the professional "imperative" requires purposeful activity. The formal training of a
professional is just one thing that adds impetus to the imperative to take action. An admonition such as "Don't just do something, stand there!" would
sound counterintuitive to all professions. Yet in development it just might
be the better approach.

Over a century ago, Thorstein Veblen went so far as to suggest that the
need for effective action in our daily work is a human trait. He called it
the "instinct of workmanship": "As a matter of selective necessity, man is
an agent . . . seeking in every act the accomplishment of some concrete, objective, impersonal end. By force of his being such an agent he is possessed
of a taste for effective work, and a distaste for futile effort. He has a sense of
the merit of serviceability or efficiency and of the demerit of futility, waste,
or incapacity. This aptitude or propensity may be called the instinct of workmanship."[6] When this instinct of workmanship is coupled with both the professional and the organizational imperatives (which gave us the short-term
development project), the result is a powerful set of forces for doing just the
wrong set of things. Consider how naturally this can occur.

During a project contract for three years, the goal of which is to help a developing country government ministry "develop," it is natural for those foreign professionals hired to "implement" the contract to want to see results.
It is extraordinarily difficult for the professionals assigned to the project to
stand by and watch mistakes being made or see consistent incompetence
and not want to intervene and do oneself the things that need to be done.

Because the salaries of the foreign professional's local counterparts are often abysmally low, they, by contrast, may not be motivated to learn. Some of
them are so inadequately motivated that they are also likely not to be physically present half the time. Thus since the professional adviser cannot live
easily with himself sitting idly by without suffering a loss of self and professional esteem, he takes over the counterpart's task and, to paraphrase the
words of Nancy Reagan, says to himself, "Just do it." He forgets very quickly
that his assignment was to "teach" and not to "do." At the end of the day the
practical reality of many third world institutions means that just to teach,
not "to do," often becomes impossible.

Then there is the problem of feedback and legitimacy for the professional
development expert. By being part of a profession with its own jargon, styles,
and associations, we give feedback to ourselves that we are connected to
some kind of legitimate body of knowledge and hence authority. But the
expert also needs feedback that she is being effective in the specific project.
If she were teaching high school math, the teacher could measure results

6. Thorstein Veblen, *The Theory of the Leisure Class*, Mentor ed. (New York: New American Library, 1953), 29.

by looking at the grades the students received on their final exam. But when the professional's job is, say, to teach a national counterpart the art of being a financial manager, the subject matter itself, the nature of the setting, and the lack of any sort of final exam greatly reduce the professional's ability to measure results, especially since she will be leaving at the end of the contracted time period. Quite easily and quickly, "Here, let me do it" replaces "I'll show you how."

Veblen's instinct of workmanship helps explain why in actual practice the complex and subtle development endeavor is constantly recast as if it were nothing more than a series of concrete objectives to be planned and completed in the same way dams and roads are. It also helps put the professionalization tendency in development in a more innocent light. But it is that very innocence that makes what happens seem inevitable.

How the Literature of the Development Profession Reinforces the Image of Development as "Rocket Science"

In most professions, the literature produced is generally intended to share ideas and convey new research (for the authors there is a career-building aspect as well). In such fields as medicine, the law, and accounting, for example, most of what is written attempts to solve known problems of considerable technical difficulty. Development is different. While the obstacles are tremendous, they are not necessarily, or even usually, solvable with improvements in technique. Yet in keeping with the tendency to "do" development, just as with many of the courses, seminars, and degree programs, much of what is written in development comes across as "how-to" prescriptions for technicians. The literature of development thus reflects in large part a sort of "faux technology," a hidden desire to make what should really be an art appear to be arcane rocket science. Consider the following titles and descriptions from one of many development publishers:

> *Measuring the Process: Guidelines for Evaluating Social Development*
> *Sustainable Development: An Introductory Guide*
> *Managing Evaluation: A Guide for NGO Leadership*
> *Doing Village Assessments: A Guide to Action-Oriented Village Research in Developing Countries*
> *Participatory Development Toolkit: Training Materials for Agencies and Communities*
> *Tools for Community Participation: A Manual/Video Package for Training Trainers in Participatory Techniques*[7]

7. *PACT Catalog no. 106* (New York: PACT Publications, 1999).

Just as often the style suggests that an earthshaking discovery or a major scientific breakthrough has been made, when what is said is self-evident. Take the following blurb from a 1999 flyer for a recently published book titled *Impact Assessment for Development Agencies: Learning to Value Change:* "Impact assessment is a major concern to all working in development, both funding and delivery agencies. This major new book considers the process of impact assessment and shows how and why it needs to be integrated into all stages of development programmes from planning to evaluation. It argues that impact assessment should refer not only to immediate outputs or effects but also to any lasting or significant changes that it brought about."[8] That we need a whole book (and at this late stage in development's history, yet) to "argue" that what impact assessment should be concerned about is lasting and significant change, suggests strongly that the walls of the development profession have become so high that many inside the profession cannot see the real-world common sense that lies outside those walls.

Or what of this excerpt from a book titled *Creating Opportunities for Change: Approaches to Managing Development Programs:* "A development program is one that is designed to (1) carry out a nation's development goals; (2) introduce change in a society or community to increase its productive or organisational capacity; and (3) improve the quality of peoples lives, including improvements in the well-being of the poor."[9] A page later, as if aware that the above is too simple, the author adds:

> There is a fourth defining characteristic of development — namely, that it is carried out in what is often a hostile environment and always a difficult one. This is a very important element. . . . One of the limitations of development plans made by economists is that economists tend to ignore . . . complexity and think of implementation as the problem. . . . The reverse problem is also very prevalent — to spend so much time documenting the difficulties of coping with environmental problems that it hard to visualize change at all. Including the nature of the setting in a definition of development suggests that when problems arise, they do not necessarily stem from poor program design or even from careless implementation. They simply may reflect the difficulties managers confront and the fact that development managers are always working under problematic conditions."[10]

Here again is a commonsense observation couched in obfuscating language and carrying the idea that there is something to be done. The culture of professionalism has so overtaken development that the recognition that projects generally take place in infinitely difficult and problematic "envi-

---

8. *Recent and Forthcoming Books from Oxfam for Development Professionals* (London: Oxfam, 1999).

9. Louise White, *Creating Opportunities for Change: Approaches to Managing Development Programs* (Boulder: Lynne Rienner, 1987), 13.

10. Ibid., 14.

ronments" is reduced to "a very important element." The author then goes on, professional that she is, to solve the unsolvable by offering six "approaches" to development management: "The goal-directed analysis approach; The anarchy approach; The bureaucratic process approach; The institutional analysis approach; The social learning approach; and The political learning approach."[11]

As the development literature has burgeoned over the years, much of it assumes that doing development is, in the end, a matter of technique. The profession at large seems obliged to make that same assumption. The majority of the books and articles on development proscribe, advise, counsel, and tinker without the least self-consciousness about the deep contradictions inherent in the way we have cast the endeavor. Even those relatively few who see through the fundamental dilemmas of development continue to seek positive ways to solve them, and always from within the profession. No one draws what should be at least one possible conclusion — that we are fundamentally on the wrong track and should close down the industry as we know it. But to say that would, of course, be "unprofessional."

We all have egos, no matter what work we do, and it is natural for humans to inflate the legitimacy, importance, or validity of their occupation, especially if they are members of a profession. But in most professions there seem to be some checks on the distance that the self-delusional tendency can travel. In development, those checks are few.

The Ease of Self-Delusion in Development

In the development industry it is easier to live solely on impressions for longer than in other professional fields. In the scientific community, for example, if one's work is false, one's peers will soon discover it. In the corporate world, the situation is more ambiguous, but there too, if one is managing a company division and that division loses money, one may well be held responsible for the loss and one's image tarnished. But obviously in development, because of its complexity and the great hubris in assuming this huge task, there is no bottom line, no proof of right or wrong, but instead a host of poor but accepted proxies for these measures. The logical framework discussed in chapter 6, for example, sets out measurable objectives at the end of the project time frame. But invariably, because the project time frame is always too short (in real developmental terms), whatever measures they are will not be measures of lasting and significant change.

It is therefore relatively easy in development to get by on little substance. The sacredness of the development task, as well as the unimpeachable motive of the individual professional in the industry — to do good for others —

11. Ibid.

helps protect the overall raison d'être of the industry from being called into question.

The language of the development literature largely reflects this blind spot. For only the technicalities (the "how-to's") are questioned, and rarely if never the underlying philosophy. This goes-without-saying quality limits debate and helps to perpetuate the industry.

Too Many Cooks

Malawi, 1997

PROFESSOR K AND BEN wait outside the office of Minister Grace Lumba. The professor, a former high official in an earlier government, now works as a private consultant, as does Ben. Ben is the "outside" consultant on this assignment, brought in by the UN Development Program (UNDP) to assess Malawi's readiness for a new program in microcredit. Professor K is Malawian, therefore he is the "local consultant." For two weeks they have gone everywhere together, and the professor's contacts — he knows virtually everyone in the capital — have made the work go smoothly.

A large, modestly dressed lady comes out to greet them, apologizes for keeping them waiting, and ushers them into her office, a square room with a dirty window looking out on an alleyway between government buildings. Immediately, a tray with six Coke bottles appears. The bottles lie side by side on the tray; there are no glasses. For five minutes or so Ben, the professor, and the minister sip Coke from the bottle and chat amiably about nothing. Having finished, Mrs. Lumba grabs her large pocketbook and the group heads down the stairs and outside to a beige nine-seater van. As the professor and Ben stand there, another large lady comes up carrying two guns. She gets in the back, without introduction. Apparently she is Mrs. Lumba's bodyguard. For the rest of the trip she says nothing.

They drive to the Office of the President in another part of town. Here they are introduced to one of the president's senior economic advisers, who will accompany the group, and also to someone who, the professor tells Ben in a whisper, is "a princess" (apparently related to an important former chief). Princess Nalinga N'dagire is a pretty, thirtyish, heavyset woman one of whose responsibilities, it turns out, is Poverty Alleviation.

As the princess and the senior economic adviser climb into the van, two more women come down the steps: One carries a notebook and will take notes throughout the trip. The other carries a video camera. She, like the bodyguard, doesn't speak but will be recording the visitors at every stop on the trip.

The entourage is now complete. The princess, the economic adviser, the minister, the camerawoman, the notetaker, the bodyguard, the two consultants, and the driver set out for the countryside. As they ride out of the city, it becomes clear that Mrs. Lumba, whose full title includes the term "economic monitoring," is a lively and sharp lady with a cynical sense of humor. And it is she who dominates not only all conversation but also the group as a whole. The "economic monitoring" suggests she would know something about the microcredit field in Malawi. But two hours of discussion with her in the car and several more in the field reveal an uninformed woman with major disconnects in her economic thinking.

For one thing, she is a fanatic about honey. "Honey can be a major foreign exchange earner for Malawi," she declares, going on at length about it being a "high-value" export crop, using the current jargon of many economic planners in the region. Mrs. Lumba's air of authority and the supreme confidence with which she continues her disquisition on the special qualities of Malawi's bees, region by region, don't permit interruption or qualification. Ben keeps silent. He has had experience with honey projects in Kenya and elsewhere and nowhere in the world is it an export commodity. Local producers in the developing world have enough trouble making money marketing honey locally, even when there is demand. Honey produced by African small farmers, cottage industry–style, faces challenges that honey producers elsewhere don't even think about—finding a reliable supply of uniform containers is one, a reliable supply of tops for the containers is another.

As they go off the main road and start to climb into the hills on bumpy red-dust roads, Mrs. Lumba finally drops the honey topic. They pass farmers and other folks along the road. Other fixations emerge from Minister Lumba: How lazy the people are, how they've lost the work ethic, how the resources they have should be better used. She amends her remarks as she warms to the topic, singling out African men for special abuse. "Useless!" she shouts, as she concludes a litany about the African male's many flaws. The professor, the lone African male in the group, feels obliged to object. Mrs. Lumba waves his remarks away, repeating, "Just plain useless!"

After an hour, the van stops for the group's visit to the first of several model farms. As the group walks into the farmyard, Mrs. Lumba stops at a banana tree trunk lying on the ground. She waits a minute until the video camerawoman has positioned herself and then stoops to pull a long fiber off one of the leaf stems coming out of the banana trunk. She holds one end out to Ben. She asks him to hold it and then, holding the other end, begins to walk away cautiously. The two now hold the thread about four feet apart. "Pull," she says dramatically. As the banana stem fiber stretches to the breaking point and then does break, she says, "See how strong it is? We are trying to figure out what we can do with this as an export commodity," she adds with considerable portent. (Ben wonders: String? Rope? He can't quite see banana fiber rope selling in the True Value hardware store back home, but then, he admits to himself, he doesn't have Mrs. Lumba's enthusiasm about things.)

Ben and the others are on this little trip because the President's Office is experimenting with providing rural credit for high-value crops. The office wants to encourage selected farmers to grow crops with potential for export and thus is offering credit on attractive terms. Exporting agricultural commodities from landlocked Malawi means exporting by air. Therefore to justify the cost and the relatively low volumes of products that can be exported by air, the crops have to be what the world of commercial agriculture now calls "high-value crops." Potatoes, for example, would not be a good idea, whereas saffron would. Perhaps the most successful example of this strategy is the export of fresh-cut flowers to Europe from several African countries, including Kenya, Ivory Coast, and Zimbabwe. In theory such a strategy is eminently sensible, hence the Office of the President's experiments and

Mrs. Lumba's dreams of figuring out what can be done with the fibers in banana leaf stems.

The theory is sensible, but it is easy for the idea to go awry in practice, and that is what Ben suspects he is about to see. That Ben has been invited (the UNDP essentially told him he had to go on this junket or it would be bad for UNDP–Government of Malawi diplomatic relations) is one of the signs of how such things go awry. Mrs. Lumba's shoot-from-the-hip approach to what commodities might be good for export is another. In Ben's experience the President's Office is not the right place in the government structure from which to implement a program or even an experiment. It might be the right place to stimulate thinking about the concept or to pass on the order to do the homework to get it happening. Delegation of this high-value crops effort by the office to people like the minister for economic monitoring suggests that the president doesn't really trust his bureaucracy to do things any better than he can or that he wants very much to be close to experiments that he initiates. And the office's invitation to Ben and the professor to come and visit when there is not much to see leads to at least two conclusions: First, Ben and the professor, independent consultants, have no power to make funding decisions, thus the President's Office has not done much to determine whether it is worth showing the fledgling project to them. Second, the lack of much to see shows a naïvely innocent hope that one can sell an idea on the basis of very little.

They have come to see what turn out to be three failed (or stalled) experiments: one in silkworm production, one in egg production, and the third, a "zero grazing" operation for farm animals.

Apparently someone from the President's Office had gone out to this rural district, contacted some farmers, and suggested that they get involved in silkworms. The idea was that the farmers would put up the houses for the silkworms (with the President's Office sending experts to tell them how) and then the farmers would plant mulberry bushes (the leaves of which the worms feed on) and receive credits for the cocoons. As Mrs. Lumba explained, the idea was initiated because somehow the President's Office had learned that the Japanese would be prepared to buy one thousand tons of silkworms, whereas last year Malawi exported only one ton. Conclusion: The market is there.

Accordingly, two fairly well off farmers had spent the Malawian equivalent of three thousand dollars each, of their own money, putting up buildings designed to handle one and a half acres' worth of mulberry leaves for the cocoons to feed on. They then planted mulberry bushes and raised them quite nicely. When they were ready for the cocoons, the government's part of the bargain — the promised credit to buy the cocoons from the government-run research farm near Lilongwe — did not appear. When asked why the credit wasn't forthcoming, Mrs. Lumba's answer was ironic: "We didn't expect these farmers to move so quickly." And this after insisting over and over again for two hours that men in Malawi sit around playing cards and drinking. Yet these two men had indeed set up something and were wondering when the promises made to them would be kept. Mrs. Lumba understood this aspect of the situation well. Half to herself and half to Ben, she said: "Well, we'll have to sort this situation out or this will be a disincentive to the farmers."

The group goes on to visit the "chicken scheme." (The word "scheme" is used unselfconsciously in many parts of the developing world by aid and government officials as a synonym for project.)

After a short drive in the van, the visitors arrive at the small farms of several women who have built elaborate chicken houses, under the direction of the agricultural extension officers who were seconded (read "diverted") to this effort by the President's Office. Each woman had invested about $400 in building the chicken coops, then bought one hundred chicks with credit (apparently), though when asked what the terms of the loan were, how long, at what rate, and so on, Ben could not get an answer. They each paid $100 for the chicks ($1 per chick). It takes six months before the chicks are old enough to lay eggs, after which one can count on an average of two eggs every three days per chick. Given a total laying life of eighteen months, that is approximately 36,000 eggs. Sold at about 10 cents each, the average local price, the gross return would be $3,600. Buying feed for two years would cost $2,800. Thus the total investment in buildings, chicks, and feed would be $3,300, for a return of $3,600, not deducting regular interest payments on the loan and the cost of transport and, of course, assuming no losses among the original one hundred baby chicks.

The women are unhappy, which becomes clear as they begin to complain to the minister about a number of problems, including having to travel far to buy feed, and with unreliable transport on bad roads to boot. The minister suggests that the President's Office might "give" credit to one of the women in the group with which she can then buy feed in bulk, store it at her place, and sell it to the others at "a small margin."

At no point was there evidence of the intricacies of finance, of the studies that have been done in the country, or of what other development assistance organizations are doing, and yet the minister said repeatedly that she thought lack of coordination of activities was one of the problems they have. Another, Ben noted, was that the women didn't know how to cost their activities.

It was also clear that the people chosen to do these initial model farm "schemes" were the very well off. One woman had at least thirty acres of land and on one plot had made five thousand dollars from cassava.

But there are no facts or figures. These "experiments" are not experimental. Knowledge is neither collected nor built. It seems as if no one has stopped to ask, "How best should we go about this?" "Economic monitoring" would seem to encompass these things. Instead there is a rush to do something, anything, "now." The word "scheme," it strikes Ben, reflects this.

Mrs. Lumba and her colleagues are for the most part well-meaning people. Mrs. Lumba could easily be a haughty, phony, or arrogant person. She is not. She has many responsibilities, one of which seems to be to admit, and act on, the truth about the past. She is worried about how to get something done after (in her own words) "everything in Malawi has failed so far."

The entourage goes on to see another experiment on the same farm, this one in a technique called "zero grazing." Zero grazing is a relatively new concept and is being tried all over the third world. Essentially it is an attempt to concentrate and control both the intake and output of the animal by putting the animal in a small space and bringing the food to it. The animal's waste products, instead of being spread haphazardly over a large area, are now collected and thus become usable as fertilizer and even as fuel. Altogether there is more return on the investment, especially for the poor farmer or family that might own only one cow or a few goats.

The visitors approach the model zero grazing scheme, which has just been completed. A small corral was built for the family cow — actually it is more like an outdoor stall. A pit for collecting the cow's manure and urine has been erected in concrete alongside the stall. It is clean and solidly built. The yard has been swept for the visitors, but an old shoe sticks out of the ground, and yellow plastic halves of jerry cans are piled in one spot. As Ben, the professor, and Mrs. Lumba's entourage walk around the area surrounding the stall there is junk everywhere. All the while they are being videotaped by the heavyset camerawoman who is intent on her work. Behind her walks the woman who takes notes. After ten minutes they come back to the zero grazing stall. Here on this farm everything is ready: the stall, the mulberries, the manure pit, the building for the cocoons (which is nicer than the main house). But Ben wonders whether once the actual cow comes to occupy the zero grazing stall, the urine pit will quickly become clogged and overflow, as he has seen happen elsewhere, and the stall will fall into disuse.

But maybe, and it *is* possible, the relatively privileged model farmer will make extra income, at least for a while. And maybe her model farm will "sensitize" the people and they too will want to plant mulberries and begin zero grazing. But then again, because the others in the community are not as well off as these model farmers, who will put up the money to make the initial investment in buildings and concrete?

Questions like these are not asked, swept out of the way by the enthusiasm of Mrs. Lumba and her dutiful entourage. The princess in charge of Poverty Alleviation has said nothing. She is treated with deference by everyone. Ben has no way of knowing whether she follows what is going on, cares about it, or takes her Poverty Alleviation brief seriously. As the group climbs into the van for the next stop, Ben hopes so.

Rhetorical Support

Netherlands, 1998

THE WOMAN BEN SPOKE with on the phone had a Dutch accent, but because the organization she represented had an English name, he didn't realize it too was Dutch. The name — World Initiative for Poverty Eradication, or WIPE — though awkward and more than a little unfortunate, sounded to Ben like those of many development organizations. He had never heard of it.

Marie Louise identified herself as the new head of research and evaluation for WIPE. She wanted to know if Ben would be interested in leading a team of consultants to look at how her organization was positioned for the future. Ben said he might, but he had a number of questions to ask first. What *was* WIPE, where was it, and what did it do?

He thought it odd that Marie Louise responded to the first by actually reading WIPE's mission statement over the phone from the Hague: "WIPE exists to fight the outrage of poverty . . . to join with the poor and the pro-poor in effective action to overcome the injustice that causes

246

poverty."[1] She explained that WIPE is based in Holland, has an annual budget of $65 million, over three thousand employees in twenty-three countries, with plans to expand in the first decade of the new millennium to Burma, Central Asia, and northern Latin America. Ben was shocked to learn that it was the second largest NGO in the Netherlands.

"But why are you calling me?" Ben asked. "It seems strange you wouldn't use a Dutch consultant for this."

Marie Louise was candid. They had lined up several Dutch consultants, but for various reasons — scheduling, other commitments — they were no longer available. Their board was now pressuring the organization to move forward with the exercise which was supposed to have been done that summer. Marie Louse had called various contacts. It was Ramesh Kirwali in India who'd given her Ben's name.

Ben now understood. As had often happened, he got work by default. The first, second, and third choices were unavailable, and so Ben got the work. And Ramesh knew that Ben was now semiretired and likely to be available. But Ramesh also knew that Ben was not easy on organizations who wanted their work evaluated. Had he told her that too? Ben asked.

Marie Louise laughed. Yes, they knew about Ben's reputation. In fact, they wanted someone who would tell it to them straight.

Ben asked who the other team members were. Marie Louise explained that they had not yet been contracted, but they had in mind using three others, all from the third world: one, a former WIPE executive from Africa; the second, a consultant from South Asia; and the third, an individual from Indonesia. They would all report to him, and she would send him their curricula vitae as soon as they had an agreement.

"OK," Ben said, "I'm interested." He then proceeded to tell Marie Louise his daily fee.

"Your fee is a bit high, but I think we can do it. But can you fly to Holland next week for two days to meet our new CEO and discuss the details?"

Ben flew to Holland and arrived at WIPE headquarters, located on three full floors of a large office building. He was immediately sent into a round of meetings with senior staff members. None of the men wore ties or jackets. Everyone worked in open cubicles, except the director of

---

1. This and the other passages quoted in the story are taken from actual documents of the organization on which the story is based. The name and other identifying details of the organization have been changed.

policy, who had a kind of playroom, a glass-enclosed space with colorful pillows on the floor and no furniture. Ben met in succession with the human resource and organizational development director, the policy director, the fund-raising director, the finance and information technology director, and the three regional directors.

By midafternoon on the first day Ben was beginning to sense some contradictions at WIPE. All the senior staff talked about decentralization and how unbureaucratic the organization was, but the number of staff positions in headquarters and the lines of authority upward to the directors in the Hague were those of a large, old-fashioned bureaucracy. By far the largest unit was the fund-raising division. Its organizational chart was a maze of functions and subfunctions. Under its director was the operations manager, under whom was the head of Dutch fund-raising, the head of German fund-raising, and the heads of two other European fund-raising operations. Separate but parallel was the International Fund-raising Development Division, under which was the manager for training and support, under whom was Systems Support and International Funding Planning, under which was the funding coordinator and two international systems officers, as well as the manager for international donor information, who had under her two communications officers and two administrators. Following a black line that moved back and forth as it went around various other boxes on the chart, Ben managed to connect the head of international media and publicity to the operations manager as well as the box marked manager, Management Information and Corporate Development. On and on it went. The fund-raising division alone had more than a hundred staff. The fund-raising policy director had thirty-two staff directly under him.

Ben was not surprised to learn that in its new, more efficient future the organization projected that its support and overhead would take up *only* 27 percent of WIPE's resources.

It also became clear to Ben that WIPE had a heavy culture of commitment to participatory process and internal consultation. People he met talked constantly about "buying in" and "ownership" — no decisions were to be made until the majority of staff had "bought in" and "owned" the concept. People talked about "task forces" and "iterations" of task force reports. Some reports, Ben learned, would routinely go through five iterations because the drafts needed to reflect the views of hundreds of staff who'd been consulted. The titles of meetings reflected this culture of getting everyone "on board." The bulletin board in the main conference room announced a meeting on the "approach to the Asia strategy" and another "to agree on the planning framework for the development of country plans." Most aspects of planning seemed to be kept permanently at one or two removes from closure.

Ben wondered if countless workshops and endless process substituted for action. As people opened up more in the two days of discussions, some began to joke (if not exactly complain) that one period of preparation for something glided imperceptibly into the next period of preparation. Not only is there the uncomfortable feeling that nothing ever gets finished, but added to it is the sense that there is no time to implement plans properly because as soon as they begin, they are revised. Everything seems to be in a state of iteration. In one WIPE country program, the country strategy preparations for the 1994–99 five-year plan, supposed to be finished by the third quarter of 1993, ended up taking all 1994, with tens of workshops, meetings, and retreats, and involved everyone.

At lunch on the second day, Ben met with the new CEO of WIPE, Philippe Mazrui. By this point Ben was beginning to get nervous about the organization's tendency to revise and "iterate," so he posed several conditions to Philippe, in the event Ben was to be offered the job. First, he explained that he would prefer to write the final report himself, taking into account the views of the other consultants. He did not want to get into the mess of trying to incorporate four separate reports into one. Second, he would write a polished first draft and would listen to corrections on factual matters, but in the end, if Ben felt that there were objections to some of his conclusions on the grounds that he was being too hard on the organization, he would not rewrite. Without discussion or objection, Mazrui smiled and agreed.

They then began talking about WIPE, beginning with Mazrui's recent appointment as CEO. Philippe Mazrui may have been brand new as CEO, but he had been with the organization for fourteen years in two of its field offices. A man from the "south" (he grew up on the island of Réunion, the son of a Lebanese father and an African mother), his placement was apparently meant to create an image of change. WIPE talked a great deal about "equity," transparency, and partnership with the south. Philippe's presence in the Hague was putting WIPE's money where its mouth was.

Like most new CEOs, Philippe wanted to chart a new course for the agency. He said to Ben that he wondered if perhaps WIPE was equipped to take on its new strategy. He handed a document to Ben. Ben read the title: "Attacking the Causes of Poverty — WIPE's strategy, 1999–2005."

Ben flipped through it quickly, pausing at page 10, where the organization's four new major goals were listed: "(1) Poor and marginalized people will increasingly be able to realize their potential; (2) The anti-poverty movement will be strengthened; (3) International constraints to poverty eradication will be mitigated; (4) Gender equity will be enhanced." Ben looked up, his brow furrowed.

"Pretty heavy stuff, if you're really serious about it. I mean this is kind of taking on the whole ball of wax all at once, isn't it? You don't even talk about anything modest like alleviating poverty or reducing poverty. You guys talk about *eradicating* it! And you're asking me to lead a team to tell you if you're equipped to take this on? Save your money. Nobody is!"

Philippe laughed. "Well, we *are* serious about it. You will come to learn how serious an organization WIPE is. And why shouldn't we be ambitious? I doubt there's any organization in development as ready as we are to do this. Wait till you meet our people. Every last one of them is dedicated to eradicating poverty."

"Has your board approved the new strategy?"

"In a way. You see, what you have in front of you is the draft. It is still being revised. But the broad outlines have been vetted over the last year and a half through scores of meetings all over the WIPE world. The board has given its go-ahead."

"But," Ben raised his eyebrows, "wouldn't it have been more logical to undertake the exercise you're hiring me for *before* deciding on the strategy? I mean, shouldn't you first take stock of where you are and what your real capacities are before throwing these enormous goals at the feet of an organization that might not be able to carry them out?"

"Well, yes, I see your point. But we *will* be able to carry them out. No one doubts that. What we expect you to do is tell us what enhancements we need to be better able to do it well."

"Oh," Ben said.

Ben then went off to a small office for an hour and a half and came out, as he'd been asked to, with a rough outline of the process and a tentative schedule. He left this with Marie Louise and took a cab to the airport.

On the plane home, Ben began calculating what this exercise was going to cost WIPE. His own trip to the Hague had cost them $3,400, including airfare and expenses. It was decided that parts of the organization would feel left out if the consultants did not talk with or examine that part of the operation. And though it was recognized that the consultants could not visit every program, they would visit seven countries, two of which were chosen because their directors were senior in WIPE and would have been insulted had they been left out. Simultaneously, four more consultancies would take place, one to look at marketing, one at finances, one at governance, and one at emergency relief operations. Ben figured all this would come to about $155,000 in fees to the consultants.

The lead consultant (Ben) was then asked to take a three-day trip to a Central American country to attend a meeting, after which all the consultants were to meet in the Hague for a week of briefings, coordination, and further "buy-in." This adds another $18,000 in travel costs. Then the four-consultant team is to take the major field trip, at a cost of over $30,000 in travel. During the trip the team is to have weekly debriefings by phone with the CEO so he can know their findings as they travel. At one point in the trip in Africa, three key persons from the regional office of the organization will fly 1,500 miles to have an afternoon meeting with the team. And on their last stop of the trip, also in Africa, the CEO and an assistant from the Hague will fly down for a day to meet the team before it disbands.

Then the team will split up to write their final reports, which Ben will read and then write his own draft. He will then be flown to the Hague for the day from the United States to discuss the draft, after which he will presumably make any agreed-on changes to the report. Then it will be presented to the board, for which Ben will again be flown to the Hague.

When Ben added the internal costs of WIPE staff time devoted to putting all this together plus the communications costs and the time involved to copy and send thousands of pages of documents for the consultants, the total cost of the exercise would be about a quarter of a million dollars.

Ben calculated that one experienced senior person using a well-chosen sample of visits and projects could do this work alone at a total cost of no more than $45,000. Was an additional $200,000 being spent basically to ensure "buying in"? Ben began to see that the term could be interpreted literally.

In the for-profit world, the concept of spending money to make money is understood. Of course, the for-profit world is not always efficient. Money, and lots of it, is wasted. To be sure, an outsider might question a trip where three employees were sent halfway around the world to attend a short meeting. And a public corporation has a responsibility to its stockholders to make money and an implicit commitment not to waste it. But what counts is, and has always been, the bottom line.

Is there a profit at the end of the day, and is that profit growing? If so, then the money wasn't wasted.

Then there is proportionality. What is cost in proportion to potential gain? This will always be a judgment call in a corporation. Feedback, in any case, will always come to answer the question of whether in the aggregate those costs were based on good judgment calls. If the feedback is negative, costs will be cut, product prices will be raised, or both.

There is also motivation. The employees of the corporation are an asset and an investment. How they perform for the benefit of the corporation will depend to some extent on the structures and procedures of the organization (that is, the organization of the organization) but to a larger extent on their motivation. In the corporation, motivation is less complex than it is in the nonprofit world of the development industry, but not without its own complexity. How one is treated is not just about money. Corporations might question a travel budget and have travel rules, but many allow business class for international travel and stays in five-star hotels. The conventional wisdom is that this promotes motivation and enhances productivity.

On returning home Ben began receiving daily overnight express packets of papers from the Hague. He quickly began thinking that if this was an indication of the next few months, he'd better add 10 percent to the cost estimate he'd made on the plane. At the end of his first ten days back he had a stack of reports, country reviews, country strategies, country budgets, regional summaries of country plans and budgets, regional strategies, resource allocation projections, audits, organigrams, three-year plans, five-year plans, minutes of recent staff retreats, briefing papers from six departments written especially for Ben, communication strategy papers, reporting timelines, personnel lists, and, finally, a series of "SWOT" analyses.

There were too many papers to stack in one pile — it would have fallen over. Ben cleared space on his floor, made three neat stacks, each about ten inches high, and left room for a fourth. Colleen, Philippe's assistant, had written a cover memo to the first packet in which she told Ben that one person had been assigned full-time to cull through the WIPE files for all documents that might be relevant to the exercise. There would be more.

Ben groaned as he came into his office on the first day he'd allocated for the work. There was nothing to do but burrow in. He began going through the stacks.

When Ben had first worked with NGOs in the 1970s, the people he'd met were the development equivalent of Marlboro men — rough-hewn, down-and-dirty, field-oriented people. They would jump into the villages of the third world and punch poverty in the nose as if it were a personal insult. "Develop first, ask questions later" would have been their motto had they had any facility at all with the spoken word. But they had not. Forget about reading and writing — they were all about action. Words were for bureaucrats and other pointy-headed obfuscators, not for real development workers.

Perhaps in the mid-1970s, certainly by the 1980s, NGOs started writing things down. As the calls for professionalization came in louder and louder, they began writing things down more and more systematically. Soon NGOs got the religion of strategic planning; they were imitating big business and government. But without the discipline of needing to make money, the documents just grew and grew. Strategy papers could be 150 pages; memos were routinely ten pages long, single-spaced, and carbon-copied to everyone. The thinking of many NGOs had always been a little flabby. Translated to the written word, it became fatuous.

Turgid writing is harder to read than good writing. As his consulting assignments always meant wading through heaps of development writing, most of which is turgid, Ben had gradually taught himself to get what the author was trying to say by skimming from beginning to end in a minute and then randomly reading a paragraph on every page or so. Still, he was unprepared for the WIPE assignment.

He opened a document: "The Strategy has been formulated to support and facilitate the overall strategy of the organization. Within this model, it draws upon intrinsic functions which are necessary for a need-based and interactive strategy."

Ben would rub his eyes. The words seemed pretty clear, but he wasn't getting it. He'd skip through the paper and then go back and read random paragraphs. He was still confused.

He opened another document: "WIPE is characterized by the intensity of its long-term relationship with poor and marginalized people and the issues that affect them. This engagement gives us a distinct perspective that encompasses a valuable diversity of grassroots experience and contact from around the world, and perspectives at the national and international level on the causes of poverty and the opportunities to overcome it. The long-term nature of our work allows us to build intimate relationships with poor people based on mutual trust, which gives an almost unique insight into the blight of poverty and insecurity. This trust enables us to take innovations and risks in meeting the challenge of poverty eradication which contribute to our learning and the learning of others."

He waded through it. Ben rubbed his eyes again and this time lightly slapped his cheeks to try to make himself more alert. He'd read only two documents. Better continue. He picked up a third and read the cover memo:

> We felt we wanted to get across that the strategy should be seen to value diversity and give people enough room to "own" their own functions. We used an analogy (for fun) of a school of sharks. They swim all over the place but stay basically together. To move them a mile to eat a large tuna fish, the leader might attempt to coerce them to follow in a straight line behind him. In that case the leader will fail or entirely squash their spirit. In any case the school will fail to see the opportunities that only just pass them by as they swim a narrow course in a docile straight line. Alternatively, the leader might simply say "there's a fat tuna over there — see you there in 5 minutes." Lastly, he might try to be a sheepdog and bustle around trying to get the frantic mass of sharks to broadly go in the direction of the tuna but of course be steering a large group which progresses on a broad front and somewhat gradually towards its goal though able to spot larger shoals [sic] of tuna along the way. At present we are probably too sheepdog-like.

Ben's chin came slowly down to rest on his palm. His head began to lean. His eyelids became heavy. He sighed once and drifted off. He was in a zoo, surrounded by sheep. No, maybe they were dogs. Or was he in an aquarium? There aren't any sharks in a zoo.

He shook himself awake. This isn't funny. I've got one week to plan for this assignment and get a handle on this organization, and I can't find a single piece of paper that describes what they actually do.

Maybe the SWOT analyses will help, Ben thought. SWOT stands for "strengths, weaknesses, opportunities, and threats." Devised originally for commercial companies, it's a simple set of headings used to help an organization assess its position vis-à-vis its market and its competition. If used well and with rigor, it can tell management what needs to be done to solve problems and improve profits.

Ben opened the SWOT analysis for WIPE's program in Indonesia, one of its largest. Under strengths, he saw written at the top of the column "competent organization," followed by "high competence in development work, with committed and hardworking staff and a good working team, with enthusiasm." Under weaknesses he read "limited management capacity at all levels; staff still lacking knowledge and experience in development work, high staff turnover; need to improve analytical capacity, staff difference in culture between expats and locals, language barriers." Was Ben missing something? Didn't the weaknesses cancel out the strengths?

He threw Indonesia's SWOT on the pile and picked up the one for the Sri Lanka program. Under strengths it was noted that WIPE/Sri Lanka "works on a broad range of issues," while under weaknesses it read that "WIPE/SL's range of activities has grown so diverse that we sometimes run the risk of spreading ourselves too thin." Under strengths was written "WIPE/SL is a thinking and learning organization, with an internal drive to change," but under weaknesses it said "WIPE/SL has not always been adequately reflective, and internalization of learning has sometimes been slow." Under strengths, "WIPE/SL is an organization that has a high capacity to manage change," while under weaknesses, "WIPE/SL has at times exhibited an inability and unwillingness to address internal problems squarely."

The pattern repeated itself as Ben whittled down the piles of documents and came upon the SWOT analyses for the other WIPE countries.

Three Months Later

The assignment had been grueling. The travel part alone had been a whirlwind of compulsive comprehensiveness. Ben and the team had covered seven countries and visited fifteen major projects, interviewed scores of villagers, dozens of officials in government, and scores of heads of other organizations, as well as over 250 WIPE staff in various capacities. Ben himself had logged over forty-five thousand air miles and bumped along in rickety trains, cars, jeeps, and trucks for another two thousand or so. He'd taken hundreds of pages of notes and used up several pens. He'd lost ten pounds.

Amazingly, despite their differences, which were not small, he and his three fellow consultants had come to the same conclusion. They generally agreed that the gap between WIPE's rhetoric and self-image and the reality of its work was enormous. WIPE was filled with dedicated and committed people but was an extraordinarily ineffective organization. Part of the reason was certainly its overblown bureaucracy and its exasperating tendency to iterate itself to death. The organization was also muddle-headed. It had no sense of when to say no, what to take on and what not to, or how to build expertise in any given area. Invariably, whenever it seemed to be getting somewhere, it would drop what it was doing and change directions, following who knows what — perhaps the wind. As a result, it threw money at problems. It spent much energy on public relations to enhance its image, and the clarity of what it told its sponsors left, to say the least, something to be desired. But worst of all, wherever it intervened, it left behind a trail of raised expectations and considerable dependency. It was not only *not* eradicating poverty but in some instances making things worse.

WIPE was not a bad organization, just overly earnest and more than a little self-deluded. The obvious challenge for Ben was how to convey all this to the CEO and the directors. But Ben had said in the beginning that he wouldn't mince words, and so he did not. In a sixty-page report, Ben distilled his own notes and the views of his three colleagues. He sent it to Marie Louise on time.

Sure enough, a week later during his postreport visit to WIPE headquarters in the Hague, appeals were made to soften his tone and perhaps be a bit less hard on the organization. Ben decided that perhaps he could make some stylistic changes. Then he flew home to make them and produce the final report.

Two weeks later he flew to Holland for the final presentation. At a large round table sat all the directors and Philippe Mazrui. Ben summarized the report. Several people then stated that they appreciated the team's candor and that many of the report's conclusions resonated with deeply felt ambivalences that a few of the directors had always felt themselves. Then, turning among themselves and ignoring Ben and his team, a lively discussion went on for the next two hours. By noon, it had been decided to form a drafting committee to write a corporate reply to the report which was to be attached to it before it went to the field programs for their review. This would take some time as it would need to be vetted by all senior staff. It was also decided to set up a number of task forces to ensure the continued forward movement of the new five-year strategy.

Mazrui closed the meeting by thanking the team and saying that WIPE was as committed as ever to continue the good work it was known for. And while some small adjustments needed to be made, it was, he wanted to reassure everyone, clearly one of the best and most effective poverty eradication organizations around.

CHAPTER EIGHT

Marketing Development

A cousin of mine in California refuses to go to funerals because they are "too depressing." She does not deny death; she knows that the people whose funerals she avoids are dead. She simply prefers not to walk up to reality in all its full-frontal three-dimensionality when she does not have to do so.

Like my cousin, the general public's avoidance of a negative message about poverty has become more urgent. Poverty *is* depressing and threatening. Polls show that Americans want little to do with poverty in the third world. Perhaps this is because of our prosperity or how tenuous we feel about its continuing. But it may also be because people can take only so much cognitive "noise" before they turn it off. Poverty is less and less a phenomenon with quick or easy answers, and the more we recognize that, the more we want to hear the opposite message. And when that message does not work, the public's next best preference is to look away.

But whatever the reasons, it seems that at the beginning of the twenty-first century the window of opportunity to explain development fully, even to the few members of the public who are potentially willing supporters of international development programs, is smaller than ever. This poses a double dilemma for the hundreds of private organizations in development that try each year to raise money directly from the public. Obviously, they have to devote more energy to inventing newer and slicker ways to "sell" poverty. But a deeper consequence is that the low tolerance for the truth is itself a threat to effective development, for in trying to sell it without the full truth, many organizations undermine what they should be trying to do.

The Power of Positive Thinking

Because of the obvious set of emotions surrounding the topic of poor children, a good entryway to the dilemma many organizations face is to look at the phenomenon of child sponsorship. And while child sponsorship is a specialized kind of approach in development, the distortions and twists that go into such fund-raising are not so different in kind from those which other types of organizations use.

Most child sponsorship organizations have Web sites and run television advertising campaigns. Here is an example of a TV campaign that appeared in the mid-1990s.[1]

> SCENE 1: A bearded white man is walking through a village somewhere in Africa. He talks about the children — about their hunger, their impoverished condition — notes that thirty-five thousand of them die every day, and then tells us that we have seen the pictures before, many times (he does not show us these, however). "But what do you do," he asks, "if little Senente arrives on your doorstep and sits down right next to you?"

> SCENE 2: The picture of a pretty, smiling little girl comes on. Her name is Senente. She is clearly poor, but she is not miserable (this is the "after" shot). "Well," says our host, answering his question on our behalf, "you feed her, you give her clean clothes, and you put your arms around her." He does not put his arm around her, perhaps because it would be perceived as patronizing (or, these days, as child abuse).

> SCENE 3: Then he explains that [name of the organization] is dedicated to "eliminating hunger and disease from the reasons children die." "That," he adds dramatically (and defiantly), "is a doable task. Your $21.00 a month provides one child with good food, life-saving medicine, and the education to extend his good fortune into the next generation."

It is hard to appreciate how "loaded" such texts as this are, since we see them, inevitably, within the framework of all present-day advertising and communication. But they rest on top of an archaeological pile of buried images of poor people, past miseries (flood, famine, disaster, war), and, above all, recurrent disappointments (if we're over forty-five we remember being told before that we can make a difference in solving problems, just as we know that these problems persist and even worsen). In the 1980s, private development agencies in America began using the word "donor fatigue" for this cumulative effect, which is what these appeals are implicitly trying to combat.

When CARE, one of the first large private organizations to solicit money from the public, began doing so in the post–World War II era, its ads simply asked the public to help by sending a package of food or clothing — hence the "CARE package." The pictures shown in the ads were of misery, plain and unadulterated: children crying, mothers struggling, and no one smiling. The appeal was easy to comprehend: war-ravaged families needed help to get back on their feet; war, the cause of the need, was also simple to understand; the people in need were likewise familiar to us; and finally, the solution itself was simple and doubtless effective.

---

1. See, for example, the Web site of World Vision (<http://www.worldvision.org>), which in January 2000 had text beginning "Changing a Child's Life." Or see the Web site of Childreach (<http://www.childreach.org>), the opening line of which in February 2000 was "What Makes Childreach Different?"

These early ads were not cleverly manipulative. They did not need to be. The text and the subtext were the same. The messages and pictures said clearly: "These people are starving. They need your help. Please give." People gave.

It is debatable whether there is more misery in the world now than there was then, or whether misery is more important now than before or in some sense of a "higher" quality. The Black Death of the fourteenth century, of which we have no photographs, must have been awful to behold, but so was Hiroshima, Vietnam, and Ethiopia in the mid-1980s famine, which we know because we have seen the photos. It is futile to compare miseries. Clearly, however, what has changed is that our own *access* to the misery of distant others has increased with photography, television, and the Internet. There is no historical analogy to this level of access. The visuals used in the above TV ad take this into account. The scenes we see arrive on top of a twenty-year history of media bombardment of the mass publics of the industrialized West.

As the competition for attention has grown in the modern world, philanthropy has not been exempted just because its organizations are nonprofit. Techniques of segmenting the "market" for philanthropic giving are highly sophisticated, and thus each viewer, each addressee, becomes a target not once but often. The sheer number of appeals, their consequent repetitiveness, and the heroic efforts to make them appear different from one another have all become transparent. In short, the sophistication of the effort to seek the caring person's help has itself contributed to donor fatigue.

Add to that the Western public's new cynicism—a knowledgeable questioning of whether these organizations really do any lasting good (the phrase "Band-Aid approach," meaning something that solves a symptom but not a root cause, has become part of our everyday language)—and the new instinct to look away from misery because it might "spoil my day," and one begins to understand the layered subtext of the various child sponsorship appeals. Message 1: The starving child is out. The smile and hope are in. Message 2: Love is in. You, the viewer, are brought into the picture (*you* are asked to imagine putting *your* arms around little Senente and are reminded of how nice love feels). Message 3: We recognize your cynicism, but it is inappropriate. You should feel slightly guilty if you are skeptical about solutions; the task *is* doable. And (here comes message 4, "the good deal") it can be done for only $21 or $24 or $26 a month. Positivity is here in spades, and with it the hope that donor fatigue can be overcome.

Every fund-raising executive in the world of poverty giving will agree that undergirding all these layers (and the best way to overcome donor fatigue) is a connection to people. That is why child sponsorship exists as the basis for many quite large NGOs. The child, any child, elicits feelings of protection and love. Just as sex, status, and power are the subtexts in much product advertising from cars to chocolate, in the world of philanthropic giving, the subtextual levers are not so different. The levers are love, a little guilt, and also power, though of a different sort — the ego gratification that comes from being thanked by grateful people.

Even when there is no direct child or people-to-people connection, development organizations find ways to create a message based on love, guilt, or ego gratification. Here, for example, is how the fall/winter 1999 newsletter sent to the donors of a small American NGO led off its appeal: "Giving Till It Feels Good. . . . Without our donors, [name of the NGO] would just be a set of good intentions. In each issue . . . one of our donors shares the motivations, experiences, and rewards that come with making possible the good that [name of the NGO] does. Here we have a moving testimonial from [name of donor]: . . . 'These are questions that burn in my belly. What does make a difference? How can I, a single human being, do something that matters? How do I give in such a way that empowers? What's the best use of my resources?'"

Accountability

The old CARE package contained the donor's own clothes or food the donor purchased at the grocery store or took off the pantry shelf. Moreover, the package was often wrapped on one's own kitchen table. This must have been a satisfying experience for the giver. The physical reality of it linked directly to the moral simplicity of the act. The clarity of that act meant that accountability was assumed and the word itself unspoken. All the organization did (in this case CARE) was set up and run the distribution system — logistics.

Two things have happened to change that earlier relationship between donor and receiver. First, the public has come to be comfortable with the notion that nothing is given away for nothing. It does not deny, as it might have in the less self-involved 1940s or 1950s, that the giver wants some kind of ego gratification in return for his or her gift. That ego gratification takes many forms, from being moved by gratitude to the simple confirmation that I, as a giver, am doing (and being) good.

Second, much of the public is aware of the possibility of corruption. No longer confined to Hollywood or to politics, corruption now shows up on the school board, in the church, at the firehouse, in the Boy Scouts. Cheating and finagling in the charitable voluntary organization sector was not a big surprise when the United Way scandal arose in the 1990s. The giving public is thus more wary. As a result, now, in addition to the expectation of an ego/emotional return on one's investment, the giver wants not only reassurance that the receiver is not going to do anything bad with the gift but also *proof* that her money will not be misused. She wants to know that it is going directly to where the ad suggests it will. She even wants to know what percentage of the donation is used to pay for the ads that will solicit other donations. The responsible giver now calls up the National Charities Information Bureau to find out what percentage of the organization's annual budget is used for administration.

This is the age of the caring donor with the green eyeshade. Givers want positivity (or at least less negativity) and at the same time are cagey squinty-eyed sorts who want to bean count and make sure you are not fooling them. Organizations that solicit the public's money for development work respond to this new demand by declaring themselves "accountable." But accountability has added further to the soliciting organizations' bind. For every field-worker for a major child sponsorship organization knows that little Senente and little Pablo are not directly receiving all these dollars each month.[2] The reason they are not is because simply feeding them, clothing them, and giving them medicine is *not at all enough*, nor will the contribution to their education extend this dubious good fortune into the next generation. The day-to-day reality of the NGO project in the field is, as ever, fraught with overwhelming complexity. NGOs know this now. While many organizations still feed and clothe and give medicine, they know better than ever before that giving things away does not, in the long run, help. If they are serious about eliminating the reasons children in the third world die, then they have to be involved in much more than medicine and food. Otherwise it is not development. It may be charity, but it is, in the end, still symptomatic relief; a Band-Aid. The problem has become that knowing this is of no great help because the rhetoric of fund-raising begins to affect what NGOs are able to do.

Rhetoric and Reality: The Negative Feedback Effect

Private development assistance organizations need to raise money. And given the state of the current market, they also need to make their messages inspirational appeals to love, guilt, and ego. But what happens to the effectiveness of development work as the result of this somewhat innocent collusion? The most pernicious thing that happens is that the necessary simplemindedness of the message gets fed back to the development organization itself, which begins to buy its own message. Ironically, in the name of accountability, the organization's work can tend to match the simplemindedness of the message.

Again, a comparison with the commercial world is revealing. When Godiva chocolates sends an advertising message of sensuality and status to the

2. See story 13 for an example of how child sponsorship is often distorted once the process gets to the field.

consumer, the company is not confused about its mission in life. The employees know they must continue to make a high-quality chocolate product that will fetch a high price. And while at a corporate retreat someone with a flip chart may get up and say to all assembled that Godiva is in the "sensuality and status" business, everyone knows they are first and foremost in the high-quality chocolate business. The demarcation lines between rhetoric and reality are clear to all.

Not necessarily so in development.

There is a wonderful Catch-22 in development fund-raising. Because the public generally gives money when the message contains one of the crucial three elements of love, guilt, and ego gratification and because there are rules for nonprofits which have to be obeyed (both formal rules set by the government and self-imposed rules of accountability that are the product of past wrongs), the recipient organization is forced to focus on relatively narrow (and hence relatively simpleminded) constructions of what development work is about. And because these organizations have colluded — however innocently — with the donors in the illusion of love, guilt, and ego gratification, they have given up the opportunity to receive open-ended, unrestricted funds, which are admittedly much harder to get. As a result, their freedom to do more real and effective development work is still further constrained. Let us look at some of the dimensions of this Catch-22.

Nongovernmental organizations are rightfully scared to be caught in a lie. So they are committed to public scrutiny and "truth in advertising." All child sponsorship organizations do try to ensure that a real child is out there and that some of that twenty-one-dollar donation is getting through to the child, in a way that would satisfy an accountant. And when such an organization invites the donor to see what his or her help is doing, it is a sincere invitation. The donor will have to see some of the benefits going directly to the child or the child's community. This aspect of accountability understandably reinforces direct transfers. But as I have shown, development — to the extent anything effective can be done by the international development assistance industry — has to be less and less about direct transfers of goods, services, and wealth and more and more about the indirect fostering of systems and institutions.

Here is an example of how the collusion of donor and NGO works to constrain the NGO. Say five thousand individual donors respond to a child sponsorship NGO's appeal over the course of a year. They commit $21 per month ($252 per year) and are assigned a child. The average donor might imagine, if she thought about it at all, that there are children by the thousands waiting to be assigned. But these children have to be located and recruited in a process that can be a rather tricky balancing of agendas for the NGO. Say the NGO wants to expand its work in a particular district, but some villages are remote and cannot be reached easily. Those villages are in fact more needy than others, but because child sponsorship usually means regular communication with the assigned children, the NGO needs to look for new child assignees in areas that are more accessible. Thus, in an odd way, the recruitment of children can be as much about serving the needs of the donor as it is about serving the needs of children.

Given the figures in this hypothetical example, the five thousand donors would make $1,260,000 available annually for direct sponsorship. Because donors have been implicitly promised that all or most of their money will go to a specific child, other moneys must be available for the administration of the local program. These come from grants and other kinds of donations. (As an average in the industry, most private voluntary development agencies figure about 4–5 percent of their income goes to administration. By comparison, about 10 percent of income is the average for fund-raising expenses. But these amounts can be substantial. For example, in 1997, World Vision's fund-raising expenditure was $38.7 million [11 percent of its total income]; in 1999, Christian Childrens Fund's fund-raising expenditure was $12.1 million [10 percent]; while the giant NGO CARE spent only $15.5 million, a low 4 percent of its income, reflecting the fact that the bulk of its money comes from government contracts.) And because of the need to ensure that most of the money — in our hypothetical case the $1.26 million from the five thousand sponsors — actually goes to the children, the volume of children needs to be high so that the small sums extracted for fund-raising and overhead can amount to something.

Suppose that in Village X in Africa there are three subprojects under way. One is a school for blind children; the second is a community health project involving water purification, midwifery, a local prescription drug distribution program, and a primary healthcare clinic; and the third is an agricultural assistance project focused on improved seeds. The total number of beneficiaries of these projects is calculated by taking the entire population of the village as well as its catchment area (since the clinic also serves other villages nearby). Let's say this total is 400 families, with an average of 6 persons per family, thus 2,400 people. Of these, the NGO headquarters may take a selection of 100 families and assign two children in each to sponsors. Thus, 200 children times $252 annually makes for a budget allocation from individual sponsors to this village of $50,400. This money might be used as follows: to support part of the costs of the clinic ($22,000); to the agricultural seeds improvement project ($18,000); and to the school for the blind ($10,400). In this way the NGO can honestly say that "your $21 per month provides food, lifesaving medicines, and education to Senente." To spend the $1.26 million at $21 per month per child, about 25 such villages need to be brought into the NGO's country program, with similar kinds of projects in each.

What is wrong with this picture? First, we can see the potential for the tail to wag the dog. Despite the rhetoric about development being "demand-driven," what actually begins to happen is that the supply of projects needs to be increased to meet the supply of donor income. But not all villages are alike, poverty in each may and will differ, and the sheer absorptive capacity for certain kinds of projects may not exist. (The real-life contextual complexities of development—lack of infrastructure, economic mismanagement, a poor policy environment, and cultural traditions that are not suited to these projects—are additional limiting realities.) But it is in the obvious interest of the agency to try to be efficient in the use of this $1.26 million. As a result, custom-tailored projects that take much longer to develop are not really an affordable option, and thus a cookie-cutter approach becomes inevitable, despite the NGO's knowledge that development should not be like that.

But why, the reader may ask, do we need five thousand donors and $1.26 million in the first place if this sum reinforces a supply-driven approach? The answer is the need to pay the NGO's overhead, and a sufficient amount can only come from volume. If, for instance, the NGO claimed that 4 percent of my $21.00 per month was to go to administration, that is only $10.08 per year from each donor. To pay the CEO, rent the headquarters building, and pay for the airplane tickets of the "project officers," a percentage strategy is not good enough—there has to be volume.

Second, to use the money in a way that promotes the message about individual children requires spending additional money that does not go to the children or the projects. Obviously, the administration of the communications connections between the child and the donor itself takes time and money. The children and their families must be met with, selected, and photographed. Then letters, photos, and regular reports must go back and forth between the child and the sponsor. All this requires staff time at both ends of the organization—the headquarters and the country program. As a donor I expect that part of my twenty-one dollars goes to fund-raising and a small part for running the organization, but do I want to pay for the letter or drawing from little Pablo that comes to me each month? That's a bit like paying my child each night for a goodnight kiss. More important, I would have to ask if this makes developmental sense.

Not only child sponsorship organizations get caught on the cusp of tricky dilemmas like these. Most NGOs do, and the dilemmas are further deepened by the latitude allowed in the laws on fund-raising. While the U.S. government is concerned with fund-raising costs, it does not specify them in detail. Nor do the two major accounting entities in the United States, the American Institute of Certified Public Accountants (AICPA) and the Financial Accounting Standards Board (FASB), such regulatory agencies as the Internal Revenue Service, or the individual states. But there is a guideline known as "the black book" in the trade: the *Standards of Accounting*

and Financial Reporting for Voluntary Health and Welfare Organizations.
This document is the source of standards to which most U.S. NGOs adhere.
It states that "voluntary health and welfare agencies are expected to report
as fund-raising the expenses of all activities that constitute an appeal for financial support. By their own nature, fund-raising efforts may include a very
wide range of activities."[3]

The guidelines are extremely wide because they take into account the realities of fund-raising. But the fund-raising agency, under scrutiny and dealing with a public that wants to have its cake and eat it too, has every interest
in using these guidelines narrowly. For most NGOs, especially child sponsorship NGOs, believe that it is in their fund-raising interest to suggest to the
public that nearly every cent of that twenty-one dollars per month goes to
Senente or Pablo or to the project, even though this is not in the best interests of development. Just at the time when thinking beyond "Band-Aid
solutions" is widely accepted, the tricky bind the NGO gets into when it
appeals to the public on the basis of love, guilt, and ego gratification and
when it promises accountability, results in having recourse largely to Band-
Aid solutions.

The Dilemma of Finding Unrestricted Money

If—and this is a big if—a development assistance agency is serious about
development as a long-term process of largely indirect stimuli and not a series of time-bound projects, it needs to seek unrestricted funding. A certain
amount of unrestricted money allows the agency the freedom to think and
plan long-term and to cover a portion of fund-raising cost; it is also crucial
in giving the development nonprofit agencies the room and the courage to
experiment.

But the tendency on the part of private donors to want to identify with
projects and programs, to want "accountability" in terms of benefits to the
community, and to want the ego gratification and love that comes with the
smiling faces of grateful poor people works against the chances of NGOs
getting unrestricted money. Many donors, small foundations in particular,
will negotiate with an NGO to see what projects they might like to "buy
into." These will be ones that appeal to their boards or to the interests of the
directors, and it is important that they be able to place a "flag" on the project. There are countless projects in the developing countries where sign-
boards are placed at a site with the words "this project is sponsored by." Unrestricted money, money that is not linked to a direct project, is thus hard to
come by. And while government agencies such as USAID do not have to

---

3. *Standards of Accounting and Financial Reporting for Voluntary Health and Welfare Organizations* (1989), 49.

produce smiling faces quite so readily, they too share the dilemma. Their moneys are not entirely unrestricted, and the complexities of accountability for a bilateral development assistance agency can even be greater than for a private NGO.

The cynic may argue that in the modern world "everything is sales." This may be true. But development assistance is one of the few industries in which the selling of the product actually feeds back negatively to the product, altering its quality and making it less effective. There are a few other realms where that kind of negative feedback occurs. One is the art market; Robert Hughes wrote about the boom of the 1980s: "The art-market boom . . . has distorted the ground of people's reaction to painting and sculpture. Thirty or even twenty years ago, amateur or expert, could spend an hour or two in a museum without wondering what this Tiepolo, this Rembrandt, this de Kooning might cost at auction. Thanks to the unrelenting propaganda of the art market this is no longer quite the case, and the imagery of money has been so cruelly riveted onto the face of museum-quality art by events outside the museum that its unhappy confusion between price and value may never be resolved."[4]

Another realm is America's public schools, with the new emphasis on accountability. Again, though the intentions behind the push for accountability are understandable and warranted, the outcome may not be desirable. The solutions under way—more testing and more uniform testing—as many critics point out, could result in a far too narrow emphasis on passing tests to the possible detriment of real learning.

The Seductiveness of Small Successes and the Denial of Complexity

The most important negative consequence of the feedback loop in development fund-raising is the denial of the complexity of development. As organizations increasingly emphasize "results," "accountability," and connections with people in their sales pitches to individual donors (and even to small foundations and other corporate donors), they are obliged to do more tangible work, aimed more directly at the poor, and hence more work that can be programmed into bite-sized projects. It is only when they work in this way that they are going to be able to report success.

Around Christmastime, many NGOs send out letters signed by their chairs, presidents, or founders. These are increasingly similar in tone. They tell of successes, of personal visits to projects and programs, and of happiness and hope in the third world. The message is that "your help has helped indeed," and you are thanked for the support and urged, not so subtly, to continue to give.

4. Robert Hughes, *Nothing If Not Critical* (London: Collins Harvill, 1990), 21.

After telling an amusing story about a visit to a village in Central America, the chair of one NGO says: "I tell you this story of two weeks ago to give you a sense of how hard your contributions to the [XXX] are working. As I visited community . . . members in village after village and talked to women like Dona Magarita and Consuelo Flores, I heard the stories of women making profound changes in their lives through their own efforts — and the assistance of [XXX] and friends like you."

A second organization, larger and more established, with projects at a somewhat bigger scale, also working in Latin America, sends its Christmas letter:

> In this 20th anniversary year, [name of the NGO] has been the focus of considerable attention. Accolades have been received and awards presented. We have been congratulated in the press and commended by foreign governments.
>
> We are grateful for the increased interest in [name of the NGO]'s work. But as [the year] draws to a close, I am reminded that it is not we who deserve the applause.
>
> First and foremost, it is the low income farmers of [country x, country y, and country z] who have brought us to this anniversary. They have invested their hearts and souls in building enterprises, and the harvest is theirs. . . .
>
> Last week I returned from a tour of [name of the NGO] projects in [district name]. I met several groups of farmers and posed a question that I've often asked in the past. "Why are you working so hard to make your enterprise succeed?" And the reply was familiar; I've heard it again and again through the years: "We are doing it for our children."

Though we know that the CEOs of these development assistance organizations did not actually write these Christmas letters themselves, the messages are surprisingly truthful in a generic sense. The poor of the third world who are in direct contact with NGOs in their villages and on their farms and who receive direct benefits in the form of seeds, loans, or advice and counseling are people who have been left out of and isolated from whatever their often corrupt governments are able to provide in the way of service, infrastructure, and support. Because they have been regularly exploited, ripped off, and lied to, it is not surprising that they now are deeply grateful for any sustained and genuine attention. They *do* have hope, and they mean it when they say they are doing it for their children.

It is the truthfulness and the moving nature of these small successes that makes them such seductive adjuncts to the feedback process. What president of an NGO or any development organization president, even the head of the World Bank, could go out to the field and hear such stories and not come away thinking "We must be doing something right"?

The problem is not that the stories are untrue. The problem is that these successes — in terms of development — are relatively meaningless. I want to emphasize the word "relatively" because I want to head off the reader's indignation at being told that the renewal of hope in a poor person's life is a meaningless achievement. It is meaningless only to the extent that this kind of story avoids dealing with the much more important and challenging realities surrounding poor people in many of these countries.

Again the reality is mixed, complex, and different, even at the very level of these stories themselves. Many of the children for whom these poor parents are now hopeful will want to migrate to the overcrowded cities, rather than be farmers. Some of those for whom the parents manage to pay the school fees will want to be bureaucrats in a nonfunctioning government and wear their fingernails long to show they are not manual laborers. A few will want to do nothing but drink Coke and watch MTV.

More important, if nothing is done to change the economic and institutional context in which these people live, these new hopes are as likely to be dashed as the ones before them were, as virtually all the evidence we have over the long term suggests. And as I have pointed out often in this book, we have not yet found a way to avoid some element of dependency creation in any direct intervention with people who are poor, and this is especially the case where the nature of the economic and institutional environment in which the interventions take place is unable to support or sustain whatever new initiatives these people may make.

The Paradox of Ambition in a Competitive Environment

While many if not most development assistance NGOs (as well as some other types of development organizations) live on the horns of these funding-related dilemmas of money versus soul, project versus process, and the seemingly inevitable negative feedback loop that they create, there is another choice. That option is to remain small, live within their means, and quietly chip away at poverty in their own way. But ambition has taken hold in the industry. Just as in the world of commerce, "grow or die" has become an unquestioned axiom of organizational life in development. The sentiment is driven in part by the self-importance that comes with years of being thanked — "these people need us and so we must do more." We must, in today's parlance, "scale up." But it is also driven, ironically, by competition, and this phenomenon has three aspects. First, competition exists for the philanthropic and the public dollar — there are more and more competing good causes outside the world of international development to which individual donor and public money is attracted. Second, there is competition *within* the industry — more organizations compete for a stable if not shrinking pie. And, third, there is competition from outside the industry — more development occurs as the result of investments by the private sector than as the result of the development assistance industry.

The magnitude of charitable giving to all causes in the United States simply dwarfs not only what U.S. NGOs receive but what the entire development assistance industry worldwide receives. In 1991, for example, all U.S. charitable contributions totaled $124.77 billion. This is greater than the entire extant portfolio of World Bank loans to the lesser-developed countries in 1989 ($114.5 billion) and almost twelve times greater than the total official assistance to the third world donated by Japan in 1990 (which had then become the largest donor in the world).

To add perspective, of the $124.77 billion in charitable giving, $103.13 billion came from individual donors (the rest from foundations, corporations, and bequests). But where did it go? What attracted these individuals? International aid was close to the bottom of the list, only slightly ahead of environmental and wildlife causes. Only $2.59 billion of charitable contributions went to the international category, while $67.59 billion went to religious organizations. The rest went to education, human services, health, public social benefit organizations, and arts and cultural endeavors.

Still, international giving went up 2.1 percent from 1990 to 1991, from $2.23 billion to $2.59 billion. This extra $360 million is, of course, a lot (the budgets of some of the largest U.S. overseas organizations such as SCF, Childreach, and so forth are in the range of $100 million per year).

But everywhere one looks for larger perspectives, the point becomes clear. The development industry is small compared with potential sources and the potential other claimants to those sources. It is this fact which makes almost all development assistance agencies feel compelled to grow in order to hold on to "market share."

Competition is also on the rise within the industry, in part because private agencies want to receive more public money, which dollar for dollar is less expensive to get than private. In the United States between 1973 and 1986, for example, USAID assistance to U.S. NGOs had a twelvefold increase, as detailed in chapter 2. The same NGOs' private-source income experienced an almost threefold increase. In effect, U.S. NGOs went from using public money at a rate of about 5 percent of their total to about 20 percent.

But it is the rise of the indigenous local NGO sector which is the biggest threat to the older private agencies in the advanced economies, for the public moneys are showing signs of favoring funding of this new sector. From 1987 on, the proportion of USAID funding to local indigenous NGOs in the category of child survival, health, and AIDs has grown steadily. As shown in detail in chapter 2, U.S. NGOs in 1987 received 4.6 times as much USAID funding as indigenous NGOs. By 1990 the U.S. NGOs received only 2.6 times as much. And while all OECD countries have increased their totals for development assistance, the pie is not expanding as fast as the numbers of organizations who want a piece of it.

More important, as noted earlier in this book, private flows of money to the developing countries since 1992 have overtaken official and voluntary contributions to development assistance. And, as the globalization takes hold, the likelihood is that the proportion of private flows to official and voluntary flows will grow. I will discuss the role of these private commercial investments in fostering development in chapter 9, but it must be said here that, at the least, the effect on the potential to increase official flows is a dampening one. This simply puts more pressure on the development industry to get a message of effectiveness out to its constituents. And to do that puts agencies even more in the feedback cycle that is so pernicious.

This industry has become one in which the benefits of what is spent are increasingly in inverse proportion to the amount spent—a case of more gets you less, both in absolute terms and in developmental terms. It is likely (this cannot be clearly demonstrated statistically) that as market share grows as the result of successful fund-raising, so do "production costs," which in effect increase the proportion of the growth that goes to the organizations themselves and can easily diminish the portion that trickles down to the poor. But, more important, as donors are attracted on the basis of appeals emphasizing "product," results, and accountability, not to mention love and connections to people, the tendency to engage in project-based direct-action development becomes inevitable. Because funding for development is increasingly finite, this situation is very much a zero-sum game. What gets lost in the shuffle is the far more challenging long-term process of development.

Unintended Consequences

Kamuli, Uganda, 1998

BEN HAS BEEN ON ROADS like this so many times that he worries he'll forget which country he is in unless he takes careful notes. He removes his steno book and pen from his shoulder bag and forces himself to start, though he'd rather doze off. While the jeep bumps along, he shakily scribbles a couple of boilerplate notes just to get his hand used to the effort: "Classic development dilemma — how can you help people become self-sufficient?" Then he looks out the window and continues: "A single-lane dirt road to a place called Kamuli, north of Jinja, thirty miles or so from Wanyange where one week ago Bill and Hillary Clinton had arrived by chopper to visit a CAVIB village banking group. Hillary Clinton's fifth visit to a CAVIB project. CAVIB is now one of her favorite American NGOs. She has seen their work on three continents. She has said that the kind of work CAVIB does is a real answer to poverty. I wonder if I'll see some things about CAVIB on this trip that Hillary did not. For one thing, Hillary and Bill sure as hell did not come out to see the Kamuli rock breakers."

Ben sees small cleared plots here and there along the road. The terrain feels surprisingly flat, since the jeep is rolling up and down through low undulating hills. Everything is green and seems densely planted. In the distance are larger hills, distinct in their separation from one another, as if they were dropped randomly down from above like so many Mason's Dots, the candies Ben used to eat at the movies when he was a kid. The farmers' plots are small and only partly cleared for planting: a hundred square meters of open land, then dense ground cover, then another clearing of the same size. A farmer might have a total of an acre or two, some coffee trees, some bananas, some root vegetables, a few goats, a few cows—not enough to call a "herd." Maybe once in a day's drive one might see fifteen lean cows. The soil is darker than the usual laterite soils in this part of Africa, but probably more fragile than it seems.

There are no villages along the road. Ben sees a few schools, all unfinished and simple, very few houses larger than a hut, and every couple of miles a small cement block church with a wooden cross on top. There are no signs of health clinics or any official government presence except the police station on the edge of Kamuli. There have been no other vehicles traveling either way in the last forty-five minutes.

The jeep pulls into Kamuli. The town is at the end of the road. Beyond is the "bush." Kamuli's insubstantial buildings give it a Dodge City aspect at first. But Ben wonders what drives the place. Unlike Dodge City, nothing is evident, such as being on the way to somewhere else or being near a mine or other resources, like cattle. Yet in a low-key way, there does seem to be movement and activity here. Amid the dust are signs of fits-and-starts private development. Ben sees buildings that look to be in midconstruction—two courses of bricks, bent rebars, a pile of corrugated sheets on the ground waiting for the roof trusses. Work on these structures has begun, stopped, continued, and stopped again. There is only one real street in the town, with rows of sewing machines, a few hardware shops, sundry supplies, and a bar at one end. But those are the formal "established" businesses. A lot more is happening off the main street.

Kamuli is a microcosm of an early mercantile economy—all petty trade, little manufacture, and what is made is local and for local consumption. It's a tiny economy, an extension of the family household, just having come out of centuries, no, millennia, of subsistence living.

But the economy is quietly humming. With little exaggeration, it seems virtually everyone (children included) has become a trader and businessperson. Everyone is a buyer and a seller. At every place where people might congregate (the school gate, the one gas station), there is an open market where traders sell.

This democratization of the marketplace is new, here as elsewhere in the country. Where once trade — both retail and wholesale — was in the hands of a few and distribution was through a few shops, now it is in the hands of many people, and distinctions between strictly retail and strictly wholesale are blurred. This rise of "penny" capitalism in the trading sector, by pushing the profit margins downward in society to more, and poorer, people, provides greater assurance that the market system will survive the kind of fluctuations Uganda had seen in its turbulent recent past.

While the financial benefits to the small trader are not large, they are nonetheless a form of redistribution. More cash is flowing more widely and penetrating the countryside's lower social strata more deeply.

Seeing all this, Ben nods. If there is peace, as there now is in this part of the country, people will take their lives into their own hands, and some kind of economy will form. He wonders how much, if any, direct help they really need to do this.

In Jinja or in the capital, Kampala, trade is robust. There is a vast marketplace where a varied range of goods is for sale. But in outlying and more rural areas, as here in Kamuli, the marketplace is basic. The same few commodities are for sale everywhere. Sellers deal mainly in food basics; soap, matches, a few cigarettes; beer and soda; occasional rickety orange-crate furniture. The biggest "service sector" business is bicycle repair (n.b., the main internal transport is the *boda boda*, a bicycle that is used as a taxi — there is no extra seat, the passenger rides on the frame, that's how basic the service sector is here). Then there is a dealer or two of kerosene, fuelwood, and timber or bricks; a slightly larger number of dealers in tin and plastic household wares; the same number in sundries; and then a still larger number of dealers in clothing, much of it second-hand. The newly minted Wharton MBA, armed with theories about value added, product differentiation, "branding," and competitive advantage, would be wasting his or her time here.

A woman purchases a sack of rice in the morning and has sold it by evening. A man patches three or four bicycle tires in a day. They have each made a small profit of fifty cents to a dollar, which they then can spend on necessities, school fees, or a school "uniform." (Ben knows from research that the women are more likely to spend this income on their families than the men.) The next day they do the same thing. Their "businesses" are marginal. The purpose is survival, cash flow, not business growth. Very little sets one woman apart from other rice sellers; likewise, nothing much makes the man's tire patches significantly better than those of the man next to him: all the rice sold is the same, there is no price competition, and there is no learning curve associated with being a specialist in rice or a tire repairer — one is as good at these trades after the first week as after three years.

This is minicapitalism in which margins are shared widely and cash (often the very same banknote) moves around so quickly and so often that it never lands in a bank. It is a people's movement to spin a thin web of commerce and enterprise, just enough to keep the cash, and hence their own lifeblood, flowing and themselves involved, albeit peripherally, in the larger world.

This is one-notch-up capitalism, the first step above subsistence, one minute into modernity.

But what do people spend money on? The same woman who trades in rice is a buyer to the woman two stalls away, who sells secondhand clothes, and vice versa. The buyers and sellers alike consume the same commodities: food, medicine, school uniforms and fees, secondhand clothes, simple kitchen utensils, beer and soda, local transport.

And though Kamuli is not on the railroad line or sitting atop some high-demand natural resource, something is driving the town. Perhaps it is simply cash and ambition. In the way that a new nation's myriad inscrutable parts begin to cohere and connect, Uganda, since the peace that Yoweri Museveni brought back to the country in the late 1980s, has become — spare and thin though it may be — a fabric of interwoven threads. Even end-of-the-road Kamuli is part of it. In fact, the road is the thread, but it would be of little use were it not for the peace, fragile though it may be. The peace has allowed ambition to rekindle. On the road, men and women travel outside to buy and sell, and men especially go far outside, to the army or to other countries, and send back money. That is the money which is behind some of the shops and which is tied up in the unfinished buildings.

But there is no wealth to be seen, other than the unfinished buildings. Everyone is still poor, though perhaps now there are three or four or six degrees of poor. That is progress. But it is also not part of the culture to flaunt. Indeed, the wealth here, to be romantic about it, is still social. There is social capital. There is family capital. And that may well be what keeps folks' cash flow uneven and why the army man wants to sink his cash into the first four rows of concrete block on one side of a building as fast as he can. One Ugandan says: "You know how it is. One minute you have some cash, then someone in your family needs help."

Ben puts away his notebook and stops writing. The jeep comes to a stop in the middle of the town. It's Saturday. The men who are not part of the trading activity appear to be idle, sitting around in clumps, two and three here and there. That's what the men do, Ben thought. They may look idle, but they are not. They are repairing small holes in the social fabric. The women are, as usual, busy working.

Ben has come here to visit some CAVIB borrowers. CAVIB, the American NGO that Hillary Clinton so admires, began offering small business loans to rural Ugandans a while back ("microcredit"), and Ben is here to evaluate the program. But what he really came to see, and is most curious about, is a new business he has heard about—rock breaking—which started up five years ago. Ben has been told by some fans of CAVIB that rock breaking is a major income earner.

All the rock breakers are on one road leading west from town. The driver asks directions, and they motor out about a half a kilometer, stopping at a small compound. In front of the house, right next to the road, are neat pyramidal heaps of quartz-filled rock broken into two- to three-inch pieces, about a wheelbarrow's worth to a pile. Ben counts seventy-five piles to the left of the compound.

This, it turns out, is Mariam's work. Mariam, the young wife of the head of the compound, has broken up these rocks with the help of her young children.

Mariam is caught by surprise. Ben has arrived unannounced and accompanied by the chairlady of one of the CAVIB groups of which Mariam is a member. Mariam, Ben guesses, is in her early thirties. Dressed in a faded orange polyester shirt filled with holes and round greasy spots and a long wraparound, equally dirty, she is standing on the edge of the compound as the jeep pulls up. Ben and the chairlady get out, and before they can say a word, Mariam laughs, raises her hands, and says to Ben, "You are welcome, sah."

The compound is clean swept, and behind the main hut stands a three-quarter-finished brick building. Some goats and children mill about.

Within seconds, four chairs appear. Ben has been visiting Africa for thirty years now, and while he makes no claims about understanding its complex cultures, he no longer worries about intruding, nor is he diffident about accepting hospitality. He sits down and explains in two sentences why they are here. Then he starts the questions right away; it's hot and he's got work to do. "Which group do you belong to?" he asks Mariam. "Kamuli Stars," she says. She joined CAVIB in May 1997, and her group consists of twenty-eight women. Other groups are called Kamuli United, Muafu Asokera, and so on; there are fifteen groups in all, and over four hundred women in Kamuli have joined CAVIB. The Kamuli Stars women are in their second loan cycle.

CAVIB stands for Community Action for Village Banking. It is an American nongovernmental organization that works in a number of countries. CAVIB's founder credits himself with having invented "village banking," a way to lend capital to poor people who have no assets and get the money back. The CAVIB approach is to go into an area, organize groups of women into borrowing groups, called village banks, lend capital to the groups, which in turn lend to their members. Ben has visited many such schemes. The theory sounds good, and the village banks themselves seem impressive in their first year or so. But studies have begun to show that problems begin to arise in the second and third years of these projects. More important, there's been no rigorous evidence yet that these loans move people out of poverty.

Ben asks to see Mariam's passbook. She returns with it in a minute, wrapped in a plastic bag, tied with a string. Mariam's first loan, like that of the others in her group, was 100,000 Uganda shillings (USH; at today's rate, 100,000 shillings is about $87). The rules for CAVIB in Uganda set the loan term at sixteen weeks. The loans must be repaid at that point, and after a week's break, the group enters the next cycle. She borrowed 135,000 shillings ($117) in cycle 2, and her latest loan, that of cycle 3, began last week when she received 170,000, or $148.

Kamuli Stars meets with the CAVIB "credit officer" every Tuesday at 8:00 in the morning. Mariam walks to the meetings. Ben asks her how long it takes. She seems confused. She doesn't know. Ben shrugs. He's supposed to find out what the client's "transaction costs" are, but if she doesn't care how long it takes her to go the loan group meeting, this may mean she doesn't perceive the walk as a "cost." He decides not to push it.

Next Tuesday she'll make her first payment of 14,025 USH, or $12. This amount represents 12 percent interest for the sixteen weeks, added to the principal and divided by sixteen; plus a compulsory savings of 20 percent of her loan, or 34,000 USH, also divided by sixteen. The savings are held by CAVIB in her name. So the total of principal, interest, and savings is 224,400 USH, divided by sixteen weeks, the amount she has written in her passbook. The dogma in the microcredit field, of which CAVIB is part, is that nothing is free. Ben asks Mariam how much she paid to buy her passbook; she paid 1,000 USH ($.87). She also had to pay a 1 percent "affiliation fee" to CAVIB International (based in Washington). That 1,700 shillings was collected on the day she took the loan, so she is really paying interest on a net of 168,300 USH, the amount she actually received. Using simple arithmetic, she is paying a "nominal" interest rate of 39.4 percent (annualized), but as she continues to pay the same rate (which is why it is called a flat rate) even though she is reducing her principal weekly, her "effective rate" (which is the rate that takes into account all the financial costs of her loan, including the cost of forced savings and the so-called time value of money) is closer to 65 percent.

The compulsory savings is one key to the capacity to pay back the loans, because it is in effect a loan guarantee. Mariam had never been able to save much before. Now she brings in, pretty regularly, her 2,125 USH ($1.85) weekly savings (1/16 of 20 percent of the loan) and some weeks even adds a voluntary savings amount. She doesn't do this regularly, few do, because her cash flow is erratic. But by the end of the sixteen weeks, what counts is that she has paid off her loan, and she has done so for two cycles in a row. The proof is that she has taken a third loan. "Do you get interest on your savings?" Ben asks. Mariam doesn't know. But the chairlady explains that Mariam's savings are pooled with the rest of the groups' money and may make 5 percent, but it isn't clear whether that is credited to her passbook. If it isn't, then one of the things she cares about (or realistically one of the things she should care about if she were sophisticated enough to know it) — a rate of interest that beats inflation — is missing.

Mariam's husband appears. He is dressed fairly well and does not look like a farmer. He signals one of his sons to help him bring up a coffee table with a large doily on it. He takes over the discussion. "We," he says to Ben, "are very grateful for CAVIB's help. CAVIB has really woken up the women around here."

He is a teacher, which in Uganda means he is a government civil servant with a fixed salary. The income from his wife's rock-breaking "business," he tells Ben, has enabled him to build the structure behind him and to pay school fees. Ben looks over his shoulder. The building seems to have been erected some time ago, probably before the CAVIB loan program started.

Rock breaking is a local business, the husband continues. Five years ago things began picking up in town and stones of two types were required. The larger pieces go for five hundred shillings a pile, while the smaller gravel-sized pieces (which involve much more work) go for one thousand. He calls a boy, who brings some tools: a large sledgehammer, a half-length crowbar, and two tools about eighteen inches long with miniature pick heads on them no more than four inches long. "See," the man says, "these are the tools." "Who does this work?" Ben asks. "My wife and the kids," the husband says.

"What exactly have you used your loan for, Mariam?" Ben asks. The husband begins to explain, but Ben cuts him off. "I want to hear *her* answer," he says, pointing to Mariam. She explains that because they are at the end of the dry season, the soil has had time to get rock hard. To get at the rocks underneath takes more work than at other times of the year. So Mariam hired laborers to dig out the bigger rocks. This cost 60,000 USH ($52).

The husband appears impatient with Ben's questions and, looking at him, says abruptly: "We need machines to do this work! We need wheelbarrows, more picks, crowbars, and explosives! You must help us." Apparently, the husband thinks Ben is a representative of CAVIB.

Ben has to see what this rock-breaking business is about. "Could we take a look at the land?" Ben asks. The group walks back into the two-acre plot. There are fifty to seventy-five coffee trees, banana trees, two other buildings (both unfinished, with nearby piles of construction brick, weeds growing between the bricks, a sure sign they have been there for some time), and five goats. The little group stops at a large deep hole about eight feet in diameter. The hole goes down ten feet into the beginning of what looks like a tunnel. Ben slips on the edge of it and catches himself. "Doesn't this fill with rain?" he asks. "No," the husband replies, "the water drains away." But Ben can see the damage. The soil here is fragile. There is already much pressure on the land. Not just for grazing but for firewood used for cooking. The deep roots of several trees are exposed on one side of the hole, and the erosion has exposed them more. "Over there," the husband points, "there are the big ones, the big rocks we cannot get out. We need explosives!"

Mariam, all smiles, nods. Ben turns to her. "How long does it take you to make a pile like the ones you have over there?" Ben points to the road side. She thinks, then appears to guess. "Two in one day," she says. Ben wants to know if she means a full day's worth of work or a day that includes the time she spends caring for her children and preparing food, but he decides not to ask. Mariam would likely be confused by the question, and anyway, Ben reminds himself that he is not here to raise women's consciousness.

They walk back. "How many kids do you have?" Ben asks the husband. "Fourteen," he says. What age is the oldest son?" "Twenty-three," he says. "Does he help in this business?" Ben asks. "He is looking for employment at the moment but does some brick making."

Ben passes a pile of concrete blocks. The pile, like the bricks, has weeds growing in the holes in the cement blocks. "What's this all for?" Ben asks. "I was going to build a latrine," the husband explains, "but one of the kids fell sick and the money we had saved to finish it we had to spend on medicines."

As they move on, Ben stoops to pick up something. "Hold on," he shouts to the husband, who has gone on ahead. "What's this?" Ben holds up a rusted pick head, about the same size as the ones the husband had showed Ben earlier, the kind he had said they needed more of. "Why is this not being used?" Ben asks him bluntly. The husband comes over and takes it. "It's no good," he says. "It's used up." Ben can't see any difference between this and the ones Mariam and her kids are currently using but decides not to second-guess the husband.

Back at the roadside, they sit down again on the chairs near the piles of stones. "When did you sell stones last?" Ben asks Mariam. "Yesterday. Two trucks came, and I sold 30 piles to one and 20 to another." Ben asks how much she made. "I made 25,000 USH," Mariam answers. Ben calculates, using some of the other information Mariam had given him. That's 50 piles, or 25 days' work, for $21.75. He guesses at the weight and figures each pile at about 130 to 150 pounds — about 3.8 tons of rock. Much hard work for a return that may seem like a lot when it all comes in at once, but — again Ben calculates — it doesn't come close to meeting the loan payment! Every week she'll have to pay CAVIB 14,025 USH, but at the rate she is breaking rock, even if she continued the work steadily every day and sold all she crushed, she'd make enough for only half the weekly payment.

Yet she had had no trouble paying back her earlier loans and appears confidant she'll be able to pay this coming Tuesday. What else is going on here? Ben wonders.

Maybe Mariam is not a lone poor African woman trying simply to earn a bit of cash. She is poor, but she is also part of a family-run microconglomerate. The husband is a salaried teacher, and one older son makes bricks; there are coffee trees and perhaps other ventures.

Remembering she'd used only 60,000 USH to pay for the laborers she'd hired, Ben wants to know about the rest of the cycle 3 loan. "What about the other 110,000 of the loan? What did you use it for?" "I bought charcoal," Mariam says, "to sell in the marketplace." "Have you sold it yet?" Ben asks. "Yes," she says.

So, Ben thinks to himself, Mariam is not just in the rock-breaking business, and a lot more is going on here than meets the eye. As the economists say, money is fungible.

Ben begins to walk to the car. The husband asks Ben if he is based in Kampala. Ben says he isn't and adds, to be more clear, that he is not part of CAVIB and doesn't even know the people who run it. The husband doesn't take in what Ben has said. "We could use a lot more help," the husband says. "We need money for electricity fees, we need wheelbarrows and machines, explosives." Just for the record, though Ben knows now that the husband can't hear it, Ben reminds him again that he is not part of, has nothing to do with, CAVIB, and that in any case CAVIB does not give things away — CAVIB makes loans. The husband keeps ignoring what Ben says. "You know," he says, "we are grateful for your help. This CAVIB, it has woken up the women. I helped get them organized, as chairman of Local Council no. 1; I was the one who introduced these women to CAVIB." Some mystery clouds begin to disappear in Ben's mind as the husband speaks. Ben pauses, shakes hands, waves to Mariam, and turns to the husband. "It's hard work your wife does, breaking rocks," he says. "Very hard," the husband says. "But the women are waking up now, thanks to CAVIB. Otherwise, they'd just be sitting idle."

The People's Program

Zimbabwe, 1999

THE COMMUNITY MEETING starts off slowly. No one seems to want to say anything.

It is getting harder and harder for Ben to sit on the ground. He kneels on one knee for a few minutes and then shifts to the other. But he is as comfortable under the circumstances as he could be. The shade under the trees is refreshing. Katerisa District is in the hills, and there's a breeze too. No one speaks, but the meeting leader isn't rushing things. No one is in any hurry.

Neither is Ben. Thomas, a Zimbabwean man whom Ben had met the week before at a meeting in Harare, had asked Ben if he would like to come out to see "his NGO." Since Ben's other work was ending a bit sooner than planned and his plane reservation couldn't be changed, he had two unexpected free days. It was nice just to be observing for a change, to be Thomas's guest.

The name of Thomas's NGO is All Is Possible in Zimbabwe, or AIPZ. Ben liked the name, not despite its sappy religious-sounding faith but because of it. It had a catchiness, like the names painted on buses and taxis in many parts of Africa and the Caribbean. They conveyed both deep-seated hope as well as the other side of things — the tongue-in-cheek, slightly self-mocking fatalism that many people use to keep their poverty at bay.

AIPZ, Ben's new friend had told him, is just five years old. It arose from the people themselves, from the communities, he had added. Of course, and Ben knew this before it was explained, it was Thomas who had really started it and who ran it, pretty much single-handedly. Thomas had brochures in his worn briefcase and had handed several to Ben. Right at the top the community role was given prominence: "AIPZ Equals Participatory Community Development — a Self-Help Assistance Program — Development That Works." This was followed by: "OUR GOAL: AIPZ is a small charitable organization with the goal to assist and build the capacity of communities in their efforts to solve their own problems by addressing a varied and broad spectrum of needs that are identified *by the community.* If given access and ownership of the needed resources, people within the community are the only ones in a position to work together to develop and improve their community in a sustainable way." Ben couldn't help but notice how many subtextual threads Thomas had woven into those few words, as if he had wanted to assure his readers that all possible ideological and rhetorical bases were covered.

"Participation": Very "in" these days. No development agency can be credible if it does not promise the involvement of the community, of the people themselves, as the starting point of all development effort. "Self-Help Assistance": Well, that one, Ben smiled to himself, that one was either clever or naïve, or maybe both. It was not as pompous as "helping others to help themselves." What Ben liked was that it left the contradiction intact but allowed for the reality that the more neutral word "assistance" conveyed. But what tickled Ben most was "Development That Works." For here was a tacit reference to the fact that it is 1999 and we now know that much of development doesn't. Could AIPZ, with its go-for-broke name, do things differently? Thomas appeared to think so.

Finally, a man in the back of the circle raises his hand. There are about 35 people sitting under the tree, almost all men and boys. Thomas acknowledges him and nods. The man stands up to speak. He hesitates for a second and then loudly and clearly tells Thomas that AIPZ has promised him a sewing machine and it hasn't arrived yet. When can he expect it, he asks.

Thomas had told Ben about the "Tools for Self-Reliance" component of the program. Ben turns to the second page of the brochure: "Tools for Self-Reliance distributes refurbished hand tools and sewing machines to rural entrepreneurs throughout Zimbabwe. These reconditioned tools are of high quality and have many years of service remaining. Since tools are just not affordable for many rural artisans, a few hand tools can have a major impact on their ability to eke out a living."

Thomas, unembarrassed by the delay in providing the sewing machine, takes out a small pad from his pocket and asks the man his name. He writes it down. "I assure you that you will have your machine within one week," he says. Ben wondered whether this was what AIPZ meant when it talked about giving "access and ownership of the needed resources."

More people now began to raise their hands. The next man to speak is agitated and considerably less polite than the first one. He has volunteered his labor on the construction of the new duplex house in his village which the community had agreed was needed to accommodate four new teachers (even though the government orders newly graduated teachers to the countryside, they often do not go because there is no place for them to stay). But the steel windows and door frames have not come when they were supposed to, and the stucco edges of the door and window openings are cracking. "Our labor is being wasted!" the man accuses.

Ben turns to page 3 in the AIPZ brochure: "In our construction projects the community provides the sand, stone, labor and locally made bricks for the buildings that AIPZ helps to construct. AIPZ provides the more costly items, such as steel window and door frames, cement, lumber and roofing materials."

Unruffled, Thomas again takes note and reassures the man that the window and door frames are on their way.

Another man speaks. He wants to know why the carpentry training course has been delayed.

Ben begins to realize that the meeting is inadvertently following the page numbers in the AIPZ brochure. He turns to page 4: "AIPZ's Rural Outreach Carpentry Training Program provides rural artisans with upgraded woodworking skills, basic small business training, and carpentry hand tools. During a four-week workshop, they are trained to build a specially designed durable wooden school desk."

Thomas responds, again calmly. The delay is due to the need to shift some of AIPZ's resources to the portable chalkboard program, which some communities have recently vowed was of a greater priority. "We have limited funds, we cannot do everything." But, be assured, Thomas tells the man, the carpentry training will resume soon.

Page 5: "The Portable Chalkboard Program provides hundreds of portable chalkboards to improve the quality of teaching when it must be done outside under trees."

Ben keeps reading this time. The brochure is 6 pages long and after he reads about the Orphan Scholarship Fund and the Computer Lab program, he finally comes to the end, where in block letters he reads: "MORE PROJECTS CAN BE ADDED TO THIS LIST WITH YOUR HELP."

Where does AIPZ get its money?

Indigenous NGOs in the third world are a relatively new phenomenon. They've sprung up everywhere since the late 1980s, with the pattern accelerating in the 1990s. Except in large and diverse countries such as India, where there is a middle class and indeed a well-heeled upper class, local philanthropy hardly exists. Raising money locally to solve local problems isn't possible in a place like Zimbabwe. When a country has enough people with enough money and conscience to donate money to local causes, it is already developed or at least well on its way. So for a new NGO such as AIPZ, a partner from a "northern" industrial country is essential.

That is what AIPZ has. In California a U.S. NGO has what amounts to a philanthropic franchise arrangement with AIPZ. It provides it with a core budget and helps it make contact with other donors. If those donors (individuals, corporations, foundations, and so on) want the convenience and security of sending the money to California instead of Zimbabwe, no problem; the U.S. NGO will see to it that the money gets to AIPZ. Moreover, the donor gets to believe that it is donating something to state-of-the-art development, because the northern partner does some of the public relations on behalf of the southern NGO and, whether intentionally or not, lends status and reputation to its partner in the south, just by association.

But Ben knows the California organization linked to AIPZ, and he cannot imagine that it could be happy with the kind of thing Ben is seeing and reading about in the brochure. Quite a few organizations in the north have learned some lessons over the years. Two prominent ones: First, giving things away to people in need is not sustainable. Second, amassing projects of many different kinds in response to people's stated needs is not a coherent approach to any kind of fundamental change.

But the irony is that the southern NGO movement has gained

strength over the years because of the currency of the idea of people's participation. Southern NGOs can claim that their indigenous status makes them that much closer to the "people" than any northern NGO could possibly be, and they are mostly right. But even if they were not, the northern organizations know that they have to turn over not just operations but all decision making to the south. The change in the 1990s has been that while the northern organizations used to try to have it both ways — the appearance of granting independence to their southern counterparts while keeping a northern hand on the management strings *as well as* the purse strings — they can no longer get away with it. The newer southern NGOs resent being told what to do, in any way, at any time. To be genuine, honest, and transparent, the northern partners have no choice but to let them do things their way and still send the money. If they stopped the flow of funds, everyone would cry foul.

As Ben closes AIPZ's brochure and tunes back in to Thomas promising yet another disgruntled community member that AIPZ will take care of his problem, he sees clearly how much this well-meaning organization is going back to what used to be done in the name of development twenty or more years ago. This is development that does not work. But Ben is Thomas's guest here, and it wouldn't be polite to say anything.

The Case for a Radical Reduction in Development Assistance

In his 1949 inaugural speech, Harry Truman proposed four major courses of action directed at undeveloped areas. He began his fourth point by saying:

> More than half the people of the world are living in conditions approaching misery. Their food is inadequate. They are victims of disease. Their economic life is primitive and stagnant. Their poverty is a handicap and a threat both to them and to more prosperous areas.
>
> For the first time in history humanity possesses the knowledge and the skill to relieve the suffering of these people.
>
> The United States is pre-eminent among nations in the development of industrial and scientific techniques. The material resources which we can afford to use for the assistance of other people are limited. But our imponderable resources in technical knowledge are constantly growing and are inexhaustible.
>
> I believe that we should make available to peace-loving people the benefits of our store of technical knowledge in order to help them realize their aspirations for a better life.[1]

This was the birth of Point Four and, in essence, the modern development establishment. About it, Truman says in his memoirs: "Point Four was conceived as a world wide, continuing program of helping underdeveloped nations to help themselves through the sharing of technical information already tested and proved in the United States. The principal item of expenditure would be the skill of our technicians teaching these people how to help themselves.[2]

Point Four was signed into law on June 5, 1950, after which the Technical Cooperation Administration (later USAID) was soon set up under the State Department. By March 1951, 350 technicians were at work on more than a hundred technical cooperation projects in twenty-seven countries. When Truman summed up progress to date in his 1952 State of the Union Address, he noted: "This is our Point Four program at work. It is working, not only

1. Harry S. Truman, *Years of Trial and Hope*, vol. 2 of *Memoirs* (Garden City, N.Y.: Doubleday, 1956), 227.
2. Ibid., 232.

in India, but in Iran and Paraguay and Liberia — in thirty-three countries around the globe. Our technical missionaries are out there. We need more of them."[3]

Though almost touchingly innocent and naïve from a distance of fifty years, there was something sound in Truman's original vision — the notion that one should transfer knowledge rather than money. But right away, the structures of the fledgling industry started flexing their imperatives, and age-old truisms came alive. One of these was that "money talks." When the recipient countries began clamoring not just for technicians but for money as well, we and others responded. And with the faith in technicians as missionaries — so blatantly conflated by Truman himself — things began to steamroll. By 1953 the original appropriation of $34.5 million had been increased to $155.6 million, and 2,445 technicians were now at work in thirty-five countries. Today, looking back over the half century since that time, it is embarrassing (or should be) to note the poor track record of development assistance.

But we are not embarrassed. Recall the criticisms made by development insiders cited in the introduction, like the World Bank's own conclusions in the early 1990s about its declining performance. Instead of embarrassment, we promise improvement. Outsider critiques, often harsher than our own, are no less inclined to propose a fix, whether it is a complete overhaul, a reorientation of vision, or a newfound coherence. Here is a 1989 *Washington Post* article: "The Agency for International Development, after spending tens of billions of dollars in 25 years of trying to help Third World nations stem poverty, has concluded that the program largely failed to achieve its objectives and suggested that a complete overhaul may be necessary."[4] And in a 1992 letter to President George H. W. Bush, Vermont senator Patrick Leahy wrote that "our international assistance program is exhausted intellectually, conceptually, and politically. It has no widely understood and agreed set of goals, it lacks coherence and vision, and there is a very real question whether parts of it actually serve broadly accepted United States national interests any longer. . . . As a whole it is failing to address adequately fundamental American interests in the global population explosion, international environmental degradation on a massive scale, and seemingly ineradicable poverty and hopelessness in the developing world."[5] But looking for the "right" formula or overhauling methods and procedures is to fall right back into the trap that has hobbled us all along: the dev biz's fundamental attachment to the blueprint thinking of the engi-

3. Ibid., 236.

4. *Washington Post*, February 21, 1989.

5. The letter, dated August 2, 1992, is quoted in Robert Zimmerman, *Dollars, Diplomacy, and Dependency: Dilemmas of U.S. Economic Aid* (Boulder, Colo.: Lynne Rienner, 1993), xii.

neering model — our structures are OK; it is our plans and methods that need changing.

There is an alternative proposition, as I have suggested in this book. Development assistance has largely failed to work because it cannot work. This is so because of human nature, the complexity of the development world's problems, and, most important, the inevitable structural distortions and contradictions within the development assistance industry. To put it another way, the organizational imperatives of the industry have generally worked against our ability to act on what we do understand about real development, rendering us not only ineffective but often harmful as well.

What We Know

The Relationship between Poverty and Economic Growth

We have always known that over time economic growth reduces poverty and creates wealth. But for fifty years the development assistance industry has devoted much moral energy, erudition, and scholarship (not to mention heavy doses of ideology) to debates about the quality of growth, the speed with which poverty is reduced, or the negative consequences of material well-being. The Swiss historian of development Gilbert Rist is not alone when he laments, "When will we realize that well-being does not come from growth?"[6]

The antiglobalization protests of 2000 and 2001 show that these debates will continue. What has been little noticed is that the poor have already cast their vote. The first thing most poor people everywhere want is material well-being. In practical terms that means they want purchasing power, which means money, which means economic growth. Only when they have this material well-being will they be able to talk about such concerns as pollution and the environment or the erosion of certain values.

Second, people who are poor want every opportunity they can to make that money, preferably jobs and, if that fails, their own businesses. And to the extent they recognize that they will need to be better and better educated to get jobs and money, they'll want education. They (or their parents) already do. (Oddly, the third world poor see the value of education seemingly more than middle-class Americans. At least they will sacrifice more for their children to have it.)

Thus we need not waste time on the debate about whether economic growth is the "correct" approach to the problem of poverty. The poor of the world have given us their answer, and their answer is the one that counts. So what are the ingredients for growth? Robert Zimmerman puts it as well as

6. Gilbert Rist, *The History of Development* (London: Zed Books, 1997).

anyone: "Sustainable economic and social development must be based on wealth created by skilled, educated, and politically empowered people in increasingly democratic political systems."[7]

Even the most poorly endowed countries have human energy. If we accept that human energy has enormous capacity for development and is one of the fundamental fuels for it, then certain conditions to release that energy need to be present. One obvious set of conditions is physical infrastructure. There has to be some minimal communications infrastructure, including transportation. A functioning and growing economy cannot grow and expand if goods cannot move and information about them cannot easily be conveyed, which means a road network, reliable electricity, a telephone system, and fuel distribution system to keep all this running. But building these things is easy. Anything physical that can be built in the advanced industrial countries can be built in a developing country. It takes money and engineers.

But what will produce the money and ensure that it is appropriately distributed to these kinds of works? Part of the answer is a system designed to increase capital (hence growth); this system would give citizens certain rights and impose certain obligations, one of which is to pay taxes on their gains, which in turn gives the government the money to build these things or to license the private sector to do so. There also has to be a generally accepted set of norms (the primacy of property rights, for instance), laws embodying those norms, and a government to enforce those norms fairly. If those things are not present, we now know, development does not happen. In short, we know that the institutional systems and the policies which govern them are primary. If those systems evolve, over time poverty will be reduced.

Complexity

Development's complexity is like the web that W. Mitchell Waldrop describes: "Except for the very simplest physical systems, virtually everything and everybody in the world is caught up in a vast nonlinear web of incentives and constraints and connections."[8] With fifty years of development assistance experience behind us, we know how complex development is. We know that in each developing country everything is intertwined in that nonlinear web of incentives, constraints, and connections.

If development assistance professionals wanted to instigate change without specifying any particular outcomes, that would be easy enough. In the film *The Gods Must be Crazy*, a Coke can dropped into the world of premodern people is like a stone dropped into a lake — change ripples every-

---

7. Zimmerman, *Dollars, Diplomacy, and Dependency*, 188.
8. M. Mitchell Waldrop, *Complexity* (New York: Simon and Schuster, 1992), 65.

where. But that kind of effect has not, of course, been the goal of the development industry. It does not want merely to drop something and then see what happens. It wants earnestly to engineer change — to control the variables, manipulate the incentives, remove the constraints, realign the connections, set the sequence and timing of things and build an orderly process by which the poor will become rich and all nations modern, free, and democratic. One of the deep dreams of the development industry, all its other agendas notwithstanding, is to hear the steady thrum of a well-oiled machine.

That dream was initially fed by a major early success. Historically, the conception of what could be accomplished through external aid was reinforced by the success of the Marshall Plan. Because of it we came to believe that external aid could be the prime mover in development. But the Marshall Plan worked because its goal was the rebuilding of previously successful modern industrial states. It did not set out to change or create social, political, and economic institutions or fundamentally alter people's values — infinitely more complex goals.

Unintended Consequences

Over the five decades of official development assistance, virtually every practitioner has encountered the unintended consequences of well-planned projects. Unintended consequences make projects backfire and undermine sustainability. The effect is a bit like squeezing a half-filled balloon hard in one place and seeing a bubble pop out in another, with the difference that we are looking so intently at the spot we are squeezing that we do not see the bubble forming at the other end. And so we are apt to be surprised by these consequences. There will always be unintended consequences of our attempts to improve things because the factors involved are not only complex but are also themselves altered by the changes induced. They are "moving" factors and thus by definition hard to "factor in." This too we know.

External Development Assistance Fuels Dependency

As with the dilemma of complexity, defining how much help is too much is difficult. Often, the development industry seems to have got the formula wrong, and the result has been the creation of dependency. This applies both to the level of individual persons and communities and to whole countries, and our experience has demonstrated the danger of dependency repeatedly.

A World Bank–sponsored study showed, for example, that countries which received the most aid performed the least well. The study clearly suggested that external funding became a substitute for "a sound diagnosis of development problems."[9] But studies aside, plain human experience and common sense should remind us that external aid can have negative consequences such as reinforcing policies that keep people poor and simply creating incentives for corruption.

Perhaps the biggest obstacle to development in many countries has been corruption. The development industry has, after all, put up money and technical expertise to build many of the infrastructural basics a country needs and has done so since the 1950s all over the developing world. But a large percentage of these finished constructions have broken down. This is not solely because there has been no technical skill available to maintain them but just as often because the funds to ensure maintenance (and often proper construction in the first place) were diverted through corruption.

Too much help given away too easily results in disincentives to solve problems in a lasting way. One of the major incentives for corruption has been development assistance itself.

Impediments to Acting on What We Know

We have not, it seems clear, been able to face the full implications of these lessons experience has taught us. What stands in the way? The structure of the relationship of the organizations in development assistance with their employees and their sources of funding bind us, almost irrevocably, to development approaches that do not make sense.

Direct Action through Projects

We have long suspected that an engineering model — a "doing" model for external development assistance — is inappropriate, yet our organizations and we as professionals are structured to take direct action, that is, to plan, justify, budget, and "do" things in measurable project-sized bites.

Money has increasingly been the driver rather than the fuel for the industry. Again, it could not have been otherwise. Money has to be sought and, in a world of extraordinarily pluralistic claims, more and more aggressively, such that development agencies have had to market their goals. And marketing (if not by definition, then certainly in practice) means some degree of image creation, which in turn means distortion, however mild. This commodification of development (and every agency from the World Bank down to the smallest NGO has been caught up in the phenomenon) has reinforced direct-action projects. Such abstractions as the idea of institution building do not sell well; to sell development requires something "bite-size."

9. Uma Lele, *Agricultural Growth and Assistance to Africa: Lessons of a Quarter Century* (San Francisco: International Center for Economic Growth / ICS Press, 1990), 7–9.

In the world of nonprofits and public funding, you need to be accountable for what you sell, and so the project, with its "log frame" and its other ersatz ways of seeming finite and achievable, fits well with the bite-size imperative, but not with development itself.

The more development became a career, the more it adhered to standards of professionalism and the more the industry began — quite naturally — to have its own self-perpetuation at stake. Careers and organizations go together. Moving upward in a career usually requires a reputation for getting things done effectively. The more projects one runs, the more one can claim to be good at "getting things done." Moving upward or having legitimacy in a career also often means having authority over other employees, the opportunity for which will increase along with the number of people working in an organization. This and other careerist tendencies reinforce the reliance on the direct-action project.

Urgency and Moral Myopia

The development assistance industry's growing concern about poverty over the years has, of course, a moral basis. But that basis has become myopic in that we have translated our moral concern too narrowly into a politically correct urgency to alleviate poverty "right now," which in turn reinforces direct action. But this urgency for solutions contradicts the most widely shared of all the lessons we have learned — development takes time.

A Reduced Capacity to Think

Promotion and advancement within organizations tend to go to safe, well-rounded people who do not rock the boat. One way to be safe is to cultivate the skill of obfuscation. Judith Tendler years ago wrote about the USAID bureaucracy, pointing out how the nature of the organization and the professionals within it de-emphasized clear writing and, with it, clear thinking, ultimately in the interests of the professionals and the organization.

> Because of [US]AID's vulnerability to outside attack, this power of the written word was to some extent based on the fear of it. If the most powerless of technicians raised a problem in writing, then the person responsible, no matter how high his position, considered it essential to produce a satisfactory response in writing. If not, he considered himself a sitting duck for the future congressional or GAO file prober who discovered the problem-raising memo in the file without a satisfactory reply sitting behind it. . . .
>
> The [US]AID technician . . . sat before the typewriter with a sense of the power of his words and his responsibility for articulating his ideas, along with a tremendous fear of his own writing. . . . Words were toned down, thoughts were twisted, and arguments were left out, all in order to alleviate the uncomfortable feeling of responsibility for possible betrayal. The writing was finished with a sense of frustration at not having articulated an argument as lucidly, honestly, and

convincingly as possible. Such a situation must have resulted in a certain atrophy of the capacity for . . . all communication through language.[10]

Disincentives for clarity and rigorous thought are real obstacles to effective development. And like the other obstacles, they are intertwined with the ways development assistance organizations and the incentives that command them work.

Less Is More

Direct action in the development industry should be reduced to basics: refugee assistance and emergency relief, with, in some cases, maternal and child care as a legitimate extension of those two realms. While these areas of direct intervention may have little to do with development, they are imperative from a moral point of view.

As for the array of what we have heretofore thought of as more truly development-oriented tasks — the many specialized sectors that have evolved with the development industry over the years — all institutionally managed efforts on the part of the OECD nations to direct or engineer development through projects should cease. Dismantle the bilateral bureaucracies and send home the people who staff them, especially the expatriates.

If there are effective things we can do that are definable as developmental, they lie in the realm of the indirect and subtle. We must be light-handed and perpetually experimental. Increasingly, we have been neither. The nice thing about a light-handed, indirect, and subtle approach to external development assistance is that it will require far less money and far fewer people. And because it will be considerably harder to sell and thus more difficult to fund, requiring less money is a good thing.

Why Do Much Less?

It is time for us to entertain seriously the possibility that development assistance is not necessary for development. And if it ever was in the past, it increasingly appears that this is no longer the case. The dev biz needs to catch up conceptually with the world as it is today. The poor have figured it out. Why can't we?

The private sector, for all the discomforts about it some may harbor, can and is being more effective at economic development than we development professionals have been. Whatever we may not like about the excesses of capitalism, the private sector will over time give the poor what *they*

---

10. Judith Tendler, *Inside Foreign Aid* (Baltimore: Johns Hopkins University Press, 1975), 50–51.

want, which is first and foremost increased spending power and the means to get it.

The poor themselves are on to us. In this globalized world, poor people everywhere have leapfrogged ahead of the development assistance industry. Millions of poor have shown that they will no longer wait around for us. For good or bad, illegally or not, they are on the move. And while those with the energy and courage to move are in the minority, the signs are that the leverage they represent (both through their example and their remittances) has unprecedented power for change. That is real people power. If anything points to the growing irrelevance of the development assistance industry, it is the contrast between our own ersatz attempts to engineer development and their having created it themselves. It may not be as pretty as what we in the "dev biz" continue to design, but it is real.

We have yet to come to terms with the underlying arrogance of the development assistance endeavor as it has been practiced for this last half century. For the ultimate hubris is to try to engineer change from outside a dynamic living system composed of different interests, passions, and affinities, all bubbling up out of a soup containing an intricate social and political structure that itself sits on top of years of history, not to mention a particular geography, climate, and set of natural endowments. The best service we development professionals can now render to developing countries is for most of us to fade away quietly and allow the era of externally provided development assistance to come to a close.

Epilogue

This book was written before the attacks of September 11, 2001. After that date, I wondered if those events had altered my conclusion that we need less development assistance money, less direct foreign aid, not more. As the book goes to press, what is happening in the world and in the development industry remains completely consistent with what I have been saying in this book, in some respects so much so that even I am surprised.

In early 2002, the subject of development assistance began to be discussed on newspaper front pages and in op ed pieces, a prominence development aid had not had for some time. The gist of the discussion has been that the deep cause of September 11 lies with the problems of underdevelopment, and if we do not pay more attention to those problems by substantially increasing development assistance funding, the United States and many other countries will continue to be at risk.

I believe that the complex problems of underdevelopment *are* behind what happened on September 11. Poverty is only the tip of the iceberg; that is a mere *condition*. More challenging is that many people in the third world are poor because of their *position* in society, a position they are usually not free to alter. They are excluded from opportunities to improve their lot because of their ethnicity, gender, or caste or because they lack a secure title to their property or for many other reasons. And to the extent that they live under regimes and institutions that discourage the rule of law, equal justice, tolerance, and political freedom, not only is their position reinforced but the condition of their poverty is exacerbated as well.

I do not believe that more money for foreign aid programs will solve those problems — for all the reasons I offer in the preceding chapters.[1]

Some months after September 11, calls for more aid money by the president of the World Bank and the secretary general of the United Nations were to be expected. But I was surprised to hear people I would have guessed to be either opposed to or cool toward foreign aid (not always for the right reasons), such as George W. Bush, ask for large increases over the

---

1. Humanitarian relief is another matter entirely. As I have said in the book, relief for people affected by disaster of whatever origin must continue.

coming years. Otherwise tough-minded commentators, like Thomas Friedman, chimed in.[2] So "politically correct" has support for increases in foreign
aid money suddenly become that the long record of our ineffectiveness
seems to have been forgotten.

But it is more disturbing that the players in the dev biz — it must be said —
have begun to take advantage of September 11 as an opportunity for growth
in the industry. I hear talk from colleagues right now (April 2002) that hotel
space in Kabul is hotly sought after by scores of NGO and bilateral and multilateral organization representatives from many of the advanced economy
countries. They are there to help, yes, but they are also there (and stepping
over each other) because Afghanistan is a hot new "market" for an industry
seeking "market share."

I see evidence within the dev biz of a rosy (if not gleeful) anticipation
that for the first time in years there will be more money available for development projects, along with a sense of relief: many of our critics have fallen
silent; we may not have to change much now; we may have a new lease on
life.

The danger is that with more money, we will be free to continue doing
what we have been doing. Old habits of thought and deep organizational
imperatives will be reinforced. And with the sense that we are again needed
will come the delusion that we are useful. But, ironically, if there is a time
when the notion of fostering change with less money and more conceptual
rigor and subtlety should come into its own, it is post–September 11, 2001.

2. Thomas Friedman, *New York Times*, March 17, 2002.

Bibliography

"Africa Is Dying." Cover story. *New Republic*, June 16, 1997.

Arndt, H. W. *Economic Development: The History of an Idea*. Chicago: University of Chicago Press, 1987.

Bauer, P. T. *The Development Frontier: Essays in Applied Economics*. Cambridge: Harvard University Press, 1991.

———. Dissent on Development. Cambridge: Harvard University Press, 1976.

———. *Equality, the Third World, and Economic Delusion*. Cambridge: Harvard University Press, 1981.

Bledstein, Burton. *The Culture of Professionalism*. New York: W. W. Norton, 1976.

Braudel, Fernand. *People and Production*. Vol. 2 of *The Identity of France*. Trans. Siân Reynolds. New York: Harper and Row, 1990.

———. *The Structures of Everyday Life*. Vol. 1 of *Civilization and Capitalism, Fifteenth–Eighteenth Centuries*. Trans. Siân Reynolds. New York: Harper and Row, 1982–84.

Bringhurst, Bruce. *Antitrust and the Oil Monopoly: The Standard Oil Cases, 1890–1911*. Westport, Conn.: Greenwood Press, 1979.

Bruckner, Pascal. *The Tears of the White Man*. New York: Free Press, 1986.

Castle, Eugene W. *The Great Giveaway*. Chicago: Henry Regnery, 1957.

Churchill, Winston S. *The River War*. New York: NEL Books, 1973.

De Gramont, Sanche. *The French: Portrait of a People*. New York: G. P. Putnam's Sons, 1969.

Dickens, Charles. *Bleak House*. Oxford: Oxford University Press, 1996.

Emerson, Ralph Waldo. *Essays and Addresses*. Chicago: Scott, Foresman, 1906.

Everyone's United Nations: A Handbook on the Work of the UN. New York: United Nations, 1979.

"Foreign Aid Largely a Failure." *Washington Post*, February 21, 1989.

Frank, Leonard. "The Development Game." *Granta Magazine*, 1988.

Glastris, Paul. Quoted in the *New Republic*, October 11, 1993.

Griffin, K. "Thinking about Development: The Longer View." Paper presented at SID 19th World Conference, New Delhi, March 25–28, 1988.

Hancock, Graham. *Lords of Poverty*. London: Macmillan, 1989.

Harrington, Michael. *The Vast Majority: A Journey to the World's Poor*. New York: Simon and Schuster, 1977.

Howe, B. "The Emergence of Scientific Philanthropy, 1900–1920: Origins, Issues, and Outcomes." In *Philanthropy and Cultural Imperialism: The Foundations at Home and Abroad*, ed. R. Arnove. Boston: G. K. Hall, 1980.

Hughes, Robert. *Nothing if Not Critical*. London: Collins Harvill, 1990.

International Council of Voluntary Agencies (ICVA). *The Reality of AID, 1997–1998*. Geneva, Switzerland: ICVA, 1998.

International Monetary Fund. *World Economic Outlook*. Washington, D.C.: International Monetary Fund, May 1997.

Jazairy, Idriss, Mohiuddin Alamgir, and Theresa Panuccio. *The State of World Rural Poverty*. Rome: IFAD, 1992.

Kaul, Chandrika, and Valerie Tomaselli-Moschovitis. *Statistical Handbook on Poverty in the Developing World*. Phoenix: Oryx Press, 1999.

Klitgaard, Robert. *Adjusting to Reality—Beyond "State vs. Market" in Economic Development*. San Francisco: ICS Press, 1991.

Landes, David S. *The Wealth and Poverty of Nations*. New York: W. W. Norton, 1999.

Lele, Uma. *Agricultural Growth and Assistance to Africa: Lessons of a Quarter Century*. San Francisco: International Center for Economic Growth/ICS Press, 1990.

Lewis, John P., and Valeriana Kallab, eds. *Development Strategies Reconsidered*. New Brunswick, N.J.: Transaction Books, 1986.

Linden, Eugene. *The Alms Race*. New York: Random House, 1976.

"Modernizing Aid." Editorial. *Toronto Globe and Mail*, March 11, 1988.

OECD. *Development Assistance Committee Report*. Paris: OECD, 1994.

———. *Development Assistance Committee Report*. Paris: OECD, 1996.

———. *Development Assistance Committee Report*. OECD online, August 2001. <http://www.oecd.org>.

Ortega y Gasset, José. *The Revolt of the Masses*. New York: Norton, 1932.

PACT Catalog no. 106. New York: PACT Publications, 1999.

"The Perversion of Foreign Aid." *Commentary*, June 1985.

Recent and Forthcoming Books from Oxfam for Development Professionals. London: Oxfam, 1999.

Rist, Gilbert. *The History of Development*. London: Zed Books, 1997.

Rostow, Walt Whitman. *The Stages of Economic Growth: A Non-Communist Manifesto*. London: Cambridge University Press, 1960.

Rush, Norman. *Mating*. New York: Vintage Books, 1991.

Schoeck, Helmut. *Envy*. New York: Harcourt, Brace & World, 1966.

Smillie, Ian. "Interlude: The Rise of the Transnational Agency." In *Compassion and Calculation: The Business of Private Foreign Aid*, ed. David Sogge, Kees Biekart, and John Saxby. London: Pluto Press, 1996.

Snow, C. P. *The Two Cultures and a Second Look*. Cambridge, England: Cambridge University Press, 1959.

Sogge, David. "Settings and Choices." In *Compassion and Calculation: The Business of Private Foreign Aid*, ed. David Sogge, Kees Biekart, and John Saxby. London: Pluto Press, 1996.

Standards of Accounting and Financial Reporting for Voluntary Health and Welfare Organizations. 1989.

"Taming the Beast of H Street." *Financial Times*, September 26, 1994.

Tendler, Judith. *Inside Foreign Aid*. Baltimore: Johns Hopkins University Press, 1975.

Thompson, E. P., and Eileen Yeo. *The Unknown Mayhew*. New York: Random House, 1971.

Thorp, Willard L. *Reality of Foreign Aid.* New York: Praeger, 1971.

Truman, Harry S. *Years of Trial and Hope.* Vol. 2 of *Memoirs.* Garden City, N.Y.: Doubleday, 1956.

Twain, Mark. *Following the Equator.* Hartford, Conn.: American Publishing Company; New York: Doubleday and McClure, 1897.

"The Twilight of Foreign Aid." *Financial Times,* September 28, 1992.

USAID. *2001 Report of Voluntary Agencies Engaged in Overseas Relief and Development Registered with the U.S. Agency for International Development.* Washington, D.C.: USAID, 2001.

Veblen, Thorstein. *The Theory of the Leisure Class.* Mentor ed. New York: New American Library, 1953.

Waldrop, M. Mitchell. *Complexity.* New York: Simon and Schuster, 1992.

"When Foreign Aid Fails." *Atlantic Monthly,* April 1985.

White, Louise. *Creating Opportunities for Change: Approaches to Managing Development Programs.* Boulder, Colo.: Lynne Rienner, 1987.

"Why Aid Is an Empty Promise." *Economist,* May 7–13, 1994.

World, October 13, 1898.

World Bank. *Assessing Aid: What Works, What Doesn't, and Why.* Washington, D.C.: World Bank, 1998.

——. "Effective Implementation: Key to Development Impact." Confidential Portfolio Management Task Force report. Washington, D.C., September 22, 1992.

——. *World Development Report, 2000–2001.* New York: Oxford University Press for the World Bank, 2001.

World Factbook 2000. Online ed. Washington, D.C.: Central Intelligence Agency, 2001. <http://www.cia.gov/cia/publications/factbook>.

A World to Make: Development in Perspective. Daedalus, special issue (Winter 1989).

Worldwatch Institute. *Vital Signs, 2001.* New York.: W. W. Norton, 2001.

Zimmerman, Robert. *Dollars, Diplomacy, and Dependency: Dilemmas of U.S. Economic Aid.* Boulder, Colo.: Lynne Rienner, 1993.

Index

accountability, 182, 260–61, 266
ActionAid, 103
African Development Bank, 100
agents of development, primary vs.
 secondary, 49
"aid fatigue," 70
Americares, 108
Appropriate Technology (AT) move-
 ment, 64, 71
Asian Development Bank, 100
Asian "Tigers," 2, 66, 68

"Band-Aid" approach, 259
"basic human needs," 64
"beltway bandits," 101–2
"big-push" strategy, 57
bilateral aid, 106
bilateral donors, 100, 104
"brain drain," 60
Bretton Woods Conference, 55

Caisse Française pour la Cooperation,
 100
CARE, 56, 65, 103, 107, 263
Catholic Relief Services, 56, 103, 107
Chemonics International, 102
child sponsorship, 257–59
 fund-raising dilemmas related to,
 262–63
Christian Children's Fund, 107, 263
classification of developing countries,
 23–27 (passim)
complexity
 as left out of development thinking, 57
 inability to come to terms with, 54,
 132, 266

recognition of, 62
consultant pay scales, 227
Coué, Emile, 50

Department for International Development (DFID), 100
dependency, 74
 as fueled by development assistance,
 290
 dimensions of, 155–58
 fear of creating, 153–54
development
 antecedents of, 50–53
 evolution of idea of, 48–74 (passim)
 as field of study, 60
 grassroots, 61
 integrated rural, 64
 as intentional effort on behalf of
 others, 48–50, 62
 metaphor for, 56–57
 primary vs. secondary agents of, 48
 as "product," 183
 role of government in, 53–54
 selling of, 183, 257–60
 time as key factor in, 132
 unintended consequences of, 2, 60,
 290
Development Alternatives, Inc., 102
development assistance
 as an industry, 4, 6, 62, 72, 98–99
 as a calling, 226–27
 as a career, 226
 as technical knowledge, 57
 effective demand for, 183
 engineering model of, 7, 57, 131
 funding, 190

THOMAS W. DICHTER has lived and worked in many developing countries over his thirty-five-year career and has observed the development endeavor from many perspectives. He has managed and designed projects, directed a Peace Corps country program, been a vice president of a nongovernmental organization (NGO), a program officer of an international foundation, a researcher for a think tank, and a consultant for many international agencies, including the United Nations Development Programme, the International Fund for Agricultural Development, the United States Agency for International Development, and the World Bank. He has worked with NGOs worldwide and studied their evolution.

Mr. Dichter holds a Ph.D. in anthropology from the University of Chicago. He has published numerous articles and taught courses on development-related subjects at Tufts, Clark University, and the Woodrow Wilson School at Princeton. He lives in Conway, Massachusetts.